Joe R. Feagin
is a professor of sociology
at the University of Texas (Austin).
Author of a dozen books, including
Discrimination American Style (Prentice-Hall, 1978)
and *Subordinating the Poor* (Prentice-Hall, 1975),
he is currently working on a book on growth
and development in Sunbelt cities.

Prentice-Hall International, Inc., *London*
Prentice-Hall of Australia Pty. Limited, *Sydney*
Prentice-Hall of Canada, Inc., *Toronto*
Prentice-Hall of India Private Limited, *New Delhi*
Prentice-Hall of Japan, Inc., *Tokyo*
Prentice-Hall of Southeast Asia Pte. Ltd., *Singapore*
Whitehall Books Limited, *Wellington, New Zealand*
Editora Prentice-Hall do Brasil Ltda., *Rio de Janeiro*

THE URBAN REAL ESTATE GAME

Playing Monopoly with Real Money

JOE R. FEAGIN

A SPECTRUM BOOK

Prentice-Hall, Inc., Englewood Cliffs, N.J. 07632

Library of Congress Cataloging in Publication Data

Feagin, Joe R.
    The urban real estate game.

    "A Spectrum Book."
    Includes bibliographical references and index.
        1. Real estate investment.   2. Real estate development.
    3. Urban economics.   I. Title.
    HD1391.F4   1983   332.63'24'091732   83-4426
    ISBN 0-13-937797-2
    ISBN 0-13-937789-1 (pbk.)

ISBN 0-13-937789-1 (PBK.)

ISBN 0-13-937797-2

A SPECTRUM BOOK

Printed in the United States of America.

10 9 8 7 6 5 4 3 2

Editorial/production supervision by Claudia Citarella
Manufacturing buyer: Cathie Lenard

This book is available at a special discount
when ordered in bulk quantities.
Contact Prentice-Hall, Inc.,
General Publishing Division, Special Sales,
Englewood Cliffs, New Jersey 07632.

CONTENTS

PREFACE

Recently in Chicago a homeless man in his thirties spent his nights sleeping in a trash compactor that was broken. One day, when the trash box was fixed without his knowledge, he was dumped and crushed along with the trash. That an affluent society such as ours cannot provide decent housing for its citizens is a human tragedy symbolized by the two to three million homeless people living in streets and parks across the nation.

Yet the homeless are not the only Americans with shelter problems. For millions in moderate-income families there is not enough safe and adequate housing that can be rented at reasonable rates. Soaring rents in cities have forced many households to spend a third to half or more of their incomes just to keep a roof over their heads. For millions in middle-income families the dream of homeownership is fading rapidly in the face of sharply inflated housing costs and cutbacks in moderate-priced home construction. Experts estimate that we are annually building 500,000 to a million housing units less than the number needed. Shelter problems have become a fact of life for many Americans.

Housing crises suggest that something is fundamentally wrong in U.S. society. Clearly decisions about investment of capital are basic to this crisis. Simply put, not enough capital is being invested in the types of housing that millions of Americans need. Powerful real estate actors—developers, builders, and bankers—blame the government for this situation. Government is blamed for taxing too much and for regulating the "free market" too much.

Yet much government spending, such as for urban renewal and for FHA mortgage insurance, has long been championed by the same real estate actors who now blame government for the housing crisis.

Interestingly, there does seem to be a lot of investment capital available for other types of real estate projects in cities—for office towers, industrial parks, luxurious shopping malls, and high-rent apartment buildings. There seems to be capital available for mergers between large corporations and for large companies to buy up smaller companies. There seems to be capital available for certain profitable industrial and real estate investments in the Sunbelt.

There is a fundamental contradiction in capital investment in the United States. The basic needs of many people in cities for better housing, as well as for other needs such as better mass transit and health-care facilities, are not being met because not enough capital is being invested in these areas. Capital is being invested in huge quantities in corporate projects and mergers that may be profitable for powerful capitalists but which do not necessarily meet the fundamental, daily-life needs of millions of Americans.

This book is about those men (few are women) and those corporations that disproportionately shape and control industrial and real estate development in U.S. cities. This is a study of who makes the investment and industrial location decisions that determine which cities grow and which decline, as well as how, where, and when internal city development takes place. The corporate rich—the developers, builders, industrial and commercial executives, and construction companies—greatly determine the economic course of U.S. cities because they control many important investment decisions. Their decisions about plant and office locations, about building construction, and about residential housing shape our present and our future. This small minority is often more important than the democratic majority in shaping the prosperity or decline of cities.

This book is also about those Americans who have organized to protest patterns of development in our cities. When we live in a city long enough, the ways of doing things come to be seen as a practical necessity. But a growing number of Americans are questioning the established ways of doing things. They are suggesting that there must be basic changes in the way urban investment and development are carried out in the United States.

My Debts.   I am indebted to many insightful readers whose comments on various drafts of this book have made it a better book than it otherwise would have been, in particular Peter Dreier, Tony Orum, Bennett Harrison, Richard Walker, Jerry Jacobs, and Steve Worden. I would like to thank Claire Mc-Adams, Gideon Sjoberg, and Walter Firey for numerous discussions that have stimulated my thinking about urban real estate issues, from the earliest days of this project. I am greatly indebted to Clairece Booher Feagin for extensive typing assistance and general support.

1
CITIES IN CONFLICT

INTRODUCTION:
PLAYING MONOPOLY WITH REAL MONEY

Buying hotels. Mortgaging whole streets of houses. Buying and selling utilities. Paying taxes on a dozen houses. Buying entire blocks of urban land to secure a monopoly. Going bankrupt because of overextension in real estate. These actions are part of the real estate game played in every American city. How many Americans regularly play this game? Not many. The only place most Americans are able to play the urban real estate game is on the Monopoly board in living room encounters with their friends. The board game mimics the real world of real estate buying, selling, and development, but the parallels between Monopoly on the board and land monopoly in city streets are limited, for in the world of urban real estate there are real winners and real losers.

Class struggle is at the heart of the game of urban real estate. Recently the people of Santa Monica, California, voted out a city council long allied with developers, landlords, and corporate executives. They elected in their place a progressive council that seemed to be determined to break with the old business-oriented pattern of city politics. The new council rejected old policies favoring developers and took action to require development projects to meet community needs.

In U.S. cities the powerful elites that control urban development—the developers, bankers, industrial executives, and their political allies—have

1

built large development projects, not just the hotels and houses of the Monopoly game, but also shopping malls, office towers, and the like—with little or no input from local community residents. Developers have typically been able to win a string of favorable concessions from city officials: cheap land, tax abatements, and utility services subsidized by the general taxpayer. In many cities developers have threatened to go elsewhere if these subsidies are not provided. Yet in the early 1980s the Santa Monica city council was trying to change this way of doing city business and to force those seeking to build new office complexes and shopping centers to commit themselves to meeting certain important needs of local citizens. One city council agreement with a developer building a million-square-foot hotel-office complex specified that it must include landscaped park areas, a day-care center, major energy conservation measures, and a serious affirmative action plan for hiring and that it must also provide one hundred rental housing units in the project or in other buildings in return for city permits.[1]

Class conflict—developers and their allies versus citizens—has long been part of city dynamics. On the one side we have the progressive city councils and the urban grass-roots peoples' movements opposing unbridled growth and development. On the other side we have the class of profit-oriented developers, bankers, landowners, and industrial executives who buy, sell, and develop land and buildings in cities just like they do with other for-profit commodities.

Some powerful developers and bankers are becoming known to the public. There is, for example, Gerald D. Hines, a Houston engineer whose corporation is one of the nation's largest urban developers. Hines' company recently marked the laying of the foundation of a Republic Bank office complex in Houston with a lavish $35,000 reception for top business and government leaders; it included a brass ensemble playing fanfares, fine wine and cheeses, and other culinary delights. The massive building itself, red granite in a neo-Gothic style, is one of at least $2 billion worth of such office buildings, shopping malls, and other urban projects built by Hines' company in cities from New York to San Francisco. Older buildings may be leveled; new projects rise out of their ashes. Developers such as Hines have been a major force in making and remaking the face of American cities, particularly since World War II. Whether most local citizens desire such large-scale development, or in fact benefit from it, does not matter. The major U.S. developers often see their projects as the "cutting-edge of western civilization." Yet the sad irony is that these massive expenditures of capital for large-scale urban development, and such things as lavish towers and parties celebrating them, occur in cities like Houston with its severe urban problems (for instance, extreme poverty, subemployment, housing shortages, severe pollution), for whose solution little money allegedly can be found.[2]

Since the 1940s U.S. cities have exploded horizontally and vertically with thousands of large-scale developments built by developers and their associates. These projects dot the urban landscape—shopping centers, office towers, industrial parks, convention centers, and suburbs. The built environments of our cities have expanded to the point that their growing, and dying, pains have become serious national problems. Trillions of dollars have been invested in tearing down, constructing, and servicing the physical structures on urban landscapes.

Cities are human creations. They reflect human choices and decisions. But exactly who decides that our cities should be developed the way they are? Who decides that sprawling suburbs are the best way to house urbanities? Who decides to put workers in office towers that look like glassed-in cigar boxes standing on their sides? Who decides that shopping is best done in highly centralized shopping centers that look like upside-down ice cube trays? Who creates the mazes of buildings, highways, and open spaces? There is an old saying that "God made the country, but man made the town." Cities are indeed manmade environments. But *which* men and women made the cities? And why? Do all the people residing in cities contribute equally to their growth, development, and decline?

Traditionally most urban analysts and scholars have argued that everybody makes cities, that first and foremost the choices and decisions by large groups of consumers demanding housing and buildings lead to the distinctive ways cities are built. But this is not accurate. Ordinary people often play "second fiddle." In the first instance, capitalist developers, bankers, industrial executives, and their business and political allies build cities, although they often run into conflict with rank-and-file urbanites over their actions. Cities under capitalism are structured and built to maximize the profits of real estate capitalists and industrial corporations, not necessarily to provide decent and livable environments for all urban residents. Today's cities are, as we will document in this book, growth-oriented machines substantially designed for private profit making. The desires and needs of ordinary working people are often a secondary matter.

In U.S. society there are fundamental social divisions between capitalists and top managers, on the one hand, and ordinary blue-collar and white-collar workers on the other. Capitalists include those powerful property and development actors, such as Gerald Hines, who own and control office buildings, industrial factories, shopping centers, and the like—the places where work and consumption occur in this society. The great class of ordinary workers, both blue collar and white collar, low paid and well paid, sell their labor to the capitalists in return for wages and salaries. The renters who elected the previously mentioned Santa Monica city council are part of the class of rank-and-file working people. Between these major classes are managers, who have some control over the labor of others but do not make major investment decisions. These classes of Americans loom large in the ongoing drama of urban conflict.

CONVENTIONAL VIEWS OF CITY GROWTH AND DECLINE

Traditional analysts see urban space as a "neutral container" of buildings and streets designed to meet consumers' needs. In this view cities are impersonal creations generated by the actions of many more or less isolated individuals.

Government-supported Conventionalism.   Recently a federal government report, *Urban America in the Eighties*, publicly articulated the traditional view, not only for President Jimmy Carter, for whom it was designed, but also for the general public. Its conclusions were hotly debated—particularly those suggesting that the federal government should leave dying northern cities alone and should at most intervene to facilitate the move of workers from them to the booming cities of the Sunbelt. Some northern mayors cursed the report's conclusions, but many southern mayors were enthusiastic. Many northern officials were concerned about the report's conclusions, and national controversy was generated. But few disputed the report's basic assumptions about how cities grow or die.[3]

Prepared under the direction of prominent business and academic leaders, this report articulates the view of cities found in many conventional arguments: that cities are "less conscious creations" than "accumulations— the products of ongoing change." Choices by hundreds of thousands of individual actors are emphasized as shaping urban landscapes. Changes in cities, such as the rising prosperity of Sunbelt cities, reflect "nothing more than an aggregate of countless choices by and actions of individuals, families, and firms."[4] Here cities are seen as the unconscious creations of a free-market system, a system with thousands of individuals and firms buying and selling land and buildings for many private uses.

This land and building market is viewed as self-regulating; supposedly it efficiently and rationally allocates land uses and thus maximizes the overall benefits for everyone living in the cities. The hidden hand of the market and the capitalist system's alleged lack of intentional design receive heavy emphasis in this conventional perspective. In their policy-oriented conclusions the authors of *Urban America* pursued this "market knows best" logic to its obvious conclusion: Those impersonal individuals and firms actively working in cities and shaping urban space know best, and government officials should thus not intervene when their impersonal decisions lead to the decline of cities in the North. Growth in, and migration to, booming cities such as those in the Sunbelt should simply be recognized, and, at most, governments should only encourage workers to move from dying cities to booming cities. Critics of the *Urban America* report resisted this do-nothing approach to urban decline; yet most did not reject the individuals-and-firms-freely-competing-in-market view of the city.[5]

Wrongheaded Assumptions. Not only are the report's policy conclusions wrongheaded; the assumptions underlying this conventional perspective on cities are also wrong. One assumption here is that the interests of the individual and society are one. This view of land and job markets in cities is a version of neoclassical economic theory; it sees urban society as the "algebraic sum of the individuals...the sum of the interests of individuals."[6] Given a free-market system, urban consumers and business firms will buy and sell. "If consumers want certain goods they will demand them. Businessmen will sense this demand through the marketplace and seek to satisfy the consumers' wishes. Everyone is happy."[7] There is a basic faith in the rightness and efficiency of buying and selling in markets, including the urban land market. The idealistic competitive market idea, Lewis Mumford suggested, was taken over from earlier theologians: "the belief that a divine providence ruled over economic activity and ensured, so long as man did not presumptuously interfere, the maximum public good through the dispersed and unregulated efforts of every private, self-seeking individual.[8] And this conventional view implies that whatever exists as the geography of the urban landscape is fundamentally good for all concerned if it results from competitive market activity.

Related to the market assumption is the idea that individual urbanites are really more important than business and corporate decision makers in shaping urban patterns, because business actors mostly react to the demands of consumers. Thus power is said to reside in the self-seeking consumer. A major study has noted the function of the American business creed: "One way of shedding awkward responsibility is to believe that the consumer is the real boss."[9] In this prevailing business creed individual workers are seen as "voting" in the marketplace with their consumer choices: Cities have been created by ordinary Americans whose demands for such things as autos and single-family houses have forced developers, builders, and manufacturing corporations to respond. Over the last few decades prominent business leaders have argued that through their consumption choices "the masses of Americans have elected Henry Ford. They have elected General Motors. They have elected the General Electric Company, and Woolworth's and all the other great industrial and business leaders of the day."[10] Moreover, the assumption that workers and consumers are by nature individualistic and selfish leads to the view that only some type of capitalism will work as the form of societal organization.

Consumers are often seen as kings and queens when it comes to urban land use and development. The conventional view sees land use and development, both in central cities and in suburbs, as resulting from individual self-maximizing behavior in a market context. It assumes that no one agent (group or individual) has a determinate influence on the urban land system. Land economists such as William Alonso and Richard Muth have argued that urban commercial and residential land markets are determined by free competitive bidding. In these theories thousands of consumers, and by extension thousands of firms, are pictured as autonomous atoms, largely without social relations and conventions, who have a "taste" for commodities, one of which is more space and housing. As their incomes grow, they will seek more space. Conventional analysts offer this as an explanation of why cities grow and expand. Actors in this competitive bidding are recognized as having different interests, even different incomes, which affect the bidding process. However, the fact that a small group of the most powerful actors can do far more to shape the land and building markets than simply outbid their competitors is not seriously analyzed.[11]

The urban land and building market is an important feature of our capitalistic system. Its operation does shape the built environment of cities. But it is not a "free" or "natural" market. It is a captive whose rules are determined by the most powerful players in the game—the array of land-interested industry, finance, development, and construction capitalists. Individual consumers and their families seeking jobs and housing do make important decisions that shape cities, but for the most part these personal decisions are of secondary importance when measured against the prior and determining actions of the capitalistic producers, whose decisions concern such things as the location development projects, mortgage rates, and types of housing construction.

Business leaders frequently see themselves as dependent, as following the lead of consumers in building cities, but occasionally even they admit their own overarching significance. One recent article in a major real estate industry journal, *Buildings*, candidly noted that "the building industry has always played a major role in determining quality of life and social groupings, whether it's in the work sector or in the provision of adequate housing."[12]

Moreover, for influential defenders of capitalism such as Edward Bernays, the founder of modern public relations, "democracy" in fact means that ordinary people should follow the lead of their "betters," such as business leaders. Bernays once commented that "the conscious and intelligent manipulation of the organized habits and opinions of the masses is an important element in a democratic society.... We are governed, our minds are molded, our tastes formed, our ideas suggested, largely by men we have never heard of."[13] And for him this mind-and-taste manipulation is a **very** good thing, because it avoids democratic participation by ordinary workers and consumers.

POWERFUL ACTORS WHO MOLD CITIES

Limiting People's Choices. Powerful real estate actors such as D. M. Carothers, retired head of Allright Auto Parks, frequently seek what they call the "higher and better uses" for urban land, sometimes losing sight of older traditions of urban neighborhoods or the needs of smaller business tenants. For many the most important tradition to honor seems to be profit. As Carothers said to journalist Elizabeth Ashton recently: "In the growth of the city, you can't take care of old traditions." Long-term tenants, small-business people, or renters are only temporary tenants in this view. "They like to think of it as a heritage that has been passed on to them, but they're living in another century."[14] The city block Carothers had in mind is the site for one of the tallest office buildings west of the Mississippi, the Texas Commerce Tower in Houston. Smaller businesses were moved out in order to build the tower. Small businesses commonly lose out in the private urban renewal done by developers and their associates.

Allright Auto Parks has made money directly from fees off parking lots on cleared central-city land. In 1982 it had 1,600 parking lots in seventy cities; it owned 2.3 million square feet in thirty-nine downtown areas. But the parking lot revenues are not its only profitable aspect. "Banking" the land for "higher" uses is the goal, as Carothers has explained it:

> We were figuring how the property could, in effect, buy itself. If we could get the old buildings off it and begin to park the cars...would income be sufficient to meet the payments? And in the back of my mind was always this extra—this icing: the eventual control of real valuable property that could be turned for a higher and better use.[15]

Selling land has accounted for much of this parking lot company's income, as the parking lots are sold at good prices to developers and bankers who recycle the land. The plan is clear. Older buildings are cleared off, and the land is "banked" in the form of parking lots until a more profitable use is found for it. In central-city areas the more profitable use is usually an office tower, shopping mall, hotel, or high-rise parking garage.

A few hundred developers and financial institutions now construct and finance most major and many smaller urban development projects, from office parks and shopping malls to suburban subdivisions. Among the nation's dozen largest developers is Century Development Corporation, which, like Gerald D. Hines Interests, builds very large metropolitan projects. For example, Greenway Plaza, a major multiple-use development, involved the buying up of several hundred of single-family houses in several large residential subdivisions not far from downtown Houston. Century had real estate agents buy houses from the local residents. Once the homes had been acquired, the houses were moved or razed. There was apparently no organized citizen protest to this destruction of residential neighborhoods in a city with a serious housing shortage. However, in other cities citizens have protested such large-scale destruction of much-needed residential housing in central-city areas. Moreover, Greenway Plaza is of such a scale that it required financing from large insurance companies. The scale of modern city developments is frequently staggering.[16]

Residential developers have shaped U.S. housing patterns in fundamental ways. The famous Levitt and Sons firm is among the 2 percent of builders who have constructed the lion's share of residential housing since World War II. Using nonunion labor, Levitt and Sons pulled together in one corporation the various aspects of the house manufacturing and marketing process, from controlling the source of nails and lumber to marketing the finished houses.[17] Levittowns were built in cities on the East Coast. Levittown, New Jersey, was carefully planned so that the acreage was within one political jurisdiction. According to Herbert Gans the company executives had the boundaries of a nearby township changed so that it was not part of the area in which Levittown would be built, thus giving Levitt and Sons more political control. William Levitt was the key figure in the firm by this time, and he reportedly built his suburbs with little concern for the tastes of his potential customers. In a detailed analysis, Gans has noted that William Levitt was not especially "concerned about how to satisfy buyers and meet their aspirations. As the most successful builder in the East...he felt he knew what they wanted."[18] Earlier Levittowns had only one house type per neighborhood; in Levittown, New Jersey, three different models were provided, including pseudocolonial and pseudo-Cape Cod styles. Profitability was the basic standard; community-oriented features were accepted when they enhanced profit.

The shift to three models per neighborhood was apparently a reaction to critics who complained of the stifling homogeneity of the new suburban areas being created by developers. When this critique spread to the mass media, Levitt reportedly became worried about sales and decided to market the new Levittown in New Jersey more aggressively. Gans points out that the choice of the pseudocolonial design was made "not because of its popularity, but because they would help them attract higher-income purchasers."[19] No surveys of potential buyers were made to determine consumer preferences, but a great deal of attention was given to advertising, marketing, and selling the houses to consumers. Friendly salespeople were selected and trained by a professional speech teacher. Buyers who were viewed as "disreputable" were excluded; and blacks were excluded until the state government began to enforce a desegregation law. Moreover, once the developments were inhabited, Levitt executives were critical of local residents who complained about conditions.[20]

Corporations such as Allright Auto Parks, Gerald Hines Interests, Century Development Corporation, and Levitt and Sons are the urban actors with the power to shape the spread and decline of U.S, cities in fundamental ways. They have indeed created their own Monopoly game, played out in the real streets of urban America.

Efficient and Rational for Whom?   The choices made by top executives in these and other powerful land-oriented companies are dominant, but they are not necessarily efficient or desirable from the point of view of most city dwellers. Ordinary citizens more or less have to accept what is in fact built and available. James Lorimer has noted that in today's corporate cities "people may *feel* free to make their own decisions about how they will live, but in fact they are restricted by the limited number [of] choices offered by developers and planners."[21]

People are not coerced into using shopping centers, office towers, industrial parks, suburbs, high-rise apartment complexes; but so much of American life is centered in these places that it is hard for urbanites not to live out some, or much, of their lives in them. Often these developments provide the only realistic working, housing, and shopping choices. Other choices have disappeared (downtown shops run by small-business people) or are allowed to decay and disappear (older row-type housing). A major assumption of conventional theories is that the "most frequently chosen location is that which is most preferred." But what if an individual worker or family has no real choice? If there is only one option, or a limited range of options, no consumer preference is truly revealed. For example, if only a few housing (or working) facilities are in fact available, the lack of availability makes individual preferences less relevant. The "tastes" of individuals develop in a social context that is fundamentally shaped by a mode of production ruled by capitalists and top managers, one that involves not only the production of goods and services but also an intricate web of relations of unequal power and wealth.[22]

In this society the production of goods and services precedes consumption, but the two processes go hand in hand. The physical structure of production builds barriers and sets limits to individual choices. To a significant degree preferences are created and manipulated by powerful people working through advertising, public relations, and the mass media. The choices, of those with moderate incomes are far more restricted than those of the rich. The inequality of money resources limits choices also. Small businesses are destroyed as real estate investors and developers shove them aside and build office towers. Much of the suburbanization literature argues that middle-income Americans express their free choice for more housing space by moving to suburbia. The implication is that the poor choose and prefer central-city locations. But this is not necessarily true. However they may be arrived at, everyone's reasonable needs and preferences are not met in this class-structured society of ours. The urban poor and the urban rich can live in central cities, but only the latter have the incomes to choose to live in central cities. Rank-and-file individual and family actions in cities do not necessarily reflect their fundamental needs or preferences.[23]

LAND AS PROPERTY

There is a limited supply of urban land. Unlike other commodities that are bought and sold, the amount of land cannot generally be increased by human action. And land is a commodity whose control and use are disproportionately in the hands of the powerful.

Creating Profits. Land is the explicit concern of the urban real estate industry. Profit accrues as land changes hands. A building is constructed. Land and improvements to land thus become an active part of the capital accumulation process. Urban land is used by some capitalists as area upon which to build profit-making offices, warehouses, and factories.

Profit from industrial and commercial enterprises can be "banked" directly in land. A major feature of modern land development is this banking aspect. Land and buildings are always important investments, but when economic growth slows in other industrial sectors, increased capital may flow to real estate. In this society both the land itself and the built environment on it become items just like other commodities, such as automobiles or refrigerators, which are developed and created with profitable sale as the objective. Yet there are differences. Real estate development at one point in time can become a barrier to real estate development later on. Buildings are relatively permanent commodities; they are fixed investments. New urban developments sometimes must be built at less valuable locations because the capital invested in already existing buildings cannot be easily abandoned.[24]

Private Property. The powerful people who buy, sell, and develop large blocks of urban land can do so because of a legal system, which protects their propertied interests. Essential to the maintenance of inequality in land decision making is the legal protection of highly individualized property ownership.

The rights of private property give owners a great deal of control over land and buildings. Within broad limits land can be developed, and buildings constructed, as owners see fit.

The unbridled use of private property has not always been predominant in the U.S. The Puritans, for example, had highly planned towns from Maine to Long Island. For two generations Puritan towns were planned by pioneer folk whose strong religious values influenced the lay out of urban areas. The private control of property was not central; communal and collective goals overrode private interests. But group-centered, folk-religious planning soon gave way to intensified private landholding, even in New England. Fee-simple (unrestricted transfer) ownership of land became central to the expanding capitalistic market system of eighteenth-century America. Early immigrants from Europe were generally hostile to landlords and vigorously sought to own their own land. Ownership of even a small piece of property was a sign of independence from landlords; many immigrants had come to the new American colonies to escape oppressive European landlords. Land was seen as a civil right in a nation with many small farmers.[25]

Yet this early and heavy commitment to the sacredness of privately held property had a major negative effect on development once the United States was no longer primarily a land of small farmers. By the early decades of the nineteenth century, there were fewer landholders and ever more tenants. In many cases, the growing number of Americans without property were seen as unworthy. Yet the heavy commitment to private property, on the part of both propertied and propertyless Americans, continued to legitimate the private disposal of property by powerful landowning factions. As a result, over the last two centuries control over urban land development has become concentrated in banks, insurance firms, development corporations, and industrial companies.[26]

There are major social costs for a system that gives owners of large amounts of land the right to use the land more or less as they see fit. Those who build large projects on central-city land have shown that they can shove certain social costs onto other people nearby. A good example is the modern skyscraper with its mirrored glass walls, which often generate heat problems for nearby buildings, and with its thousands of workers whose egress in the evenings can create massive traffic jams. These social costs of skyscraper development usually are not paid for by the developers and owners of the buildings. Private control of property, particularly of large blocks of land and development projects, can create enormous urban social problems that cannot be solved without violating the long-established right of private property owners to dispose of property as they see fit.

NAMING THE CORPORATE PRODUCERS

If ordinary individuals and families play a secondary or opposing part in the decisions shaping cities, who plays the primary part? The primary decision makers are the capitalistic producers, the key actors in the real estate industry. Today real estate capitalism is organized around a complicated network of entrepreneurs and corporations of varying sizes and functions.

Private and Public Decisions. An approximation of the size and complexity of the urban development industry can be gauged from Exhibit 1, which lists real estate producers and associated government actors.* The categories refer to sets of major decisions that are critical to urban development projects.[27]

EXHIBIT 1 Urban Development: Decision Categories and Corporate Actors

Private Actors

1. Industrial and commercial location decisions
   Industrial companies (including service industries)
   Commercial companies

2. Development decisions
   Development companies (developers)
   Land speculators
   Landlords and landowners

3. Financial decisions
   Commercial banks (including trust and pension funds)
   Savings and loan associations
   Insurance companies
   Mortgage companies
   Real estate investment trusts

4. Construction decisions
   Architectural and engineering firms
   Construction companies (contractors)

5. Support decisions
   Chambers of commerce
   Real estate brokers
   Leasing and management companies

(continued)

---

*In this book the term *corporation* will be used for the various organizational arrangements (including partnerships) capitalists utilize in profit making, whether or not they are legally incorporated.

1. Utility services, building code, zoning, tax decisions
   City councils
   County officials
   Zoning and planning commissions

2. Subsidized housing and urban redevelopment decisions
   U.S. Department of Housing and Urban Development (HUD)
   Local and state government agencies

Looking at the private sector, we see that Category 1 encompasses those corporations whose location decisions (for example, northern or Sunbelt city) often set the other actors into motion. Category 2 covers the developers, land speculators, and landowners who buy, package, and develop land for use by industrial corporations and others. Category 3 encompasses those financial corporations that make the loans for construction and land purchase. Category 4 includes the various design and construction actors who build urban projects. Category 5 covers a variety of supporting actors.

Such a listing can be somewhat misleading. In the first place, one modern corporation often includes within itself a development subdivision, which not only develops projects but also engages in land speculation; a real estate brokerage subsidiary; and an architectural subsidiary. Or a major insurance company may have a financial department as well as its own urban land development subsidiary. Large vertically integrated companies are involved in major decisions in more than one category in Exhibit 1.

Second, there is the issue of scale and region. Local developers, realtors, and bankers are critical decision makers in land development; studies of community decision makers show clearly the role and power of local business people in all types of cities in the North and South.[28] However, major real estate decisions are made not only by powerful local real estate companies but also by powerful regional and national companies, which also determine the shape of U.S. cities. There are complex interconnections between powerful interests external to cities and those that are part of the internal power structure of a particular city. An example would be a major insurance company, such as Prudential Life Insurance Company, which in connection with other local and national companies finances and owns real estate and development projects in many cities across the United States. There is indeed a complex urban puzzle lying behind the development and ownership of the modern city.

Close Ties: Business and Government.   There are the close ties between developers and government. Government plays a critical support role. For

14

example, a Dallas mayor was recently quoted in the *Wall Street Journal:* "The system probably works better when a poor man is not in office." A major local developer, this mayor may have had in mind the working of the urban property and development system. When he was Dallas mayor, he was also a president, vice-president, partner, manager, or board member of many businesses. Many American cities have been directly governed by individuals with real estate or banking interests that are fostered by the decisions they make as government officials. Moreover, government officials without direct development connections make decisions supportive of the urban development industry.[29]

In the United States real estate capitalism has not been able to supply all the conditions for its profitable existence. Much government activity has developed substantially because of the continuing problems of capitalism, including the constant need for new capital and the persisting class conflict between capitalists and workers. Local and federal governments help provide an aid system (including urban renewal and special development loans) to facilitate profit making in urban development. Governments subsidize by means of taxes the services, such as roads, sewers, and utilities, critical to urban development. Urban land is valuable because it is usually not raw but "serviced." Human labor has been expended on it. Services are usually provided by governments out of ordinary people's taxes. Thus much urban land has taxpayer-subsidized features, which add to its value as a marketed commodity.

The U.S. market system often leads away from profitability in land use; early capitalist cities had a freer land market and little government regulation but also severe water, sanitation, garbage, utility, and related problems, which hurt land development. Supportive government intervention brought greater profitability back into urban real estate patterns. Inefficiency, pollution, and congestion in cities increase as capitalists and their minions seek the locations that maximize profits; so government, again and again, is pressured to intervene.[30]

OPPOSING DEVELOPERS: PEOPLE'S MOVEMENTS

Unlike the game of Monopoly, the game of urban real estate has its countervailing forces—people's movements that periodically force developers and governments to make concessions and changes in their plans. Well-organized groups of workers and consumers can sometimes make a difference in patterns of urban development.

This chapter opened with the dramatic example of well-organized worker-renters in Santa Monica, California, who threw out a developer-oriented city council and replaced it with a council seeking to restrict developers to projects meeting at least some community needs. Other people's movements have also pressed for changes in urban development projects. Portions of many major expressway projects in cities such as Boston, New York, Philadelphia, and Washington have generated organized citizen protest. In the early 1970s local and state governments in Massachusetts rejected certain long-planned expressways in the Boston area and committed the state to spend $2 billion on mass transit because of organized citizen protest. Intense opposition to urban redevelopment projects has come from a variety of people's organizations in cities from Seattle to Boston. In Washington, D.C., the Capital East Community Organization and the Adams-Morgan Community Organization joined together to fight speculative real estate development; these citizens' groups pressured the city council to pass a bill called the Real Estate Transaction Tax, which would restrict speculative buying and selling.

There have been numerous attempts, and a few successes, by citizens' groups seeking to stop large mall developments. One was in Burlington, Vermont, where the citizens fought on environmental grounds against a nearby mall to be built by a major shopping center corporation. Citizens protested against the traffic congestion and accelerated decline of the downtown area that the new mall would bring. In Hadley, Massachusetts, another citizens' group took on a national mall development corporation. At issue were the questionable need for another mall in this small town and the air, water, soil, and traffic problems that a mall would create. In recent years renters' and tenants' movements have grown up, protesting condominium conversions by developers, the lack of development of moderate-rent housing, and the ever-rising rents that the now short supply of housing seems to generate. Rapid growth in tenants' organizations can be seen in states like New Jersey, where they began in earnest in the 1960s. By the 1970s the New Jersey Tenants' Organization had organized many large-scale rent strikes. A majority of the strikes were effective in reducing rent levels and improving apartment conditions.

CONCLUSION:
PUBLIC BALANCE SHEETS?

In this chapter we have examined conventional perspectives on urban land use and development and have seen them to be substantially grounded in major assumptions of conventional (neoclassical) economics. These perspectives put heavy emphasis on a "free" land and property market, on private property, on efficient land use, and on the benefits that markets in land allegedly bring to all urbanites. But the realities are not what these perspectives suggest. There are no free competitive markets in cities, because land purchase and development is disproportionately controlled, if not monopolized, by powerful capitalistic agents and interests. Real estate capitalism shapes the major development projects in cities—the shopping centers, suburbs, industrial parks, office towers, and apartment complexes. Once the decisions of the powerful are made, smaller-scale builders often build around the larger-scale projects. Consumers choose within the limits provided. Worker-consumers must endure the many social costs of this capitalistic development system, which have been enormous.

But class struggle is also at the heart of capitalist cities. Some of those in people's movements have suggested new ways of looking closely at the *social* costs of private development. One of their tools is the *public balance sheet*, simply a way of tallying up, as David Smith puts it, the "tangible, measurable, quantifiable costs being imposed on citizens individually and collectively by the actions of the private sector."[31] The social costs, the social inefficiencies, of urban development take a variety of forms: a shortage of rental housing at reasonable rents, displaced families without suitable housing alternatives, racial segregation, added tax costs for rank-and-file taxpayers because of local development bonds, traffic congestion and air pollution, and highly constrained choices for consumers because of developer decisions about what housing will or will not be built. As we will see in detail in the last chapter, Smith and others have argued that these social costs of private enterprise should be calculated, and factored into the overall costs of urban development projects. Progressive people's movements in cities today are pressuring developers to compensate communities for the broader community costs that urban development creates.

NOTES

1. This discussion is based on copies of developer-council agreements in author's files. See also Dave Lindorff, "About-Face in Santa Monica," *Village Voice*, December 2-8, 1981, p. 20.
2. "The Master Builder," *Newsweek*, August 31, 1981, p. 45; Joe R. Feagin, "Sunbelt Metropolis and Development Capital," in *Sunbelt/Snowbelt: Urban Growth and Restructuring*, edited by Larry Sawers and William Tabb (Oxford University Press, forthcoming, 1983).
3. President's Commission for a National Agenda for the Eighties, Panel on Policies and Prospects, *Urban America in the Eighties: Perspectives and Prospects* (Washington, D.C.: U.S. Government Printing Office, 1980).

4. Ibid., pp. 12, 104.

5. Shoukry T. Roweis and Allen J. Scott, "The Urban Land Question," in *Urbanization and Conflict in Market Societies*, edited by Kevin R. Cox (Chicago: Maaroufa Press, 1978), pp. 46-47.

6. Quoted in Stephen E. Harris, *The Death of Capital* (New York: Pantheon Books, 1977), p. 64.

7. Ibid., p. 65.

8. Lewis Mumford, *The City in History* (New York: Harcourt, Brace and World, 1961), p. 452.

9. Francis X. Sutton et al., *The American Business Creed* (Cambridge: Harvard University Press, 1956), pp. 361-362.

10. Edward A. Filene, *Successful Living in the Machine Age* (New York: Simon and Schuster, 1932), p. 98. This is quoted in Stuart Ewen, *Captains of Consciousness* (New York: McGraw-Hill, 1976), p. 92.

11. William Alonso, *Location and Land Use* (Cambridge: Harvard University Press, 1964); Richard Muth, *Cities and Housing* (Chicago: University of Chicago Press, 1969); Richard A. Walker, "The Transformation of Urban Structure in the Nineteenth Century and the Beginning of Suburbanization," *Urbanization and Conflict in Market Societies*, pp. 165-212.

12. Lillie Mikesell, "Challenges of the New Community," *Buildings* 74 (January, 1980), p. 47.

13. Edward L. Bernays, *Propaganda* (New York, 1928), p. 9, as quoted in Ewen, *Captains of Consciousness*, p. 93.

14. Elizabeth Ashton, "Houston's Doctor of Urban Decay," *Texas Business Review*, March, 1982, p. 53.

15. Ibid., p. 52.

16. Century Development Corporation, Greenway Plaza brochures and fact sheets, in author's files; interview with senior research official, Rice Center, Houston, Texas, May, 1981.

17. Herbert Gans, *The Levittowners* (New York: Random House, 1967).

18. Ibid., p. 6.

19. Ibid., p. 11.

20. Ibid., pp. 5-13.

21. James Lorimer, *The Developers* (Toronto: James Lorimer and Co., 1978), p. 220.

22. Eric S. Sheppard, "The Ideology of Spatial Choice," in *Papers of the Regional Science Association*, edited by Morgan D. Thomas, vol. 45 (1980), p. 206.

23. Ibid., pp. 206-297.

24. Leonard Downie, *Mortgage on America*, (New York: Praeger, 1974), pp. 6-7; Maria B. Nofal, "Fixed Capital in the Built Environment," paper presented to Conference on New Perspectives on Urban Political Economy, Washington, D.C., American University, May, 1981, pp. 6-7; cf. C. P. Bradford and L. S. Rubinowitz, "The Urban-Suburban Investment-Divestment Process: Consequences for Older Neighborhoods," *Annals of the American Academy of Political and Social Science* 422 (November, 1975), p. 79.

25. Sam Bass Warner, *The Urban Wilderness* (New York: Harper and Row, 1972), pp. 16-17. See also pp. 8-18.

26. Ibid., p. 18.

27. An earlier version of this exhibit appeared in D. Claire McAdams and Joe R. Feagin, "A Power Conflict Approach to Urban Land Use," Austin, Texas, University of Texas, unpublished monograph, 1980. I have also been influenced here by D. Claire McAdams, "Powerful Actors in Public Land Use Decision Making Processes" (unpublished Ph.D. dissertation, University of Texas, 1979), chaps. 1-3.

28. John Walton, "A Systematic Survey of Community Power Research," in *The Structure of Community Power,* edited by Michael Aiken and Paul Mott (New York: Random House, 1970), pp. 443-464.

29. John Fullinwider, "Dallas: The City with No Limits," *In These Times,* December 17-23, 1980, p. 13.

30. Roweis and Scott, "The Urban Land Question," pp. 57-63.

31. David Smith, *The Public Balance Sheet: A New Tool for Evaluating Economic Choices* (Washington, D.C.: Conference on Alternative State and Local Policies, 1979), p. 2.

2
"WE HAVE TO CLOSE THIS PLANT": CORPORATE LOCATION DECISIONS

CAPITAL FLIGHT

GE CLOSES PLANT IN LOS ANGELES. THOUSANDS OF WORKERS AFFECTED. FORD PLANT CLOSING, THOUSANDS UNEMPLOYED. AUTOMAKER BLAMES HIGH COSTS, MOVING TO MEXICO. AREA ECONOMY DEPRESSED BY TEXTILE COMPANY LAYOFFS. NEW ENGLAND TOOLMAKING COMPANY MOVES TO SOUTH CAROLINA. STATE GOVERNMENT TO REDUCE TAXES TO KEEP INDUSTRIES FROM MOVING SOUTH.

Headlines such as these are regularly repeated in newspapers across the nation. All regions and most cities have been affected by a company closing down a facility. According to recent estimates, between 1970 and 1980 alone, 32 million jobs were lost because of plant, store, and office closings; another six million jobs were lost because of permanent cutbacks short of closure. Many areas have experienced shutdowns and lost jobs. This is part of a disinvestment process being aggressively carried out by the leaders of American capitalism. Some areas are actually losing plants, called runaway plants, to other areas. But in many cases plants, offices, and stores are closed in one area and the investment capital is moved elsewhere—to the Sunbelt or Third World countries. In the 1970s twelve states lost more jobs from closings than were added by new businesses starting up. Capital flight from one city to another or from the United States to overseas can be part of a broad corporate plan to run from

20

taxes, or to find cheaper land, or to find cheaper and less militant workers. The withdrawal of capital from an area has often been the work of large firms. In a New England study, Barry Bluestone, Bennett Harrison, and Lawrence Baker found that large companies were responsible for half of the jobs lost in that area by plant closings between 1969 and 1976. Such a withdrawal has disrupted communities, cost workers their homes, increased health problems, and remade the face of the industrial heartland of America.[1]

This scenario recurs in the United States. In the fall of 1979, U.S. Steel closed down operations in Youngstown, Ohio—with 3,500 jobs lost. In the spring of 1980, Ford closed its Pico Rivera plant in Los Angeles—with 2,000 jobs lost. In the winter of 1982, General Electric laid off hundreds of workers at its Ontario, California, metal iron plant. That corporation's capital is being reportedly invested in plants in Singapore, Brazil, and Mexico—areas with much lower wages. The Ontario plant was profitable, but in the corporate view not profitable enough. In the spring of 1982 it was announced that the famous Seth Thomas clock factory, resident in Thomaston, Connecticut, for more than 160 years, would be moving its operations to Atlanta, Georgia. The president of General Time, Inc., the parent company that owns the factory, was quoted to the effect that relocation to Georgia would mean lower operating costs. As a result, most of the plant's 175 workers will lose their jobs.[2]

Milking Plants. A major example of corporate relocation was the closing of a large steel plant in Campbell, Ohio. In 1969 this profitable Youngstown Sheet and Tube Company plant was bought by Lykes Corporation, a large conglomerate. Before its sale to Lykes, the plant had received millions in annual investment, but Lykes reportedly dropped the investment substantially, allowing the quality of the facilities to deteriorate. Apparently Lykes used the profits from the Ohio plant to pay off other debts and to buy non-steel companies. After eight years most of the Campbell facility was closed as unprofitable. Many conglomerates buy up profitable companies and slowly "milk" them for capital to be used for other investments. Local workers and communities pay a heavy price for this disinvestment. In the Campbell case the local community lost millions of dollars in tax revenues and even had to borrow money to run its schools. In addition, 4,900 jobs were lost. The total social cost of the death of this plant has been estimated at $72 million over the first few years in terms of increased welfare and food stamp costs, related governmental expenditures, and lost taxes to government. Ripple effects, including the loss of thousands of jobs in other local businesses, could be seen across the area.[3]

Human and Social Costs.   A conventional business perspective on plant or capital relocation from one area of a city to another or from northern cities to southern cities suggests that unregulated corporate mobility is necessary for the health of the U.S. economy. Capital must be free to move. Corporate executives do not wish governments to intervene, except to facilitate capital mobility with tax incentives and other subsidies. They see no harm coming to working people from unrestrained capital mobility. Some even suggest that working people should simply follow corporations wherever they or their capital go. New jobs may, or may not, be created in abandoned areas.

The United States is the only advanced industrial nation that allows this mobility for corporate enterprises. Western European nations, for example, limit the ability of corporations to move plants and offices; governmental permission is usually required.

Corporate flight from one U.S. city to another is not just a matter of money. It involves serious social costs: broken lives for working people, who lose jobs and livelihoods as well as homes and their consumer goods. Whole cities, such as Youngstown, Ohio, become economically depressed when companies leave. There are no longer enough firms and people to pay taxes for good schools and city services. People who are permanently laid off, particularly older workers, can have great difficulty in finding new jobs. Corporate flight and plant closings have ripple effects across the faces of cities. Taxes decrease because companies leave and unemployed workers pay fewer taxes. Money for urban services is reduced. Police officers and fire fighters are laid off. Local small businesses, grocery stores, taverns, gas stations go bankrupt. Downtown shopping areas become ghost towns, with many stores boarded up. Cities are left to die.[4]

A union song written by Karl Jenkins signals the troubles that corporate mobility generates for American workers.

> *The corporation bosses with bloody arrogance*
> *Say "profits aren't high enough,*
> *We have to close this plant.*
> *We're moving to a town where we won't have*
> *   to pay these rates,*
> *We're moving our factory to a non-union state."*

We heard about the closing on the company bulletin board.
They gave us two weeks notice, said "pack your things and go.
We'll try to find a job for you in another of our plants."
But with layoffs all across the land — we've got one
hell of a chance.

Some been working here for thirty years, some been working
here for less,
What have we got to show for it but our life that's now a mess.
What about our families, our homes, our bills, our car?
The unemployment payments aren't going very far.[5]

Anger and pain are clearly evident here.

THE WORLD AS A MONOPOLY BOARD: LOCATING FIRMS FOR PROFIT

Conventional Views.   There is an extensive economics and business literature on how companies make location decisions. This literature is highly
technical, but its assumptions are simple. Location decisions hinge on profitability. One of the founding fathers of industrial "location theory," August
Lösch suggested that industries should locate at the point of maximum
profits, where the total income exceeds total costs by the greatest amount.
Cutting costs is a critical aspect of location decisions.[6]

More recently, Melvin Greenhut has traced out the conventional
business view of location decisions and listed major factors that influence
decisions.

1. Cost factors at the location: transportation costs, extent of unionization, wage
   costs, taxation
2. Demand factors at the location: extent of competition by other firms
3. Cost-reducing factors: cities that specialize in one type of industry (presumably
   including governmental subsidies)
4. Revenue-increasing factors: areas that especially need the product made
5. Personal interaction factors: advantages from interaction with other companies
   and executives[7]

Conventional location analysts see a huge market of smaller autonomous
companies competing with one another for space. Their model is one of
smaller companies, no one of which has coercive or dominant market power.

But this is the major error in the assumptions of these analyses. The cost and profit factors they identify are generally accurate, but the theories ignore the rise of large companies *(monopoly capitalism)* and, most dramatically, neglect the social and human costs of corporate location decisions.

Big Capital and Little Capital.   The rise of big corporations has changed corporate location and capital mobility decisions significantly. Big companies, such as a manufacturing corporation, can more easily abandon a community and reduce wage or materials costs by moving than smaller companies.

Before 1880 most capitalist companies were small. By the early 1900s mergers of companies were creating giant corporations, first in the oil, steel, and grain industries, later in the auto industry. In 1901 U.S. Steel, a company formed from mergers, already controlled $1.4 billion in the form of hundreds of industrial plants. Decentralized capitalism was on the decline. Industrial concentration was the trend. And the trend continues today. Every week newspapers detail mergers of corporations, which create ever greater concentration and centralization of wealth in many industries. Today only 500 companies control 80 percent of all the manufacturing plants and related assets in the United States. This means economic and political dominance for larger companies.[8]

Location decision making is shaped by the size of a corporation and its access to capital. Many large companies have the internal profit-generated funds to expand and relocate without borrowing a great deal; large corporations can use their credit worthiness to secure capital from lenders for new development projects. Large size gives corporations the ability to plan and build long-term projects; and large size enables companies to separate their operations spatially with greater ease because such companies have the resources to reintegrate operations using transportation and communication networks, even across wide areas of the United States or the world. Many firms have put part of all of their administrative operations in office towers in downtown areas of cities such as New York, Chicago, San Francisco, and Houston; they have placed research and development facilities in suburban rings or regional cities; they have located their manufacturing operations in dispersed areas, including Sunbelt cities, suburban or rural areas, or towns and cities in Latin America or Asia.

Large-scale building projects in U.S. cities reflect a dispersion of corporate functions. Industrial parks house the manufacturing facilities of large corporations and related smaller companies. Office towers contain managerial and information (for instance, computerized accounting) processing; they have thus become the administrative centers for corporations. Shopping centers are filled with retail corporations, which sell the products of the manufacturing firms. Downtown office tower development exploded only when corporations became large enough to separate their administrative and production operations. Sometimes downtown development is explained in terms of the need of businesspeople to have much face-to-face contact. But ˌˌˌ business need ˌ existed well *before* downtown skyscrapers began to iˌˌˌ dramatically ˌ numbers. It was not until the 1910-1925 period thaˌ ˌˌˌ national corporaˌˌˌˌs could afford to separate administrative heaˌˌˌˌ ˌˌˌˌˌˌˌˌ ˌˌˌˌˌˌˌˌˌˌ fˌˌcilities.[9]

ˌˌˌˌ ˌˌˌˌˌˌˌˌˌˌˌˌ ˌˌe often built by development and construc-
tioˌˌ ˌˌˌˌ ˌˌˌˌˌˌˌˌ ˌˌˌˌˌˌ ˌˌˌment buildings, to house those who work
forˌ ˌˌˌˌˌ ˌˌˌˌˌˌˌˌˌˌˌ ˌˌˌ ˌˌˌˌ ˌˌaller businesses dependent on them. Today's
citˌˌˌ ˌˌ ˌˌˌˌ ˌˌˌˌˌˌ ˌˌˌ ˌˌˌˌˌˌˌnt functional components of national and
muˌ ˌˌˌˌˌˌˌˌˌˌ ˌˌˌˌˌˌˌˌˌˌˌˌ ˌˌ ˌˌhe geographical layout and location of deˌ
veˌˌˌˌˌˌˌˌˌˌ ˌˌˌˌˌˌˌˌ ˌˌˌˌˌˌˌˌ ˌffice towers, industrial buildings and parks,
anˌ ˌˌˌˌˌˌˌˌ ˌˌˌˌˌˌˌˌ

ˌˌˌ ˌˌˌ ˌˌˌˌ ˌˌˌˌ ˌˌˌˌ ˌˌˌˌˌˌˌ ˌˌpact of urban development and corporate
loˌˌˌˌˌˌ ˌˌˌˌˌˌˌˌˌˌˌˌ ˌˌˌˌˌˌˌrs and workers. Large-scale investments gen-
erˌˌˌˌˌ ˌˌ ˌˌˌˌ ˌˌˌˌˌˌ ˌˌˌˌ ˌˌˌut in fact lead and shape the movements of
coˌˌˌˌˌˌˌˌˌ ˌˌˌ ˌˌˌˌˌˌˌˌˌˌ ˌˌe are what Michael Smith calls "mobility-
inˌˌˌˌˌˌ ˌˌˌˌˌˌˌ ˌˌˌ ˌˌˌ ˌˌ ˌovement of industry and shopping facilities
toˌ ˌˌˌˌˌˌˌ ˌˌ ˌˌˌˌ ˌˌˌˌˌ ˌˌas a significant effect on workers, consumers,
aˌˌ ˌˌˌˌˌ ˌˌˌˌˌˌˌ ˌˌˌˌˌˌ ˌˌey must move. And downtown business and
reˌˌˌˌ ˌˌˌˌˌˌˌ ˌˌˌˌ ˌˌˌˌ may decline as a result.[10]
sˌˌˌˌ ˌˌˌˌˌ ˌˌˌˌˌˌˌˌˌ ˌˌ by large companies shape the decisions of
sˌˌˌˌˌ ˌˌˌˌˌ ˌˌˌˌˌˌˌˌˌ ˌˌ hem. For example, the location of major oil
aˌˌˌ ˌˌˌ ˌˌˌˌˌˌˌˌ ˌˌˌˌˌˌ cities such as Houston has brought thousands
cˌ ˌˌˌˌˌ ˌˌˌˌˌˌˌ ˌˌˌ ˌˌˌl companies and smaller oil companies, law
fˌˌˌˌ ˌˌˌ ˌˌˌˌˌˌˌˌˌ ˌˌˌˌ ˌo locations nearby. And many retail (for in-
sˌˌˌˌˌ ˌˌˌˌˌˌˌˌˌ ˌˌˌˌˌˌˌˌ ˌave located there to serve the thousands of
ˌˌˌˌˌˌ ˌˌˌ ˌˌˌˌˌˌˌ.

ˌˌˌˌˌ ˌˌˌˌ ˌˌˌ ˌˌˌˌˌˌˌ *Philanthropy?*   In recent decades many companies have decided to locate their manufacturing and other operations in the "better business climate" of outlying suburbs or in Sunbelt areas. They cite strong unions and expensive (in tax dollars) city services as problems for doing business profitably in central cities. This view may not be shared by ordinary working people, who see worker organizations such as unions as a way to protect themselves from greater employer exploitation.

Traditional social scientists view the suburbanization of industries as both normal and good.

> Directed by the sixth sense of profit, entrepreneurs of blue-collar industries have sought alternative, more cost-effective sites in the suburbs, exurbs, and nonmetropolitan areas which are far better suited to today's advanced transportation and production technologies and which avoid what have become serious negative externalities of inner-city locations.[11]

Here is a sign of the corporation-biased assumptions that underlie much contemporary urban analysis. Profit is described as a unique human sense, a "sixth sense," which drives entrepreneurs to avoid the "negative externalities" (that is, the human problems) of inner-city locations. What is really being said is that owners and top executives follow the profit logic of a capitalistic system; this system's rules of profitability dictate that the needs of working people in cities for such things as decent-paying jobs be more or less ignored in the never-ending quest for expansion of the profit rate.

A survey by the Fantus Company, a firm providing major location assistance to industrial corporations, found that *only* 112 of 700 companies would even consider building a plant in or near poverty areas in cities. These firms would not build in such locations without the following conditions:

1. A large docile labor pool
2. Lack of well-organized opposition from unions and community groups
3. Ample land and adequate utilities and roads
4. Lower taxes
5. Absence of massive housing deterioration
6. Government-subsidized training programs and services

The Fantus report summed it up: "These companies are interested in good publicity and profits. None of them indicated any interest in philanthropy."[12]

Do Regulations Hurt?   Government red tape and regulations, including environmental standards, are not major considerations in most company decisions about plant and office locations inside and outside cities. Even though corporate officials complain about regulations, they generally do *not* cite these as the significant factors affecting their siting of new plants and offices. Moreover, many government regulations reflect a compromise between the interests of businesses and local citizens' pressures.

Unless citizens mobilize and organize to protest, the routine behavior of most government officials is to enforce local regulations to the degree that business leaders will accept. Variations from zoning laws protecting residential areas from commercial development are granted; environmental reports are filed and ignored; development permits are granted without the studies required by law. Unless local citizens protest, property development interests in cities get much of what they want. For example, in the late 1970s Dow Chemical Company dropped its plan to build a half-billion-dollar petrochemical plant on the metropolitan fringe of San Francisco because a coalition of community groups, a labor union, and environmental groups threatened lawsuits and forced officials to enforce local environmental laws, which Dow decided would be too costly to obey. Still, this corporate retreat may be an exception, because of the lack of citizen protest in other cities. For the most part, government regulations seem to have a minor effect on corporate location decisions.[13]

USING UP CITIES AND MOVIN' ON: UNEVEN URBAN DEVELOPMENT

Cities grow and die largely in response to the needs of capitalism. Cities are old inventions, but their character and existence have always reflected the choices of powerful decision makers. Over the last century those decision makers have been corporate owners and top executives. Regional "flights" are only one type of corporate location decision. Where corporate executives decide to locate their production and distribution facilities, directly or indirectly, affects the lives of most Americans, whether the choices involve locating a new facility in a suburb, deciding on a downtown location for an office tower, or moving investments from northern cities to the Sunbelt.

Waves of Urban Growth. Large corporations have sought out the most favorable places for their operations — the central cities of large metropolitan areas. By the 1920s metropolitan cities dominated most states, even though a majority of the population lived outside them. Virtually all industrial production was located in factories in the top twenty-five metropolitan areas; New York City, Chicago, Philadelphia, Cincinnati, Pittsburgh, and Milwaukee were the dominant manufacturing areas. Many cities were specialized centers. Albany made shirts; Troy, shirt collars; New Bedford and Fall River, textiles; Waltham, watches; Bridgeport, furniture; Dayton, cash registers; Detroit, automobiles. These centers in turn attracted skilled and unskilled American workers.[14]

Typically, a few key industries are at the heart of each successive epoch of industrial growth. Usually the location decision of any one company does not give a city its characteristic industrial structure—rather, the set of decisions made by several, dozens, or hundreds of companies are involved. In each distinctive period of U.S. industrial growth older industries, such as steel or automobile production, do not necessarily die out. They are just less dominant. And each new wave, such as today's computer and electronics industries, is reflected in distinctive urban development.[15]

However, there can be inertia in the urban environment. Iron and steel industries, for example, have been highly localized; in the 1920-1960 period most steel was made in the areas around Pittsburgh, Cleveland, Detroit, Youngstown, and Chicago. There has been a slow shift westward in steel-making, reflecting western demand for steel and new sources of ore and coal. But this shift has been gradual. The high cost of fixed capital equipment, of land and buildings, can shape locational decisions and enforce stability for a long period of time.[16]

New industries frequently locate in new cities, such as electronics in Sunbelt cities. Older cities may continue as before or they may stagnate and die, as Detroit seems to be doing. Some older cities may capture part of the newer industries; yet others may actually lose their industries, as when New England towns lost their textile factories to southern cities. Older cities tend to give way to the dominance of newer cities.

Designing Cities for Worker Control.   David Gordon has noted that U.S. cities have been shaped by the changing character of capitalism in three periods: commercial capitalism (1750-1850), industrial-competitive capitalism (1850-1900), and monopoly capitalism (1900-). The cities that grew dramatically in each of these periods tended to be of different kinds. In the commercial period merchants' activities generated and influenced cities; ports became major cities as trade expanded. New York became the dominant commercial metropolis. Central cities were diversified in terms of income, but poorer workers generally lived outside the central areas. Merchants engaged in land speculation; the lot-and-block grid system across many cities was first implemented by these early land speculators.[17]

Later, from 1850 to 1900 industrial capitalism and the factory system dominated city structure. Factories required large numbers of wage laborers, so it is not surprising that the crowded central cities became centers of industrial capitalism. Traditional discussions of capitalistic location have emphasized that transportation and communication efficiency and access to other companies are among the most important factors in city location. But these industrial cities grew well beyond the point where transportation and access were efficient. Cities became greatly congested. Gordon suggests that a primary concern of capitalists was labor control, that is, keeping cheap workers available in large numbers. The impersonality of cities as large as New York and Chicago, in the beginning at least, made it more difficult for workers to organize successfully. During this period factories were located in downtown areas; segregated working-class residential areas — tenements — sprang up nearby. Higher income urbanites tended to leave the downtown centers, moving farther out to suburbs as streetcar lines expanded. Gordon argues that these industrial cities became clogged not because of technological necessity, but because the dominant capitalists there required a concentrated mass of relatively impoverished workers to make their enterprises profitable.

The twentieth-century city, in contrast, grew up under a monopoly capitalism dominated by a few hundred huge corporations; it is characterized by significant decentralization of manufacturing, the movement out of central city areas. Modern technology is usually offered as the reason for this change: trucks and telephones made manufacturing in outlying areas possible. But Gordon notes that this decentralization had already begun in 1900, well before the truck was an important factor. Manufacturing decentralization was to a substantial degree a reaction to the militant labor unions and growing class conflict. Companies able to finance plants outside the central cities moved out to find cheaper labor and to reduce the ability of workers to organize. Large-scale union organizations and rebellion in major central cities took place in the 1870-1915 period, and this contributed to the decentralization of much industry to outlying city areas.[18]

Shift to the Sunbelt.   The 1980 census revealed major population losses for major northern cities; St. Louis, Cleveland, Detroit, and Pittsburgh suffered dramatic losses of more than one-fifth of their populations over the 1960s and 1970s. Chicago, Boston, Newark, and New York also lost significant proportions. Substantial manufacturing and other employment have shifted from the northern states to the South in the last two decades. This Sunbelt shift began in the 1960s considerably before the well-publicized fiscal crisis of northern cities such as New York. These crises are substantially the result of that shift, not its cause. Between 1960 and 1980 "capital stock" (new plant and equipment) grew at twice the pace in the South as in the North. In roughly the same period the North lost a total of 800,000 manufacturing jobs, even though the nation gained 2.3 million jobs. Moreover, the shift of jobs from the North has been faster than the shift of population.[19]

Why the tilt to the Sunbelt? Why have many companies chosen to invest in new operations or expand existing operations in this area? Several explanations have been offered. Some have argued that capital movements to the South have followed workers seeking more attractive life-styles, an argument contradicted by data on jobs moving faster than populations. Even more often, business and allied political leaders talk about "fiscal responsibility," "balanced budgets," and "good business climate" in describing what are for them "good" and "bad" cities. What does the phrase "a good business climate" mean? It is a code for lower wages, moderate living costs, fewer unions, lower taxes, and a cooperative (in other words, conservative) governmental environment, as outlined by a handbook of the Urban Land Institute, a major development industry think tank.[20]

There are other reasons for Sunbelt growth. From the beginning Sunbelt cities have not had as many physical barriers to new industrial development. Most were initially smaller, less built up, with open spaces. They did not have the older industrial structures of Frostbelt cities.

How does the shift to the Sunbelt work? Some multilocation corporations disinvest by delaying maintenance or ignoring machinery replacement needs in a northern plant, store, or office facility. Then they invest the savings in new and different operations in the Sunbelt. Or sometimes facilities may be moved from plants being phased out to expanding plants already in the Sunbelt. By various means the profits from northern operations can be rechanneled. An estimated 2 percent to 5 percent of manufacturing changes result from the actual physical relocation of the same plants. John Rees's study of location decisions by manufacturing firms in the Sunbelt cities of Dallas, Fort Worth, and Houston found that nearly 6,000 such plant decisions were made in the 1960-1975 period. Of these, four in ten were plant expansions, and just over one-third were new plants. Only one-seventh of these decisions were plant relocations from outside the area; the rest were acquisitions. The majority of plant location decisions did not involve relocating existing plants. Major causes of Sunbelt growth have been the expansion of existing companies and the creation of new companies. However, an important component of this process is the shifting of operations by a large multilocational company from one region to another, expanding employment in one region—the Sunbelt—and contracting employment in another—the Frostbelt.[21]

Manufacturing and other business growth stem mostly from capital shifts into businesses distinctive in the Sunbelt. The six pillars of this Southern development, according to Kirkpatrick Sale, are defense, oil, advanced technology, real estate and construction, tourism, and agriculture—all industries that are relatively new that have seen a dramatic new infusion of capital since World War II. The Sunbelt reflects a new round of corporate profit making in cities.[22]

Most Sunbelt cities have good business climates in part because the federal government has channeled financial aid to them and away from northern cities. This began in the 1930s under the New Deal and accelerated with major military expenditures in World War II. In the last few decades substantial federal expenditures have gone to support military—industrial complexes (e.g., Dallas-Ft. Worth), as well as to subsidize highway, sewerage, electric, and other services, providing the support structure necessary for expanded corporate development in the South. In the last decade or two federal resources (military and civilian) have been dispersed disproportionately to cities in the South and West, to the disadvantage of cities in the North. These expenditures make it clear that the rise of the Sunbelt cities is closely tied to government action. Some even speak of this regional conflict over federal aid as the "second war between the states."[23]

The Government's Urban America Report.   A 1980 report sponsored by the Carter administration suggests that the federal government should go further still in aiding corporate growth in Sunbelt cities, to the point of letting northern cities stagnate or die. This report, prepared by the President's special Commission for a National Agenda for the Eighties, calls on government to stay away from the declining cities of the North such as New York and Cleveland and explicitly notes that "contrary to public wisdom, cities are not permanent." A basic idea is that the federal government should not try to create jobs in the declining central cities of the North but rather should keep "hands off," or at most help people migrate to the Sunbelt, where corporations are generating new jobs.[24]

The *Urban America* report views the Sunbelt as an area of "economic viability, benefitting large numbers of poor southerners." But the business climate is not necessarily good for poorer working people in the Sunbelt. Robert Firestine notes that demographic data show that "despite the dramatic income expansion in the Sunbelt in recent years, this economic growth has apparently done little to alleviate the relative extremes in income distribution which have marked the South, at least for decades."[25] Census data indicate that extraordinarily large proportions of inner-city residents in Sunbelt cities remain very poor in spite of the region's heralded prosperity. Incomes are almost as unequally distributed in the South today as in the past, particularly for blacks and Chicanos. The South is on the whole much less generous than the North in educational, health, welfare, and other social service expenditures. Part of the price workers and their families pay for business prosperity in the South is less desirable working conditions and lower quality of services, not only for the poor, but for middle-income workers as well.

Nor is business development in the southern cities necessarily permanent. Surprisingly, the South is losing certain manufacturing jobs. Recently for every 100 new manufacturing jobs created in the South, 80 manufacturing jobs were lost. Yet in the North for every 100 jobs created, 110 were lost, so the net gain in the South was clearly better. The balance is favorable for the South, but why does it also see plant closings? The *Urban America* report is quite candid on this point: "Industrial activity that was attracted to the South since the 1950s by lower wages, greater labor control, and lower energy costs is often found relocating outside the United States to achieve even lower production costs.[26]" Capital will flow from Sunbelt cities when profitability dictates that it do so, without regard to the human costs.

Shifts within the Sunbelt.   Some movement out of Sunbelt cities is already observable. To take one recent example, advertisements in the Houston area have boldly proclaimed the advantages of good schools, good jobs, less pollution, and fewer traffic jams *elsewhere*. These ads are not intended to seduce workers to Houston from other cities. Rather, they are intended to attract firms and people out of Houston to outlying cities within a hundred-mile radius. Even southern business leaders and publications, such as the *Houston Business Journal*, have come to recognize that "a city, like a macrocosm of businesses that create it, can reach a point of diminishing returns."[27] Houston's traffic, pollution, and poverty-related crime—all creatures of unbridled Sunbelt capitalism—have escalated business costs. Thus companies such as Brown Oil Tools, Inc., an old Houston firm, are moving out from the "shining new" metropolis to small towns such as Huntsville. The views of a former top company executive were recently summarized by a business reporter:

> He doesn't hedge when he gives reasons for moving Brown to Huntsville: traffic, equality of life and the availability of high quality labor. ... The time element in commuting is become an important consideration for workers, and he contends that Houston is making too little progress in its public transportation system and in the congestion of its freeways.[28]

Even the industrial heartland of the North may come back into fashion as a place for profitable investment. Gentrification in certain areas of northern cities will be discussed in Chapter 5. By the early 1980s some real estate investors were saying that big money was to be made in northern cities and their suburbs. One investment consultant noted that moderate growth areas outside the Sunbelt do not have the increasing Sunbelt problem of supply (e.g., new development projects) exceeding the demand. Developers in the Sunbelt are too optimistic and are overbuilding and outpacing demand, "so that they're not really reaping the benefits of growth—because the supply is so ample."[29] This investor recommends urban areas where developers are not building so aggressively. He suggests investing in the suburban areas of Boston, Columbus, and even troubled Detroit.

This uneven oscillation of investment shows clearly that corporations have no commitment to urban communities anywhere. They do not exclusively prefer rural or urban areas, or the Sunbelt or Frostbelt as places to make profits; rather they will move freely from one place to another, even encouraging competiton between local communities bidding for their jobs with tax incentives and other subsidies, with little concern for human costs.[30]

GOVERNMENT SUBSIDIZES BUSINESS

The *Urban America* report put the federal government's seal of approval on corporate mobility whatever its social costs. But governments do a lot more than create commissions to make life easy for corporations.

Welfare Assistance for Capital.   Government officials in many cities and states have competed vigorously to entice companies to their areas. Thousands of local agencies and officials compete, with government grants and subsidies, for corporations seeking to move their investments. City and state governments play a type of "Russian roulette" to attract businesses; businesses pit one government against another for the best deal. The result is a broad array of tax and other subsidies that are in fact unnecessary, making taxpayers shoulder more and more business risks.

In a recent speech a senior vice-president of a major industrial location firm emphasized his company's success in winning $30 million of subsidies in Canada for one of his client corporations, including "a free, fully serviced site with heavy utilities in place, reduced local property tax levies, a federal grant of over $10 million, [and] a provincial training grant."[31] Similar packages have been worked out for companies in many areas of the United States.

Some state governments, especially in the Sunbelt, have restricted unionization with right-to-work laws. Texas, Virginia, and Oklahoma have advertised that "labor-management relations are excellent" and that "wage rates are considerably below those found in major manufacturing areas." Northern states such as New Hampshire have also advertised this lack of unionization. North Carolina has proclaimed in a promotion brochure that its right-to-work law "*guarantees* employee freedom" and "*preserves* right to manage."[32] And a recent advertisement for plant location in Florida ran as follows:

> *Got Labor Pains? Central Florida Delivers!* Florida's "right-to-work" laws contribute to a low incidence of labor un-rest and work stoppages. We are ranked 43rd among the fifty states, with less than 13 percent of non-agricultural labor unionized.[33]

This ad was placed by a county development group in cooperation with the Florida State Department of Commerce.

Enterprise Zones: Company Towns?   Federal government subsidies for business have been quite substantial. They have included major programs for urban renewal in central cities and other public investments that cleared land for new business developments. We will consider urban renewal programs in Chapter 9. Here we can note one major proposal to redo central cities that was developed in the early 1980s. In 1982 the Reagan administration presented its first serious program for dealing with cities, an "urban enterprise zones" proposal to deal with poverty-stricken central-city areas. The basic idea was to entice companies back into cities by providing an incredible array of giveaways. For companies setting up shop in central-city areas there was to be a sharp reduction in taxes, including investment tax credits, payroll employment tax reductions, income tax and capital gains tax reductions, and numerous others. Also proposed was a significant reduction in governmental regulations in the areas where companies relocate. Eligible areas, in the final Reagan proposal, would be chosen on the basis of poverty and unemployment levels, and local governments would apply to the federal Department of Housing and Urban Development for designation as urban enterprise zones. Seventy-five zones in the first few years were suggested. (An estimated 350 cities have areas that could meet the criteria.)[34]

The Reagan administration's 1982 Enterprise Zone Tax Act was presented to Congress in a form substantially different from the original proposal, which was far more extreme in its attempt to do away with minimum wage, health, environmental, and civil rights regulations for firms locating in the enterprise zones. The original proposal was called by some "frontier" capitalism because of its throw-the-workers-to-the-wolves philosophy. It was an attempt to assist companies in making a profit in central-city areas. The proposal would attract some companies seeking to make superprofits, although judging from similar past programs the corporate commitments would be temporary. These proposals are in line with the Fantus survey of corporations mentioned earlier. They include many items on the shopping list of concessions corporate executives want.

An official of a public employees' union called the Reagan urban enterprise zone proposal "an excuse for the creation of company towns." Such proposals do reflect the profit needs of corporations in seeking out locations. Jobs for ordinary working people are thereby created, but at the heavy social cost of letting corporations dictate the terms. In this sense, then, urban enterprise zones would be company towns built with federal assistance.

CONCLUSION

U.S. cities are changing, as industrial and commercial corporations make decisions to abandon one area and move to another. This constant threat of job loss has made many American working people fearful. Their community, their city may be next. Bluestone and Harrison have articulated the dynamics succinctly:

Working people's feelings about this are not without foundation. Deindustrialization is occurring—on a surprisingly massive scale. It can be seen from North to South and East to West. It is happening as the largest, most powerful corporations in the nation shut down older plants in the industrial heartland (*and* in the Old South) to move to new industrial zones in the New South and overseas...in an effort to maximize their profits and increase their span of control over the global economic system.[35]

NOTES

1. Barry Bluestone, Bennett Harrison, and Lawrence Baker, *Corporate Flight* (Washington, D.C.: Progressive Alliance, 1981), pp. 12-13; "Capital Moves: Who's Left Behind," *Dollars and Sense*, April, 1981, pp. 7-8; Barry Bluestone and Bennett Harrison, *The Deindustrialization of America* (New York: Basic Books, 1982), pp. 9-30.

2. "Capital Moves," p. 7; "Seth Thomas," *Austin American Statesman*, April, 1982, p. A7.

3. "Capital Moves," p. 8; David Smith, *The Public Balance Sheet: A New Tool for Evaluating Economic Choices* (Washington, D.C.: Conference on Alternative State and Local Policies, 1979), pp. 3-4.

4. Bluestone, Harrison, and Baker, *Corporate Flight*, pp. 24-35.

5. Karl Jenkins, "Don't Let Them Close This Plant," quoted in " 'Big Three' in Mexico," *Labor Today* 19 (June, 1980), p. 6.

6. August Lösch, *The Economics of Location* (New Haven: Yale University Press, 1954), pp. 28-30.

7. Melvin Greenhut, *Plant Location in Theory and Practice* (Chapel Hill, N.C.: University of North Carolina Press, 1956), pp. 175-285. I am drawing on the summary in David M. Smith, *Industrial Location*, first edition (New York: John Wiley and Sons, 1971), pp. 144-146.

8. E.K. Hunt and Howard J. Sherman, *Economics*, fourth edition (New York: Harper and Row, 1981), pp. 112, 575-579.

9. M. Storper, R. Walker, and E. Widess, "Performance Regulation and Industrial Location: A Case Study," *Environment and Planning* 13 (1981), pp. 321-338; David M. Gordon, "Capitalism and the Roots of Urban Crisis," in *The Fiscal Crisis of American Cities* (New York: Vintage Books, 1977), pp. 104-105.

10. Michael P. Smith, *The City and Social Theory* (New York: St. Martin's Press, 1979), p. 240.

11. John D. Kasarda, "The Implications of Contemporary Redistribution Trends for National Urban Policy," *Social Science Quarterly* 61 (December, 1980), p. 385.

12. The report is quoted in Richard A. Walker, "A Theory of Suburbanization: Capitalism and Construction of Urban Space in the United States," in *Urbanization and Urban Planning in Capitalist Society*, edited by Michael Dear and Allen J. Scott (London: Methuen, 1981), p. 401.

13. Storper, Walker, and Widess, "Performance Regulation and Industrial Location," pp. 325-327.

14. Diana Klebanow, Franklin L. Jonas, and Ira M. Leonard, *Urban Legacy* (New York: Mentor Books, 1977), pp. 157-158.

15. Alfred J. Watkins, *The Practice of Urban Economics* (Beverly Hills, Calif.: Sage Publications, 1980), pp. 130, 154.

16. Smith, *Industrial Location*, pp. 350-360.
17. Gordon, "Capitalism and the Roots of Urban Crisis," pp. 93-94.
18. Ibid., pp. 94-102.
19. President's Commission for a National Agenda for the Eighties, Panel on Policies and Prospects, *Urban America in the Eighties: Perspectives and Prospects* (Washington, D.C.: U.S. Government Printing Office, 1980), pp. 18, 27, 42.
20. Urban Land Institute, *Industrial Development Handbook* (Washington, D.C.: Urban Land Institute, 1975), p. 229.
21. John Rees, "Regional Shifts in the U.S. and the Internal Generation of Manufacturing Growth in the Southwest," paper presented to Conference on the Committee on Urban Public Economics, Baltimore, Johns Hopkins University, May, 1978, pp. 11-13; John Rees, "Manufacturing Change, Internal Control and Government Spending in the Growth Region of the United States," Paper presented to the 24th North American Meetings of the Regional Science Association, Philadelphia, November, 1977, pp. 1-7.
22. President's Commission, *Urban America in the Eighties*, pp. 41-42; Kirkpatrick Sale, *Power Shift* (New York: Random House, 1975).
23. President's Commission, *Urban America in the Eighties*, p. 78; Felix Rohatyn, "The Older America: Can It Survive?" *New York Review of Books* 27 (January 22, 1981), pp. 13-16.
24. President's Commission, *Urban America in the Eighties*, pp. 18-42; see also "Burning Up the Snowbelt," *Time*, January 12, 1981, p. 19.
25. Robert E. Firestine, "Economic Growth and Inequality, Demographic Change and the Public Sector Response," in *The Rise of the Sunbelt Cities* (Beverly Hills: Sage, 1977), p. 199; c.f. also Peter A. Lupsha and William J. Siembieda, "The Poverty of Public Services: An Analysis and Interpretation," in *The Rise of the Sunbelt Cities*, p. 174.
26. President's Commission, *Urban America in the Eighties*, p. 42.
27. "Corporate Flight to the Suburbs," *Houston Business Journal*, January 12, 1981, p. 1.
28. Ibid.
29. Steven Lewis, "Institutions Will Dominate Development in 1981, Predicts White: Money Market to Remain Volatile," *National Real Estate Investor* 23 (February, 1981), p. 60.
30. Robert Goodman, *The Last Entrepreneurs* (New York: Simon and Schuster, 1979), p. 49.
31. Robert M. Ady, "Shifting Factors in Plant Location," *Industrial Development*, November—December, 1981, pp. 16-17.
32. Quoted in Goodman, *The Last Entrepreneurs*, p. 37.
33. Advertisement in Conway Publications, *Site Selection Handbook/78* 23 (February, 1978), p. 70.
34. John Herbers, "New Urban Program," *New York Times*, March 28, 1982.
35. Bluestone and Harrison, *The Deindustrialization of America*, p. 47.

3
DEVELOPERS, BANKERS, AND SPECULATORS

PLAYERS IN THE REAL ESTATE GAME

One of the pioneers in large-scale urban development was Bill Zeckendorf, who from the 1940s to the 1960s became involved in many office, hotel, shopping center, and apartment projects in both the United States and Canada. "Real estate is one of the few businesses," Zeckendorf once commented, "in which you can get into the big-time without much money." Zeckendorf followed his own prescription and built a multinational real estate empire from a small beginning. By the 1950s his development corporation, Webb and Knapp, had half a billion dollars in construction and was probably the most important real estate developer in urban renewal areas in U.S. cities. According to Zeckendorf's autobiography, his company packaged and built the first giant suburban shopping center in New York, started a Denver construction boom with an office complex and a hotel, built a famous multiple-use (office and shopping) center in Montreal (the Place Ville-Marie), and fathered large-scale reconstruction projects in Washington, D.C., Philadelphia, Pittsburgh, and numerous other cities across the nation. Zeckendorf packaged the land for the Chase Manhattan Bank Plaza, and in his heyday he owned numerous New York office towers. He was a real estate capitalist who hobnobbed with the rich and famous, including President Dwight Eisenhower and the queen of England, as well as many bankers and other financial backers who helped get Zeckendorf projects started and developed.[1] He was a wizard at leveraging—buying and developing property with other people's cash.

38

In the late 1950s Zeckendorf's company ran into financial trouble, in part because of construction problems and the extensive borrowing for which he was famous. Zeckendorf sold land and buildings. Reportedly conservative British bankers bought some of his projects, and millions of dollars were consequently lost by the British. Ever resilient, Zeckendorf survived this fiasco to become involved in real estate operations again.[2]

Ironically, the corporation that is often considered North America's largest urban developer got a boost from Zeckendorf's financial troubles. By the early 1980s Olympia and York Developments, Ltd., a corporation still unknown to most Americans, owned 50 million square feet of space in cities on three continents, altogether an estimated $4 billion in assets, or more than the assets of General Motors. Headed by Albert and Paul Reichmann, this company grew from a small operation to a $4 billion enterprise in just three decades. The Reichmann brothers started out building warehouses and other industrial buildings, then branched into office buildings in the early 1960s, when they were able to buy land cheaply from Zeckendorf's troubled company. That land in a Toronto, Ontario, suburb is the center of a major industrial and residential district. Olympia and York has built many major development projects in the United States. They include a $350 million redevelopment project in downtown San Francisco, as well as major projects in Boston, Miami, Hartford, and Dallas, and it is scheduled to develop the largest private construction project ever built in the eastern United States, the $1 billion Battery Park City in New York City. With several huge office towers, this project will be larger than four Empire State buildings and make the Reichmann brothers New York's biggest landlord. The Reichmanns have avoided reporters and kept themselves out of the limelight, yet this one corporation has had a major impact on the face of U.S. and Canadian cities.[3]

Construction is the largest U.S. industry. And the variety of *urban* development projects account for much of that construction. Developers such as Zeckendorf and the Reichmanns, together with major construction companies and banks, are indeed the shapers of our cities. It is not sufficient to discuss the character of cities, their growth, or their demise primarily in terms of ordinary workers and consumers, for as we shall see consumer choices are limited in many ways by business producers.

WHAT DO DEVELOPERS DO?

The age of the large-scale property developer began in earnest after World War II not only in the United States but also in Canada, Britain, and other European countries.

Developers as Catalysts.   Developers commonly see themselves as the conceptualizers, organizers, and supervisors of real estate development projects. They package the process. Developers act as catalysts, notes James Lorimer, as they

> look for sites to erect a profitable apartment building or shopping center or suburb, they assemble the site, draw up some kind of plan for the project, get the necessary approvals from governments and public bodies, line up tenants if this is appropriate, line up mortgage lenders to lend them the bulk of the cost of the project once it's built, get the architectural plans for the scheme drawn up, hire the contractors to do the construction, and arrange to rent or sell the building once it's finished.[4]

Some developers have their own construction subsidiaries to do the actual building, but many hire major construction companies. Many developers are organized as a new type of business—the property development corporation.

A recent report on development in Sunbelt cities notes that "the location, timing, and form of future urban development is determined in the project planning stage of the development process." It is the private developers and their associates, the report further notes, who make the land tract and purchase decisions, taking into account highway patterns, regional growth patterns, the availability of utilities, and the general "feasibility" (that is, profitability) of the development project. Typically the developers also decide on the financing, such as Federal Housing Administration (FHA) guaranteed loans or conventional loans for a suburban subdivision. The developers arrange for the necessary governmental permits and approvals, such as approval of sewage and other waste disposal arrangements. Developers arrange for utility provision, securing governmental assistance in subsidizing the provision of new utilities. Developers secure the construction and long term financing, bringing banks and other financial institutions into the picture. Depending on the type of development, developers may sell off what they build, as in the case of suburban developers who sell off serviced lots to smaller builders, or they may retain ownership and lease out space to tenants, as in the case of developers of office buildings.[5]

Major Developers.   There are different types of land and property developers. Some are diversified; they build and manage a variety of urban projects, including office towers, shopping centers, warehouses and plants, hotels and motels. In recent years top developers, in terms of construction put in place, have included Trammel Crow (Dallas), Urban Investment and Development (Chicago), Gerald D. Hines Interests (Houston), Vantage (Dallas), Daon Corporation (Newport Beach), Century Development Corporation (Houston), and Maguire Partners (Los Angeles). Many of these are based in the Sunbelt, although they build in many cities. Other developers tend to specialize in certain projects, such as shopping centers or multifamily housing. Major shopping center developers include the Edward J. DeBartolo Corporation, General Growth Companies, and Ernest W. Hahn, Inc. These companies own and manage millions of square feet in shopping centers.

Larger developers tend to dominate particular types of urban construction. For example, Trammel Crow, in recent years one of the largest U.S.—based developers, has dominated the commercial warehousing market as owner and manager of a $2 billion (in 1982) empire. Its warehouses are usually located in industrial parks near major traffic arteries.[6]

Many developers started in one specific type of construction, such as warehouses or shopping centers, then diversified into other projects such as office towers, apartment buildings, houses for resale, and land development to maximize profits. Today's profits from land sales, housing sales, and shopping centers, may be invested in tomorrow's apartment and office buildings.

Shady Connections. Developers can be inventive in pursuing their goals. Most operate above board, but others press against ethical limits. Lorimer's analysis of some Canadian developers suggests that some who built high-rise apartments used the tough methods often associated with organized crime.[7] And in her book *Sweethearts*, Catherine Wismer has traced the ties between legitimate businesspeople, the developers and contractors, and organized crime in the development boom in Toronto, a city that between 1950 and 1980 became a forest of office towers and apartment buildings. Wismer documents the role of organized crime in providing both labor for apartment projects and cash to finance buildings. An in-depth study might reveal similar ties in the United States, but that study remains to be done.[8]

A few developers press ahead vigorously and run roughshod over others, sometimes bribing politicians and harassing local residents to get them to move out. Parking-lot blockbusting has been used by some developers and land speculators seeking to force homeowners to sell to them. To displace a whole neighborhood of homeowners one may buy a few houses here and there and let them run down or bulldoze them and replace them with noisy parking lots. Eventually other residents will be forced to leave by the adjacent deterioration.[9] Under developer pressure, the government-controlled zoning can be changed; then new high-rise development can replace the older healthy neighborhoods of low-rise housing.

Reorienting Cities: Early Entrepreneurs.   Real estate developers can have profound effects on cities. Take, for example, the powerful nineteenth-century capitalists Marshall Field and Potter Palmer, whose real estate operations remade the face of Chicago. At the end of the Civil War, the Lake Street area was the central retail district. A single powerful capitalist, Potter Palmer, rechanneled this business growth to another section of Chicago. The area he chose, around State Street, was run down. Palmer bought up much of the property, pushed for a wide street heading into the area, and then developed a plush hotel to entice businesses there. He succeeded in relocating the center of Chicago business activity, a result signaled by the sharp rise of property values there. After the great Chicago fire, Marshall Field made decisions that again relocated substantial business activity in the city. As did Palmer, Field avoided former business centers and chose another dilapidated area inhabited by the poor. Field rebuilt his large retail store in a poor Irish area, displacing the residents. Numerous businesses followed his lead, another indication of the early importance of capitalists in shaping urban patterns. Field made his real estate investment and speculation more profitable than his retail business operations. However, Palmer and Field were not as centrally involved in real estate development in and for itself as are modern developers.[10]

DEVELOPERS BUREAUCRATIZED

Individuals and Corporations.   The real estate development industry is complex; there are many sizes of developers, and their internal organizational structures vary significantly. Most developers in the decade after World War II started as relatively small, aggressive entrepreneurs and used profits to move into one land enterprise after another. The small entrepreneur has frequently been seen as the crucial risk taker, the one who seeks to invest and reinvest in new business enterprises. However, in recent decades bureaucratized corporate capitalism has come to replace many individual entrepreneurs in the real estate industry as elsewhere.

Many large development corporations like those of Zeckendorf and the Reichmann brothers have grown up around one or two powerful individuals.

Sometimes these men (few are women) keep a low public profile. In other cases the developers are better known to the public. Some are colorful figures who wheel through deals and social life with a flair for publicity. Many have built their empires with entrepreneurial aggressiveness, with opportunity for success and failure. Thus a recent article in the Houston *Chronicle* shows a developer of apartment and commercial projects hovering eagerly, with hands shaped into claws, over a model of a new multi-million project; he is quoted as saying, "I have a little problem with ambition. I want to do more. I want to get bigger."[11]

Another entrepreneurial example is Robert Campeau, the head of a major Canadian-based development company, who entertains Canada's leading citizens and top politicians, including Prime Minister Pierre Trudeau, in his mansion in Ottawa. A driving capitalist who started as a homebuilder, Campeau has put together one of North America's largest development corporations; it has three-quarters of its new development projects in the United States, including office buildings and shopping centers. According to a recent newspaper article, Campeau plans to diversify into oil and gas properties. The article depicts Campeau as an aggressive developer; an associate is quoted as saying that "he knows what he wants and goes for it, and if he doesn't get it, he fights back."[12]

Cadillac Companies. However they got started, most development corporations, large and small, are today bureaucratized with multiple levels of managers and other white-collar employees, associated professional experts like architects and lawyers, numerous divisions, and complicated rules and regulations. Large corporations have come to dominate much urban real estate development and financing. The land and development industry was once dominated by relatively small entrepreneurs and corporations. But since the 1960s numerous smaller firms have merged to form larger ones, large firms have bought up smaller ones, or small builders have expanded into larger-scale commercial development. Large development companies, such as Trammel Crow, Gerald D. Hines Interests, and Cadillac Fairview, grew rapidly, some by acquiring other companies, such as building supply firms. Large companies, with greater access to capital sources, have shoved aside or taken over smaller firms.

There are various building and development specialties: constructing itself, manufacturing prefab houses or parts of houses and other buildings, packaging and subdividing land, financing, and managing ongoing income properties such as office towers and shopping malls. Some development companies incorporate several functions. Many of the largest development corporations active in North American real estate are unknown to the general public—for example, Cadillac Fairview Corporation, one of the largest and most diversified development companies operating in the United States. It was created by the merger of several smaller companies. Typical of the large developers, Cadillac Fairview has engaged in several categories of projects.

1. *Corporate rental projects*, including development and operation of office buildings, shopping centers, apartment buildings, and industrial plants
2. *Residential projects*, including development and selling of single-family homes and multifamily housing
3. *Land development projects*, including development and sale of land for housing and commercial projects

In 1981 the company controlled thirty-three office towers and multiple-use projects, forty-four shopping centers, ninety-four industrial buildings, and fifty residential properties. These projects were located in such cities as New York, Philadelphia, Atlanta, Houston, Los Angeles, and Seattle, as well as Toronto and Vancouver in Canada.[13]

The complexity of a modern corporation is indicated by the eight operating units of Cadillac Fairview as of 1981.

1. Corporate Financial Group:	Financial services Treasury and taxation Planning
2. Land and Housing Group:	Condominiums Single-family homes Large planned communities
3. Shopping Centers Group:	Shopping center management New shopping center construction
4. Construction Services Division:	Construction services
5. Urban Development Group:	Office towers Multiple-use projects
6. Industrial Division:	Industrial parks Industrial buildings
7. U.S. Southern Region:	All types of development
8. U.S. Western Region:	All types of development

Cadillac Fairview is involved in virtually every type of urban project. In 1981 the total rental income for Cadillac Fairview was $302 million; the company's income-producing assets were about $2.7 billion. Yet the fortunes of such companies ebb and flow. In the 1982 office glut this international corporation tried to sell off a large share of its real estate holdings to reduce its debt.

In the early 1980s Cadillac Fairview was one of the eight largest Canadian developers. The others included Olympia and York and the Campeau Corporation. About half the (book value) assets of these eight developers were located in the United States; the scale of their development projects in U.S. cities was growing rapidly because of limitations on development in Canada. Only a few U.S. developers, such as Texas-based Trammel Crow and Gerald Hines Interests, have been large enough to compete in the same league with these billion-dollar companies.

By the 1970s many of the largest U.S. multinational corporations were moving into some aspect of the real estate development industry. Three hundred of the top 1,000 corporations had real estate departments and subsidiaries, including those in the oil, food, chemical, paper, and machinery industries. Thus 250 major corporations replying to a 1971 survey already held $25 billion in real estate. Specialized housing companies have been bought and sold by major corporations, including Boise Cascade, Aetna Life and Casualty Company, and Bethlehem Steel.[14]

The troubled auto company, Chrysler Corporation, set up a real estate department in 1967. Three years later its holdings exceeded $300 million and included a wide range of real estate projects around the country, from urban town houses and office buildings to a Montana ski resort. Aerospace companies, major utility companies, timber corporations, and oil companies have gotten into urban development projects. Big companies have also become involved in huge "new towns," massive suburban projects such as Reston, Virginia (Gulf Oil) and Rancho, California (Kaiser Aluminum).[15]

Behind this dramatic expansion of non-real estate corporations into the development industry has been, noted Richard Walker and Michael Heiman, the "search for profitable outlets for surplus capital, product diversification, tax benefits, and the use of surplus land. Large-scale development, in particular, absorbed large blocks of capital, allowed internalization of profitable neighborhood effects, and promised monopoly control over local housing markets." Foreign companies with surplus capital to invest have in recent decades invested in urban real estate. Canadian-based developers have moved into U.S. real estate in a major way. In mid-1970s Olympia and York bought several New York City office buildings in the middle of a depressed real estate market, including buildings whose rents more than doubled from 1976 to 1982. The acquisitions included the headquarters buildings for Harper and Row, Chemical Bank, and ITT.[16]

Oil Capital into Real Estate.   Oil company profits have been invested in urban development. We have noted Gulf Oil's Reston, Virginia, satellite city project. Another project, one of the largest satellite cities in the world, is The Woodlands, on 23,000 acres north of downtown Houston. This development is the brainchild of an oil capitalist, George Mitchell, who has moved some of his oil-generated capital (plus other financial resources) into a new investment: the building of a multi-billion-dollar city of his own design. Built by Woodlands Development Corporation, a subsidiary of Mitchell's oil company, this planned development housed 13,000 residents and 200 businesses in 1981. By the time its thirty-six-year master plan is completed in the twenty-first century, however, it will have 160,000 residents and 25 million square feet of office space. Schools, shopping malls, apartments, single-family homes, churches, and transportation lines are to be provided.[17] The Woodlands represents Mitchell's vision of how urban problems are to be solved. He views his corporate development as providing a better quality of life. As he has said,

> Energy is a very fast moving business on pay-out. I have to drill a well every seven years because the well's gone by then, produced out. But if I build a building, it has a slow pay-out of maybe 10 years, but it has a 40-year life. The long-term economics are what make it look interesting.
>
> If we do this well and build human resources and make a profit, then other people will have to do the same to compete with us.

The Woodlands, Mitchell further notes, is "not Utopia, but it's a step better than anything done in the past."[18]

A Monopoly Trend?   Traditionally a few key rationalizations have been used to defend the domination of fewer and fewer corporations in major U.S. industries. One such rationalization in urban real estate development is that large corporations provide better planned developments than smaller ones. Lewis Goodkin notes that the smaller "entrepreneurial builder, short on bankroll and long on leverage, has to follow a hedgehopping pattern of suburban development, so large-scale development can mean less hedge— hopping and less sprawl."[19]

Over the last two decades the trend in the development and land industry has been toward accelerated control by fewer companies. Inflation creates tighter profit margins, forcing many smaller developers and builders out of business. One report on construction and sales by publicly owned homebuilding companies found that thirty-seven firms delivered 19 percent of all the single-family homes sold in the United States. Two dozen of these companies sold more than $100 million in homes in 1980, with U.S. Home, Jim Walter Homes, Ryan Homes, Centex Corporation, and Weyerhaeuser Real Estate leading the list of superbuilders. A number of the top homebuilding companies are subsidiaries of large non-real estate corporations. Ponderosa Homes is part of Aetna Life and Casualty Company; Arvada is a subsidiary of Penn Central; and Mission Viejo is part of Philip Morris.[20] By one estimate 200 major developers will be in control of most suburban housing projects by the end of the century.

Still, there have periodically been major setbacks, which have slowed the penetration of non-real estate multinational corporations into real estate development. The 1974-1975 and 1980-1982 recessions, and other declines in the economy since 1960, have hurt corporate investments in land and urban housing; periodically, many large conglomerates have reduced their real estate involvements. Many smaller developers and builders lost out, and some large corporations pulled out of real estate entirely, but the larger independent developers, such as Trammel Crow and Olympia and York, and the large multinational corporations, such as Gulf, Penn Central, Aetna, and Exxon, have remained important in the real estate industry in the 1980s.[21]

Many real estate development companies do not want to be well known to the general public. They fear that bad publicity may generate citizen protest harmful to their interests. They often prefer to operate behind front names, lawyers, or dummy corporations, so the landowners with whom they deal will not raise their prices, as they might if the true identity of the purchaser were known. Henry Aubin's study of real estate ownership in Montreal, Quebec, found that numerous owners of important real estate projects in that city were actually dummy companies with "front" offices in the small European country of Liechtenstein. Dummy companies and other legal complexities can permit the real owners of city real estate to remain secret if they wish to do so. Public awareness of the role of large corporations in building, buying, selling, and financing real estate development in cities has been limited. This has made it easier for developers and contractors to operate with little public scrutiny. To a surprising degree cities are shaped by people who are relatively unknown, not elected, and largely beyond the control of the electorate.[22]

Profitability.   Substantial profits are to be made in development projects. Inflation in building prices, with buildings financed at fixed-interest loans, brought large profits to hundreds of developers in the decades after World War II, enabling some to grow much larger. Reported profits are not always actual profits; some development firms have been known to massage their corporate reports to suggest a rosy financial picture. Some have underestimated or overestimated by creative bookkeeping, that is, have disguised true profits.

One analysis of selected North American development company profits found that companies were making from a low of 9 percent to a high of 430 percent returns on shareholders' investments. In addition, because most developers own property that is appreciating, they may eventually make high profits from the sale of that property, income that is not figured into annual profits until projects are sold. Depreciation write-offs (special tax deductions for building owners) make the profits in the reports of many development companies appear small. Some even show losses. But this is only a paper phenomenon. Except in recessions, the financial returns on real estate development projects have generally been good.[23]

BANKERS AND INSURANCE COMPANIES: THE LEVERAGE ACT

To understand how developers can make substantial profits one has to understand complex financial arrangements. Cash and borrowed funds make various types of urban development possible. Money may come from selling shares to stockholder-investors, profits earned and kept from previous projects, and loans from financial corporations. Equity investors and debt lenders are critical actors in most large urban projects. A developer's own funds or those of friends and relatives may provide the basic equity capital. But this is only a small part of the money needed for most projects. The necessary debt capital is usually provided by institutions such as banks, insurance companies, and other investors such as real estate syndicates (tax shelter firms).

Finance Capital: Clout and Resources.   Banks and insurance companies make up what are sometimes termed *finance capitalists*, the complex network of organizations that make profits by trading in various types of financial instruments, including bonds and certificates of deposit, and by servicing clients with loans and mortgages.[24] Finance capitalists tend to operate behind the scenes; there is little research on the handful of organizations which finance the larger urban development projects. Developers as a group are closely tied to them, because a major function of developers is to piece together the financing for projects. Bankers tend to view real estate property as a good investment; its worth has generally stayed ahead of inflation. But this is circular, as Peter Ambrose and Bob Colenutt noted, "because it is finance capital which is partly responsible for stimulating demand for property in the first place, by its own needs for office space, by lending money to developers and by pouring money into property as a hedge against inflation."[25]

In making investments banks have considerable power to shape how, and whether, urban communities grow. When they decided to loan to corporations building office towers in central cities, they contributed to the growth of administrative centers. When they decided not to loan to black homeowners in ghetto areas (called *redlining*), they hastened the decline of housing in such low- to moderate-income areas.

Banks tend to prefer bigger developers and industrial corporations as borrowers, particularly in metropolitan areas, because they figure a big company is less likely to go bankrupt than a small one. In this way they contribute to concentration and centralization in the real estate industry.

Mortgages provide one type of borrowing developers use to get most of the cash they need in return for a legal agreement whereby they pay interst and principal payments over several years to the lender. A mortgage loan is a written agreement in which the borrower pledges the physical property as security to the creditor to receive the loan. The lender has a lien against the property, which allows the lender to take title or sell the property if mortgage payments are not made. Put another way, the lender has the building as collateral for the loan. Ordinarily mortgage loans provide the majority of the long-term money for development projects. Mortgage insurance and other protection for finance capital provided by the federal government since the 1930s have made it more profitable for banking corporations to loan money to developers and builders.

Developers prefer to use other people's money for their projects. This process, called *leverage*, gives the developers a lot of clout beyond their own resources. Thus developers need little of their own money, because banks finance the land costs, construction costs are paid by banks and building contractors, and a bank or insurance company provides a long-term mortgage. Leverage is the mechanism that allows the pyramiding of large real estate operations, such as those of Bill Zeckendorf, on a small initial investment.[26]

The property developed serves as collateral, and real estate operators need less of their own money to get into the business than entrepreneurs in other businesses. They can borrow more of the total purchasing price of their projects from banking institutions than if they purchase industrial equipment. And for those developers who buy land and older buildings, build new apartment and commercial buildings, and rent them out, there are several ways to profit from their actions. One business analyst notes that, "There is not only the prospect of leverage at a high ratio but also of shielding the resultant profits through the liberal tax shelter permitted to owners of income-producing property in the form of depreciation allowances, as well as other expense deductions associated with development and ownership."[27]

Active developers constantly search for new loans. A loan comes due, and money must be found to cover it. "Prepayments on huge [property] loans create a constant demand for cash so that the only ways in which profits can be made are by raising additional mortgages and selling off buildings and land."[28] Yet borrowing can create problems as well as profits, as can be seen in the mid-1970s default of developer in Los Angeles. He had borrowed a large amount from a Beverly Hills bank. When the developer defaulted, the bank's worried customers began withdrawing money. The U.S. Comptroller of the Currency intervened, and the bank was sold to another large-banking corporation.[29]

Today many finance capital corporations expect leasing commitments from important tenants as the basis for long-term financing of developers' projects, such as office towers and shopping centers. Many developers cannot get into actual land packaging until they have these leasing commitments. In addition, mortgage lenders tend to be conservative and prefer to support proven types of real estate projects, such as traditionally designed shopping centers. They check the profit expectations of the developers' projects, as well as possible problems created by the construction and management of the projects. In this way financial institutions can control the character and type of much urban development.

Banks and other lenders set limits on development by requiring certain conditions to be met before they will loan money. Financial institutions can even dictate such conditions as size and scope of projects, type and frequency of financial statements, interest rates, bank access to company records, legal fees, and even access to mass transit. In the case of smaller developers, finance capitalists can dictate virtually all important conditions. New mortgage arrangements have appeared in recent years. Lenders are requiring more interest for their loans and a share of ownership as well. Many mortgage lenders require a large share of a project's equity ownership, as well as high interest rates, refore they will make a loan.[30]

A Potpourri of Lenders. Over the last few decades the sources of loans for developers of properties have included commercial banks, savings and loan institutions, insurance companies, real estate investment trusts, wealthy individual investors, and pension funds. Commercial banks often provide the interim and construction financing for major development projects.

Construction loans are usually paid back by another loan, a long-term mortgage, when the building is completed. But these arrangements sometimes fall apart. In the mid-1970s several Nw York banks put together a $62 million loan for an office building and later had to take ownership of the building when the developer was unable to get long-term financing.[31] Banks would rather not hold long-term mortgages, preferring other lenders such as insurance companies to assume such responsibilities. Mayer notes that knowledgeable bankers go into the field to check on the progress of construction developers and builders:

> Ancient wisdom in banking urges the visitor to the loan department to look at the shoes of lending officers: if nobody has mud on his shoes, it means nobody is out visiting the construction projects, and the builders are stealing the bank blind.[32]

Because lenders loan the money to other real estate actors, many lending executives maintain close ties to local and national development companies. Local banking officials, as one Long Island study documents, may even get into land speculation partnerships themselves; and some bank officials may serve on zoning and planning boards, to which their developer friends and clients apply for permits.[33]

Real estate syndicates are devices to obtain money for development and to provide tax advantages for well-off investors. Real estate syndicates have helped generate money to put up office skyscrapers, the depreciation on which buildings attracts highly paid professionals such as doctors, and other outside investors seeking tax shelters. Real estate syndicates become increasingly commonplace in the 1970s. In 1972 real estate syndicates accounted for one tenth of new security offerings offered by Wall Street firms. Supreme Court Justices and U.S. Senators have been involved in real estate syndicate ventures in the Washington, D.C. area. Banks sometimes put together syndicates for wealthy individuals seeking to put $100,000 - $1 million into large-scale ventures. A number of these syndicates have gone bankrupt, and the luster they once had for the wealthy has to some extent worn off.[34]

A similar real estate financing device is the Real Estate Investment Trust (REIT). This arrangement permits smaller investors to go together and invest in land and buildings. The trust funds are like mutual funds. By the early 1970s stocks in REITs were "hot properties" on Wall Street, with volume $20 billion. The REITs accounted for one-fifth of the money loaned out for development and construction. Major banks including Wells Fargo and the Bank of America launched trusts of their own; even insurance companies such as Massachusetts Mutual were involved. The largest trust was Chase Manhattan Mortgage and Realty, for which the Rockefeller bank Chase Manhattan was investment adviser. But in 1973-1975 several large developers went bankrupt, sending a number of the REITs backing them into financial trouble. Shares in many REITs dropped to one-fifth of their former value.[36]

Joint ventures between industrial companies and developers have also been important in project financing in recent years. For example, in the early 1980s Royal Dutch Shell went into a joint venture with Gerald Hines Interests to build a $100-million office building in Chicago. In such cases the eventual user of the project provides some control and financing.

Insurance Companies.   Many long-term mortgages, especially for larger projects, have been provided by life insurance companies. These companies have had a love affair with real estate investments for many decades. As early as the 1920s the country's largest insurance companies, Metropolitan Life and Prudential, were putting $50 million into home and apartment loans, funneling the funds through 150 local banks.[36] By the early 1980s, according to the *Life Insurance Fact Book*, insurance companies were third among all institutional investors in the amount of mortgage loans made. Mortgage loans held by life insurance companies totaled $138 billion, constituting a little more than 26 percent of insurance company assets. Back in 1958, fully 70 percent of all mortgages held by insurance companies were for single-family and multi-family housing; but by 1968 that proportion was down to 59 percent. And by 1981 only 26 percent of insurance-financed mortgages were for urban residential loans. Nonresidential, nonfarm mortgages now made up well over half (64 percent) of all mortgages held by insurance companies. These mortgages cover a wide variety of development projects, including shopping centers, office towers, industrial factories, and medical centers. In 1981 life insurance companies had more than $86 billion in these mortgages.[37]

One qualification should be noted. Life insurance companies reduced their net dollar investments in new commercial mortgages in 1982, in step with the general reduction in commercial mortgages made in that recession year. Changes in real estate market conditions, such as general recessions, can reduce lending activity by all lenders, including insurance companies. However, reduced lending does *not* mean a reduced role for life insurance companies. In recent years, including recession years, they have made about 25 percent to 35 percent of commercial mortgage loans. That market share is likely to continue into the future, given the attractiveness of such major loans.

Interestingly, life insurance companies sometimes see themselves as doing "good works." James Oates, onetime board chairperson of the large Equitable Life corporation, wrote that

> with the great housing boom which followed World War II, the life companies again directed their reserve assets into this area of financial need. .... Later, the flow of mortgage funds emphasized industrial and commercial properties, as shopping centers emerged to serve a growing suburban population and as office buildings dominated urban construction... life insurance funds have been highly mobile both in responding to and, to some extent, in anticipating the needs of a rapidly growing and changing society.[38]

Note that profitability for the insurance companies is not listed as a dominant motivation for this major, and oscillating, involvement in real estate. Nor is the negative impact on home loans of this shifting to commercial loans considered.

In addition, life insurance companies have owned a great deal of real estate directly—altogether $18 billion in 1981, up from $3.8 billion in 1960. About 80 percent of this is real estate investment property, not their own office buildings. Life insurance companies have bought all or part of apartment buildings, skyscrapers, and shopping centers. Sometimes they have played a role in directing construction as well. According to a recent article in *Business Week*, life insurance companies are putting the money they hold from clients and from pension funds they control into office towers, shopping centers, apartment complexes, and industrial parks so fast that at the current rate they and similar financial institutions may own the majority of such real estate by the twenty-first century.[39]

In 1981 an estimated 90 percent of commercial property sold was reportedly being bought by life insurance companies and other financial institutions managing pension funds. Insurance companies have not only purchased existing buildings and other real estate but also have developed commercial projects alone or as partners with developers. Independent developers have sometimes been crowded aside or forced into joint ventures with insurance companies. Some corporate executives see independent developers as eventually becoming part of the large finance corporations on which they now depend. One executive quoted in *Business Week* put it this way: "What's to prevent Prudential or Equitable or Metropolitan from hiring developers, with the institution retaining 100% ownership?"[40] Still, caution must be exercised in forecasting the dominance of real estate markets by life insurance companies and other companies managing pension funds. Indeed, in 1982 the office building glut led many pension-fund managers to cut down their real estate investments, including life insurance companies. Cycles in buying and selling commercial real estate suggest that there may not be the long-term trend toward dominance that some have forecasted.

Total pension fund money was well over a half-trillion dollars by 1980 and was expected to be one trillion dollars by 1990. Yet banks, insurance companies, and financial management companies control the investment decisions for most pension funds, even including 80 percent of the union pension funds. Half of the 192 union funds in one AFL-CIO survey were invested by only four companies: Morgan Guaranty Trust, Bankers Trust, Equitable, and Prudential. For the most part, these companies have invested the funds as they see fit, including investing union pension funds in nonunion construction projects. According to one report Prudential used union pension funds to finance a building for the National Right to Work Committee, an organization opposed to unions. A number of building trade unions have organized, in states from California to Florida, to take back control of their pension fund money, to put more control into the hands of the workders themselves. Some of these struggles have been successful, and the future is likely to see more union-finance capital battles over who will manage pension funds and how their money will be used.[41]

Pension funds are not the only source of other people's money that finance capitalists use for their own purposes. Banking institutions loan the savings and other deposits of millions of people to developers. Government programs have encouraged this financing with mortgage loan insurance programs and special tax breaks. Frequently the areas getting the loans are not where the people live whose savings are being loaned. For example, one study of depositors' funds and mortgages found a surprising pattern. A mid-1970s study of large savings and loan institutions in New York found that 70 percent to 90 percent of their deposits came from city residents, but only 15 percent to 17 percent of all the mortgages they held were on properties in the same city area.[42]

Foreign Investment. Capital for development flows across national boundaries. Some U.S. companies have been heavily involved in mortgage loans in Canada. In the mid-1970s Prudential Life Insurance Co. and the Rockefellers' Metropolitan Life Insurance Co. were reportedly among the top ten lenders in Canadian real estate. Developers and other real estate actors who have had trouble getting loan money for projects seen as risky by Canadian lenders have gone to U.S. and other foreign lending corporations. A significant portion of Canada's urban real estate is owned or financed by U.S., German, Italian, British, and other foreign interests. Canadian companies have, in turn, invested heavily in U.S. real estate. For example, Olympia and York Developments, Ltd., bought several New York skyscrapers for $350 million, and the Cadillac Fairview Company has invested in a number of major projects in cities across the nation. Since the 1970s many Canadian developers have been eager to move to the United States, where profits are higher because of, acccording to developers, lower labor costs, better interest rates, and less government regulation.[43]

Capital shortages for urban development projects have become a serious problem for U.S. developers. As a result, they have sought overseas capital to fund their projects, and foreign banks, investors, and pension funds have provided significant financing. Not only Canada but also the United Kingdom, West Germany, the Netherlands, Saudi Arabia, Japan, and Hong Kong have been involved. During 1980 alone, according to official reports, foreigners invested $6.9 billion in U.S. real estate; half of this was by Canadians, with the United Kingdom and the Netherlands accounting for most of the rest. The total held by foreigners is estimated by the Homer Hoyt Institute to be in the $125-$190 billion range and growing rapidly.[44]

A Note on Related Actors Often coordinated with industrial firms, developers, and lenders, a variety of other land-interested actors play key supportive roles in the drama of urban growth, development, and decline. Among these are construction companies, real estate agencies, architectural firms, and engineering companies.

Construction companies are critical to development projects. Those that are not subsidiaries of developers are often closely held companies that do not publish much information on themselves. The public view of construction is one of a lot of little companies. Yet large construction companies do a great deal of commercial and residential construction in the United States. For example, in an examination of New York City, N.R. Kleinfield noted that "only a smattering of general contractors regularly build tall office towers in New York City. ... They are the hired hands, the ones that for a flat fee take the dream of skyscraper and wrench it into reality."[45]

Real estate brokers and agents are another category of lan-interested actors whose decisions, often in coordination with developers and bankers, have shaped cities. Some specialize in selling commercial real estate space; others, in residential sales. Real estate associations were organized in larger cities prior to 1900, but it was not until 1916 that the forerunner of the National Association of Real Estate Boards (NAREB) was created. The NAREB (later renamed the National Association of Realtors) has been one of the most powerful and effective lobbies in Washington, D.C. Together with the National Association of Home Builders, they have fought for certain types of government housing and banking assistance programs, and against others. In later chapters we will see the role real estate organizations played in securing government assistance for the home mortgage industry—and thus for suburbanization.

DEVELOPMENT AND LAND SPECULATION

One of the major consequences of urban land development under modern capitalism can be seen in the patterns of landownership. One noteworthy phenomenon is *land banking*. Developers, particularly large developers, their financial associates, and large landowners, own or control an increasingly large percentage of urban land. Development corporations can buy up land and hold it in land banks, waiting for its value to rise from adjacent development, including the building of highways. They can become involved in joint ventures with other owners and financiers of land. Billions of dollars in land assets are held in this fashion by land development and allied companies. This land can serve several purposes. It can be held for future development by the company holding it, and it may be a speculative investment. Developers, as well as other land-oriented capitalists, not only shift capital from one real estate sector to another—as from land in downtown areas to land in suburbs and back—but they also bank capital drawn from commercial or manufacturing operations in land holdings. This banked profit and wealth can be returned to development or industrial activities when future profitability dictates. But investment in land is not productive, that is, it does not increase the goods and services available in the society.

Great amounts of money can be realized in urban land holding, buying, and selling. The creation of money value, often on paper, occurs as land ages and changes hands, often many times, in its life span. Land developers and other real estate investors acting as speculators are at the heart of this recurrent processing. A real estate investor is an entrepreneur or corporate entity that purchases land (or land and buildings) with the hope of a profit from rising property values. But a speculator can be seen as a distinctive type of real estate investor, one who is primarily interested in the unearned profits from property values and thus less interested in developing the land for productive uses or in managing buildings. Some speculators are not interested in holding property for a long time. Of course, in everyday practice it is difficult to tell where ordinary land investment ends and speculation begins —the two are closely related.[46]

The Nineteenth Century.   Rural and urban land speculation by individuals and corporations has been characteristic of capitalism since the early days of this nation. In the first centuries of North American development real estate speculators and developers, often merchants, large farmers, and railroaders with wealth and means, launched or shaped city development from Washington to Omaha and San Francisco, setting the pattern for much future growth. Acting legally and illegally, they bought lands, pressured legislatures, and bribed officials in their quest for profits.[47]

In the nineteenth century the growing railroad corporations were among the first capitalistic enterprises to become heavily involved in real estate speculation and development, rural and urban. Actions taken by railroad executives had a significant effect on land use and development in the West. Many railroad lines were extended into unoccupied territory primarily for land speculation. Railroad capitalists received huge government subsidies to expand lines westward, the most significant of which were large grants of land along the railroads. These gifts of public land rose in value with the growth of railroads and towns along the railroads, often leading to large land profits for railroad corporations, even to the present day. For example, in 1850 the federal government gave 2.6 million acres to the Illinois Central Railroad. Later the Northern Pacific Railroad was given 47 million acres.

Surprisingly, land sales and development were often a greater source of profit than railroad building. By 1900, 183 million acres had been given to the railroads, compared with the smaller figure of 80 million acres sold to the better-known 600,000 pioneering farmers.[48]

The growth of some midwestern and western cities was significantly accelerated or depressed by the actions of railroad capitalists. Sometimes railroad corporations developed towns. But even when they were not directly involved in building towns they had a profound effect on urban development. Because the placement of railroads heavily shaped land values, some railroad companies even sought private bribes in return for putting the towns on a new railroad line. Railroad capitalists and their subordinates sometimes negotiated with town developers or promoters to get the best bargain in terms of right-of-way land and direct city monetary contributions. Towns and cities usually had to pay the fee or face serious economic troubles, possibly even death, if the railroads bypassed them.[49]

Urban promoters were very important in town and city development as the frontier of the United States moved westward. Urban entrepreneurs promoted growth. Town promoters, argues Richard Wade, were the real pioneers who opened up the West.[50] They chose many town sites. Most promoters were heavily involved in local landownership, speculation, and development. Many were local businesspeople, such as merchants, looking to expand their clientele or invest surplus profits. "Boosterism" has been important since this early period. Local officials and promoters with real estate investments lobbied railroad corporations to come their way. Cities such as Kansas City and El Paso became major because of railroad company decisions to deal with local promotors. In Los Angeles, local land promoters gave a major railroad $600,000 and other subsidies to secure a railroad route.[51]

The Impact Today.   Today land speculation continues to be a critical part of profit making on the urban fringe. It may be done by developers, bankers, or industrial corporations. Many developers of shopping centers, suburbs, and industrial parks are actively involved in land speculation. They seek profits not only from building and leasing but also from buying land near their developments and around the city fringe. Some passively wait for their land values to rise, but others work actively to increase those values, such as by aggressively seeking governmental subsidies in the form of utilities for their lands.

Developers and speculators can be the real planners of a given urban area. Some operate by looking a decade ahead, trying to predict the next round of urban or suburban sprawl. Other developer-speculators become involved when development seems imminent, making a profit by getting the necessary rezoning and other political decisions for a parcel of land. There are intimate relationships between real estate capitalists and industrial capitalists. Sometimes industrial capitalists lead the development process by their own site location decisions. At other times, property capital makes strategic land purchase decisions that shape development by attracting industrial corporations. One Long island study by Mark Gottdiener, for example, clearly documents the role of land investors and speculators in channeling urban growth there in distinctive directions. Moreover, central-city land speculation helps drive prices high and thus encourages outward expansion of the city. Transitional areas "slums") near existing central-city development are major targets of speculation; they may be bulldozed and banked, for example, as parking lots, until the right time for profitable further further development.[52]

Land banking and speculating have negative consequences. Bruce Lindeman argues that speculation actually alters the nature of the land commodity itself, by restricting the supply of land and forcing prices *above* what they would have been without speculative activity. Market prices can rise to absurd levels. Higher-than-necessary prices result in part from the expensive financial arrangements into which speculators enter, as well as from the speculative pricing proves itself. These costs are passed along in the form of higher prices for the actual users. Restrictions on land supply also arise because of the complex legal and financial arrangements that a series of speculators, one after another, can bring to a given parcel of land. Complex legal entanglements later hamper the sale of land to developers and builders. Encumbered by mortgages, land changes its character as a commodity. One result of this speculation is an acceleration of urban sprawl as developers try to leapfrog land tied up by legal or financial complications or by speculators holding out for higher prices. Suburban sprawl might even be defined as the recurring flight of speculators and developers to cheaper land farther out.[53]

One of the few discussions of land speculation in the United States appears in *Progress and Poverty*, a provocative yet neglected book by the nineteenth-century reformer Henry George. George argues that it is the work and effort of an *entire* community that really brings a steady advance in land values, *not* the efforts of land speculators. He notes that "this steady increase naturally leads to speculation in which future increase is anticipated." The land speculator thus secures, unjustly and without productive effort on the land, the increased value generated by the whole community's efforts. By control of land, the speculator ultimately secures hard-earned dollars from working people who must later rent or buy what is developed on the land.[54]

CONCLUSION:
THE SOCIAL COSTS OF DEVELOPMENT

We have examined developers and their allies, the large landowners and financial institutions, and noted their impact on cities. Control over the physical environment of cities comes with control over medium- and large-scale developments. A development corporation may build a large office park; smaller developers often develop the areas surrounding large projects, such as by providing condominium buildings. A large city area thus changes, and viable older communities and smaller businesses may be destroyed.

Actions of developers contribute to inflation for consumers. New projects can mean higher housing and apartment costs, ranging from 10 percent to 40 percent more. Profits from shopping centers and industrial parks also put upward pressure on the consumer prices charged by the companies who rent and use these facilities. Major developers often do not reduce their project prices and rents when sales are slow; they have the market power to hold their price levels and wait until conditions improve.[55]

The United States development system extracts huge resource surpluses and thus redistributes wealth according to its own logic of inequality. Who gains, and who loses? The retail and industrial corporations, developers, and finance institutions gain. Those worker-consumers in need of reasonably priced goods and housing often lose. New development may make a central city look more glossy and modern, but the slum or housing problems there are not solved.[56]

Cities are zones of conflict between competing claims for land use, and those with less wealth and power usually lose in the competition. Development projects, large and small, benefit some people and cost others. The conflict over land use and development is a barely hidden class conflict—between those who build office towers, shopping centes, and the like and those who need better schools and better housing; between development and finance capitalists and ordinary working people.

The development industry has absorbed much investment capital during periods when those resources could have been available for other projects to meet more basic societal needs. Is the capital used by development companies put to productive use? Yes and no.

If it is all used to build new factories, schools, or hospitals one can see that it has been a productive investment, provided of course the new buildings are quickly put to use. If it is used to tear down an old, but perfectly usable, office block and replace it with another, or to produce a large building that stands empty for years, society may doubt the wisdom of the system.[57]

Property developers go where the profits are, not necessarily where the human or societal needs are. Societal resources used to meet luxury needs, such as for expensive suburban subdivisions or downtown condominium apartments, cannot be used to increase the supply of low-income or middle-income housing, a persisting social need.

NOTES

1. Leonard Downie, *Mortgage on America* (New York: Praeger, 1974), p. 69; William Zeckendorf, *Zeckendorf* (New York: Holt, Rinehart and Winston, 1970), pp. 5-10.

2. Oliver Marriott, *The Property Boom* (London: Hamish Hamihou Press, 1967), pp. 199-202.

3. "Aloof Canadians Put Mark on U.S. Skylines," Dallas *Morning News*, September 27, 1981, microfiche 106, G6-7.

4. James Lorimer, *The Developers* (Toronto: James Lorimer and Co., 1978), pp. 61-62; cf Marriott, *The Property Boom*, p. 24.

5. Rice Center Research and Development Corporation, *Houston Initiatives: Phase One Report* (Houston: Rice Center, 1981), pp. 1-15.

6. "Straight Talk from a Master Builder," *Housing* 59 (June, 1981), p. 29; "How Building Better Makes Crow Tops in Warehouses," *Building Design and Construction* 20, August, 1980, pp. 68-72.

7. Lorimer, *The Developers*, pp. ix-x.

8. Catherine Wismer, *Sweethearts* (Toronto: James Lorimer and Co., 1980), pp. ix-xi.

9. Downie, *Mortgage on America*, pp. 79-80, 181-196.

10. Dana L. Thomas, *Lords of the Land* (New York: G. P. Putnam's Sons, 1977), pp. 137-175.

11. Don Mason, "Ambition Drives Apartment-Builder Watson to Commercial Construction," Houston *Chronicle*, July 19, 1981, sect. 3, p. 20.

12. Susan Goldberg, "Campeau Not Afraid to Speak His Mind," Dallas *Morning News*, September 29, 1981, microfiche 109, F9-10.

13. This discussion is drawn from *Cadillac Fairview, Annual Report, 1981*; and Michael V. Prentiss, "Canadians Setting the Pace in the U.S.," Speech to the National Association of Real Estate Investment Trusts, New York, October, 1981.

14. Lewis M. Goodkin, *When Real Estate and Homebuilding Become Big Business: Mergers, Acquisitions, and Joint Ventures* (Boston: Cahners Books, 1974), p. xv.

15. Ibid., pp. 20-22.

16. Richard A. Walker and Michael K. Heiman, "Quiet Revolution for Whom?" *Annals of the Association of American Geographers* 71 (March, 1981), p. 71; the survey is reported in Goodkin, *When Real Estate and Homebuilding Become Big Business*, p. xv.

17. Woodlands Development Corporation fact sheet, in author's files.

18. Interview with George Mitchell, originally published by Ginger H. Jester in *Houston North Magazine*, November, 1980, revised and published as a brochure for Woodlands, p. 5.

19. Goodkin, *When Real Estate and Homebuilding Become Big Business*, p. 20.

20. "The Public Builders in 1980-1981: Hanging Touch against Mounting Odds," *Housing* 59 (June, 1981), pp. 10-15.

21. Walker and Heiman, "Quiet Revolution for Whom?" pp. 76-77.

22. Henry Aubin, *City for Sale* (Toronto: James Lorimer and Co., 1977), pp. 35-41, 64, 383.

23. Lorimer, *The Developers*, pp. 70-71; "Still an Inflation Haven, with the Right Deal," *Business Week* (December 29, 1980), pp. 140-142.

24. Peter Ambrose and Bob Colenutt, *The Property Machine* (London: Penguin Books, 1975), p. 41.

25. Ibid., p. 127.

26. Lorimer, *The Developers*, p. 62.

27. Goodkin, *When Real Estate and Homebuilding Become Big Business*, p. 6.

28. Ambrose and Colenutt, *The Property Machine*, p. 58.

29. Martin Mayer, *The Bankers* (New York: Ballantine Books, 1974), p. 407.

30. Urban Land Institute, *Downtown Development Handbook* (Washington, D.C.: Urban Land Institute, 1980), pp. 233-234.

31. Mayer, *The Bankers*, pp. 265-266.

32. Ibid., p. 267.

33. Mark Gottdiener, *Planned Sprawl* (Beverly Hills, Calif.: Sage Publications, 1977), p. 110.

34. Downie, *Mortgage on America*, p. 76-78.

35. Anthony Sampson, *The Money Lenders* (New York: Viking Press, 1981), pp. 135-136; Thomas, *Lords of the Land*, pp. 285-290.

36. Pearl Janet Davies, *Real Estate in American History* (Washington, D.C.: Public Affairs Press, 1958), p. 141.

37. American Council of Life Insurance, *1982 Life Insurance Fact Book* (Washington, D.C.: American Council of Life Insurance, 1982), pp. 80-84.

38. James F. Oates, Jr., *Business and Social Change* (New York: McGraw-Hill, 1968), pp. 44-49, as quoted in Karen Orren, *Corporate Power and Social Change* (Baltimore: Johns Hopkins University Press, 1974), pp. 89-90.

39. Ibid., p. 84; "Lenders Rush into Ownership," *Business Week* (April 13, 1981), p. 158.

40. "Lenders Rush into Ownership," *Business Week* (April 13, 1981), p. 163.

41. Marc Erlich, "Building Trades Aim for Union Control over Pension Fund Investments," *Labor Notes* 30, July 28, 1981, p. 11.

42. Jack Newfield and Paul Dubrul, *The Abuse of Power* (New York: Viking Press, 1977), pp. 101-103.

43. Aubin, *City for Sale*, p. 319.

44. Prentiss, "Canadians Setting the Pace in the U.S."

45. N. R. Kleinfield, "Boom Times for the Builders of New York," *New York Times*, July 26, 1981, Section 3, p. 1.

46. Gottdiener, *Planned Sprawl*, pp. 104-108.

47. Aaron M. Sakolski, *Land Tenure and Land Taxation in America* (New York: Robert Schalkenbach Foundation, 1957), pp. 53-55.

48. Aaron M. Sakolski, *The Great American Land Bubble* (New York: Harper and Brothers, 1932); Edward P. Eichler and Marshall Kaplan, *The Community Builders* (Berkeley and Los Angeles: University of California Press, 1967), p. 15.

49. Thomas, *Lords of the Land*, pp. 70-87; Sakolski, *Land Tenure and Land Taxation in America*, pp. 163-174. Dee Brown, *Hear That Lonesome Whistle Blow* (New York: Bantam Books, 1977), pp. 244-268.

50. Richard C. Wade, *The Urban Frontier, 1790-1830* (Cambridge: Harvard University Press, 1959), pp. 27-40.

51. Charles N. Glaab and A. Theodore Brown, *A History of Urban America* (New York: Macmillan, 1967), pp. 119-120; Sam Bass Warner, *The Urban Wilderness* (New York: Harper and Row, 1972), pp. 19-22.

52. Cf. Gottdiener, *Planned Sprawl.*

Bruce Lindeman, "Anatomy of Land Speculation," *Journal of the American Institute of Planners* 42 (April, 1976), pp. 149-151.

54. Henry George, *Progress and Poverty* (Reprint ed., New York: Robert Schalkenbach Foundation, 1962), pp. 264, 268.

55. Lorimer, *The Developers*, p. 223.

56. Ambrose and Colenutt, *The Property Machine*, pp. 142, 159.

57. Ibid., p. 36. See also p. 127.

4
THE MANHATTANIZATION
OF AMERICA:
SKYSCRAPERS AND MXDS

A SKYLINE OF TOMBSTONES

Rape, Manhattanization, inhumanity, plastic environment. These and harsher terms have been used by city dwellers to describe the widespread development of high-rise towers in their cities. In earlier decades the public had quietly accepted high-rise architecture as a vertical sign of progress, but by the 1970s and 1980s a growing number of citizens' groups had come to question the process, as one group put it, of "burying our city under a skyline of tombstones."[1]

With its increasingly obscured scenic views of bays and hills, San Francisco has become a national symbol of discontent over the Manhattanization of cities. By the mid-1970s a substantial majority of citizens there were in favor of high-rise building controls. A local initiative petition to have every high-rise building approved by the general public was supported by 40 percent of the voters. The battle in San Francisco started in the 1960s with the construction of curved high-rise apartment buildings, the Fontana Towers, which were built on the shoreline and blocked the view of the bay from major sections of San Francisco. Other giant buildings constructed over the next decade became targets for public hostility, including the prominent Bank of America building (1965-1966), cursed for its dark color.[2] Environmentalists were increasingly joined by large numbers of middle-income neighborhood residents. One advertisement by a citizen's group opposed to developers building more skyscrapers put the public view forcefully: "San Francisco was once light, hilly, pastel, open. Inviting. In only twelve years it has taken on the forbidden look of every other American city. Forty more skyscrapers are due in the next five years. They are as great a disaster economically as they are aesthetically."[3]

People in other cities have also begun to question the dominating skyscraper architecture, from Boston, where one major tower has many cracked windows and pieces of facade falling off, to New York, where skyscrapers have created numerous sunless canyons for the urbanites below. For an increasing number of citizens skyscrapers are dramatic symbols of the takeover of cities by large industrial, retail, and development corporations.

And they are correct. Large industrial and commercial corporations increasingly dominate cityscapes. They organize the development process. Developers and associated construction firms are at the heart of high-rise developments. Working to house industrial and commercial corporations, they build office towers and office parks as well as hotels and industrial buildings. They build such projects as hospitals and government buildings for government agencies. They also build shopping malls and housing facilities for those who work in the towers, parks, and hotels. And they build apartment buildings and suburban subdivisions.

Today certain projects, such as office towers, tend to be located in central-city areas and reflect a concentration of business activities. Other major urban development projects, such as industrial parks and suburban subdivisions, tend to be located outside the central cities and represent a decentralizing tendency in urban development, a shift outward from central areas. These contrasting trends are part of the broader process of uneven and oscillating urban development, a process tied closely to the investment decisions of an elite group of private-sector decision makers.

CHANGING SKYLINES: SKYSCRAPERS AND OTHER OFFICE BUILDINGS

Shifting City Faces. The dominance of skyscrapers is rather new in American cities. Most of these glass and steel boxes have been built since World War II. Mostly office buildings, the skyscrapers are built to house corporations and to make profits. Many conspicuous symbols of who runs our cities—very large corporations. In building industry handbooks office buildings, large and small, are sometimes described as structures where services are provided or where information is processed. But they signal much more than that. The largest office buildings, in particular, reflect the shift from an older ("competitive") capitalism of smaller firms to a modern ("monopoly") capitalism dominated by larger firms.

There is a close relationship between the character of capitalism in a particular historical period and its urban form. Manhattan-scapes of high-rise towers, hotels, and apartment buildings are a new invention, for until the 1940s and 1950s most cities had only modest-sized buildings either downtown or in outlying areas. Going back into the mid-nineteenth century, we find cities mostly composed of buildings less than five stories high and organized around the needs of merchants and early manufacturers. Take a major city of the day—Boston. In 1850 Boston was a walking city of small buildings stretching only two miles out from the city hall. Hills had been cut down and marshes filled in, and developers were building three- and four-story homes for the small, prosperous middle-income sector. Wharves were built along the coast. Warehouses and manufacturing buildings were concentrated in low-rise structures in certain sections. Residences and manufacturing facilities were near each other. That would soon change.

Within a few decades urban development in such cities created ever more functional segregation, with areas for factories, railroad yards, suburban housing, and office buildings, most of which were larger-scale projects than before. The increasing domination of the urban scene by ever-larger corporations in the late nineteenth and early twentieth centuries reshaped the cities.

Interestingly, the development of the technology necessary to skyscrapers, for instance, electric elevators, had already preceded the great expansion of high-rise construction by several decades. Modern steel skeleton skyscrapers, rising higher than the eleven to twelve-story limits of the older stone wall construction, were first built in New York and Chicago in the 1880s. But it was only after 1900 that the demand for skyscrapers began to increase dramatically. Skyscraper building began in earnest between 1905 and 1930 in New York and Chicago, which became major nerve centers for the new supercorporations. In New York there was the Singer Building (1908, forty-seven stories), the Metropolitan Life Insurance Building (1909, fifty stories), and the Woolworth Building (1913, fifty-five stories). This increase was related to the emergence of large national and multinational corporations whose control over widespread industries required centralized administrative centers. For several decades now, high-rise office buildings have been seen as necessary for housing the large groups of white-collar workers required to coordinate and administer (the paperwork of) large corporations. Skyscrapers thus emerged with the rise of large corporations in the modern period of monopoly capitalism. Earlier capitalism did not require such centralized office facilities.[4]

A New Breed: Skyscraper Builders. Rising in prominence alongside the high-rise buildings have been the major development corporations. In Chapter 1 we noted the dramatic reception Gerald Hines gave at the foundation-laying ceremony for a large bank-and-office tower in Houston. Since the 1950s Hines's company has built 273 projects, altogether about 55 million square feet of space in cities from coast to coast. Among his famous projects are the Galleria (multiple-use) shopping mall and the Texas Commerce Tower (one of the nation's tallest buildings) in Houston. Hines's company has built office towers, manufacturing facilities, warehouses, shopping malls, and some residential housing.

Hines became nationally famous for hiring prominent architects to design some of his buildings. A *Fortune* story notes that he "did so because he thought well-designed buildings would make more money for him and his partners."[5] Monumental constructions by architects such as Philip Johnson and I.M. Pei were generally shunned by developers until Hines decided these projects could be undertaken at reasonable cost. Hines has also brought high-powered marketing techniques to the selling of his office buildings. Prospective business tenants reportedly get a grand tour, called the "processional" in the firm, during which they are presented with huge models of the building under construction, a slide-show presentation on multiple screens, and the implied message that this architecture is the cutting edge of Western civilization. A sad irony is that these lavish displays of large-scale urban development occur in cities with massive urban problems.[6]

BOOM AND BUST:
CYCLES IN OFFICE CONSTRUCTION

Periods of Shortages and Surpluses. From at least the 1960s to 1981 there was heavy demand from corporations for office space. Office towers and other office buildings were springing up in key cities, North and South. In the 1975-1981 period major cities, including Seattle, San Francisco, Los Angeles, Phoenix, Dallas, Houston, Denver, Atlanta, Miami, Washington,

Chicago, and New York, were experiencing shortages of downtown office space. According to a major survey, the average vacancy rate in buildings in the United States and Canada declined over the 1970s, then rose a little in 1980-1981.

However, in 1982 the office construction boom was replaced by a bust in numerous cities. Owners of new office buildings in many of these cities were having difficulty in finding tenants. Even big real estate developers and investors were caught in the general economic recession. They had invested with the idea that continuing inflation would guarantee them profits in the leasing and eventual sale of their office buildings. By 1982 the recession forced many industrial companies to cancel plans to expand, to move into new offices, or to move to new areas of the country. Those that could still move were seriously considering office space outside the more expensive downtown areas. These decisions meant less demand for the formerly soaring office building construction and leasing. Journals such as *Newsweek* and *Business Week* were heralding a long-term "office glut."[7]

In the middle of this glut were major Canadian corporations, such as Cadillac Fairview and Olympia and York, which had rushed into U.S. real estate in the previous five years. Investing $15 billion in U.S. real estate, these companies often had little experience with local U.S. land and markets and paid very high prices for their office building and other real estate investments. In the 1979-1982 period the Canadian companies controlled one quarter of all new office construction in the United States. But these Canadian companies began selling off a large share of their investments when the office glut became a reality. This selling in turn triggered others to sell their office buildings, and the glut increased.[8]

Office building development, like other development, has moved up and down with movements in the larger political economy of modern capitalism.

Towers in the Sunbelt: The Houston Example.   In the office building boom of the 1960s and 1970s cities such as Los Angeles, Denver, Atlanta, and Houston were stand-out stars in construction and leasing. Supported by the inflow of capital, development corporations put up many office projects.

The city of Houston, for example, became the construction capital of the nation with billions of dollars in construction. When compared with that in other major cities, real estate development in Houston has involved less governmental involvement, such as urban renewal projects, and profit rates have ranged from good to tremendous. The lack of zoning in Houston can reduce development time, because of fewer government permits, and speed the realization of profit. Much urban development has been centered in office buildings or multiple-use developments (MXDs) that combine office buildings with such features as shopping centers. The construction of large office buildings (100,000 square feet or more) in Houston began in the pre-World War II period; yet only two dozen of the 280 largest buildings now standing were built before 1952. Most large buildings have been built in the last decade and a half. Office construction has been scattered all over town and includes the tallest building west of the Mississippi.[9]

By the early 1980s Houston had 100 million square feet of leasable office space. Yet the majority (62 percent) of Houston's office space is outside the immediate downtown area. The office and retail space in just two outlying centers (the Post Oak and Greenway areas) taken together is twice that of the office space in *downtown* areas in such major cities as Baltimore, New Orleans, and Minneapolis. This suggests the incredible scale of office (and related retail) development in Sunbelt cities in the last decade. In Houston a few dozen large development corporations, oil companies, and financial institutions dominate much of the office tower and office park business.

Yet the office glut that plagued developers in other cities also hit Houston in 1982. Campeau Corporation, a major Canadian developer, was one of several to cancel or postpone major office projects in Houston. With the oil and gas industry in economic recession, there was less demand for office space. Lending institutions were becoming more conservative in loaning money for skyscraper projects. Even so, there were many skyscrapers and smaller office buildings under construction. As a result, the already growing and relatively high vacancy rate for office buildings (11.4 percent in 1982) was expected to increase further before declining again in the future.

Not even booming Sunbelt cities have been immune from the periodic recessions in real estate development.

Efficiency and Profitability.   Except in times of recession, over the last two decades among the most successful and profitable real estate projects have been office buildings. A common explanation for the downtown office construction is couched in terms of improved business efficiency; that is, this clustering of corporate offices increases access for businesses, their executives, and ordinary workers. But the massive traffic jams in downtown areas suggest the major inefficiencies in centralized office towers as well. Various factors lie behind this concentration: the desire for spatial dominance, the differentiation of administration from production in larger corporations, the interaction of capitalist and managerial elites from several companies, and a desire for a prestigious image, a type of conspicuous consumption by corporate elites seeking to be housed in the finest new buildings. Office building centralization did not involve a vote of the working people who work in these central cities—the life-shaping decisions were made by top corporate executives.[10]

Generally speaking, office buildings are measured not by their contribution to the community but by their height, pizzaz, and profitability. Larger buildings require major developers together with their various business partners. In the development of office buildings developers work with bankers and construction executives. The operations and negotiations may be secretive and may involve dummy corporations to conceal the true corporate involvements from competitors and the public. The first step is gaining control of the land where the building is to be constructed. A second major step is securing prior leasing commitments from companies to occupy space in the new building, for lenders often require these. Another step is to get the necessary planning and zoning approval from government officials.

Office buildings are sometimes favored by developers over other projects because their business tenants can more easily pass rental costs on to consumers and are unlikely to press for rent control. Once the buildings are in successful operation, as a rule, rising office rents more than cover mortgage and operating expenses and provide developer-owners with a high rate of return on their investments. Office buildings are marketed by the managing firms in much the same ways as are other commodities. One office building advertisement, for example, emphasizes the following: (1) its "prestige" address; (2) flexible floor plans; (3) its central atrium and panoramic views; and (4) its special climate control system. Expensive color brochures and advertising techniques are used to build interest in a new office building among executives of possible tenant corporations.[11]

The larger development projects set the pattern within which much smaller-scale development takes place. Hotels and apartment buildings built by other developers are constructed near office towers and office parks. High-rise luxury apartments are sold as condominiums for better-off urbanites.

HIGH-RISE HOTELS:
THE GAME IN ACTION

In the board game of Monopoly people buy and mortgage little plastic hotels as they develop their properties from Marvin Gardens to Boardwalk. Rents charged to passers-by determine a player's success. In the real world of Atlantic City, New Jersey, from which the Monopoly game's property names are drawn, the huge hotels are located on property owned by a few major corporations. High rents charged to visitors, many of whom come to gamble, enhance the profits of hotel chains, as well as of the developers and general contractors who constructed the high rises. New casino hotels earn gambling profits as well. But Atlantic City is not alone. Interspersed among office skyscrapers, new high-rise hotels dot many central-city skylines.

Large international corporations often own or control these hotels. For example, in the early 1980s the Hilton company owned or leased 17 hotels, managed 31 more, and collected franchise fees from 165 additional hotels that use its name. More than 200 hotels, mostly large ones, rose up under the Hilton name, which covered real estate assets estimated at nearly $2 billion. In recent years this type of high-rise construction has been very profitable for developers, owners, and managers. Hotel chains can increase profits and keep up with inflation by raising room prices, a practice that makes little effect on occupancy rates. As Barron Hilton, head of the Hilton company, said recently: "That pricing flexibility has been one of the most favorable aspects of our business. We can change rates overnight."[12]

Today's complicated ownership and financing for many hotels can be seen in the way the Hilton company operates. In the mid-1970s the company sold half interest in six of its largest hotels to the Prudential Insurance Company for $83 million, with Hilton collecting the management fees for running the hotels.[13]

FINANCING HIGH-RISE DEVELOPMENT

Financial Institutions. The financing of office building projects by development companies is usually complicated. Developers of office building projects compete with other users of credit for the limited loan money available; alternative investment opportunities for lenders affect their interest in office projects. As with other types of development projects, lenders often require not only interest but also *points*, that is a lump sum payment to the lender at the time of loan closing. Points and other lenders' fees increase lenders' profits. Construction loans are short-term, high-interest loans necessary for actual construction. Permanent financing, usually from another lender, such as an insurance company, replaces the construction loan; until recently permanent financing has typically involved twenty-five- to thirty-year pay-out (amortization) and a lower interest rate. Variable rate loans and roll-over loans have, more recently, been written so that lenders can raise (or lower) interest rates as the loan market changes; in this way lenders are not tied to a fixed interest rate for twenty-five to thirty years. Over the last decade or so instability in finance capitalism, signaled in part by sharply rising interest rates, has made such loans necessary.[14]

A developer may go in with a bank or insurance company as a major financial partner on a particular project. Once silent financial partners, today lenders frequently wish to own a piece of the buildings they help finance to enhance their own profits. Many financial corporations will provide long-term financing only if they receive a portion of the equity.

Large insurance companies have been important in financing office tower projects. For example, in 1980 Prudential Insurance and its PIC Realty subsidiary held $2 billion in real estate assets in the city of Houston alone. Prudential is involved in a number of office buildings; in recent years it has emphasized shorter-term real estate loans and participation as partial owner in the projects it finances (equity participation). During periods of construction glut, such as the office glut of 1982, insurance companies and other lenders have been able to get better deals for themselves. In 1982, a vice-president of Metropolitan Life Insurance Company noted that his company usually demanded 50 percent to 75 percent of the equity, and thus of the income generated by leasing, in major real estate projects.[15]

In the 1970s and 1980s a new trend could be seen in the close organizational ties which were developing between some lending organizations and developers. One Chicago developer, Metropolitan Structures, became allied with the Metropolitan Life Insurance Company. The limited partnership gives the developer a dependable source of financing and the insurance company a close linkage to what it regards as better investments. A similar relationship was developed between Equitable Life Assurance Society and a major urban development company in New York. Business Week has described this in terms of insurance companies adding "in-house developers." A number of developers have expressed their fears that they are becoming too dependent on financial institutions such as Prudential and Metropolitan

Life; they as developers may become subordinate, or even extinct, as lending corporations organize their own development subsidiaries.

Many financial institutions are beginning to require other development restrictions. For example, when one large developer in Houston went to financial backers to see about expanding a multiple-use office park by another several million square feet, he was reportedly told that the backers would only finance another one million square feet if some type of relief for severe traffic problems were provided, such as a public mass transit system. Concerned with their own profit, financial institutions have imposed a type of urban planning on developers, formerly accustomed to operating without this type of control. Mass transit has become necessary from finance capital's point of view in cities with extreme traffic congestion. Ironically, conservative bankers and developers can now be found begging for more government intervention, at least in the form of mass transit.

Foreign investment money has been also channeled into office buildings. Foreign banks and other corporations have put surplus profits into this and other U.S. real estate. In some Sunbelt cities a fifth or more of all new investment money for such development has come from foreign sources, much of it hidden from public scrutiny.

Government Assistance.   Government officials play a role in downtown office development, providing money for services such as new roads and sewers, giving away public land by closing streets and by urban renewal projects, and constructing business-oriented projects such as convention centers and parking garages. Office building developments in central business districts receive tax and utility benefits. Local public services and utilities for the corporations to be housed in the skyscrapers may be partially subsidized by smaller commercial and residential customers in the central-city areas, because the latter pay proportionately higher tax and utility rates.[16]

Most residents in New York are aware of the two 110-story World Trade Center towers in lower Manhattan, the tallest buildings in a forest of giant structures. Those high-rise columns cost a billion dollars and house tens of thousands of employees and visitors on a typical weekday. Eight hundred tenants, when the buildings are fully occupied, will sprawl across 9 million square feet of office space, linked by ninety-five elevators. Tenants include international import and export companies, international bankers, U.S. and New York government trade agencies, and world trade organizations.

The idea for the World Trade Center came from the Downtown-Lower Manhattan Association, a business group organized and led by David Rockefeller, then head of the Chase Manhattan Bank. Its goal was to raze older structures in the area and create a new center of business prosperity in Manhattan, with a public agency (the Port Authority) picking up the tab for construction. In this case, governmental subsidies for office construction were used to build a project.

THE OPPRESSIVENESS
OF HIGH-RISE DEVELOPMENT

High-rise building development can have serious negative effects. Smaller retail corporations and other small businesses may be displaced from downtown areas by development. Owners of older buildings may have to sell because of the competition with large office towers. Older but much-needed residential housing is sometimes destroyed by downtown development of new office buildings, apartment towers, and hotels. A study of Calgary, Alberta, found that 65 percent of the buildings demolished in downtown areas were single-family houses. In other cases, a new office building replaces an old office building that would be serviceable for many more decades because greater profit is to be made from new construction with its depreciation advantages. New buildings mean more space to rent and, generally, more profit.[17]

A New Climate?   Office towers can even create their own weather and seasons. Sam Bass Warner observes that the "skyscrapers shut off light and air from the passing pedestrian...[and] the lofty height of the towers creates a special microclimate of high winds in winter and sizzling streets and oven-hot masonry walls in summer."[18] Indeed, the expression "twenty-three skiddo" came from the wind-generating feature of New York's Flatiron Building, an early skyscraper built on Twenty-third Street. The winds there played havoc with women's skirts, to the delight of male passers-by. Since the 1950s the "international" style of office building architecture has flourished—boxy concrete, glass, steel, and aluminum structures. This "glass box" architecture is widespread in North American and European cities. Before 1960 most high-rise buildings had modest windows with exteriors of concrete, brick, and metal, but since then there has been a dramatic shift to high-rise buildings with walls made substantially of glass, often coated to look like "a man with opaque wrap-around sunglasses." Because the windows usually do not open, many open-air shafts are needed for expensive, energy-consuming air conditioning systems. And because glass as a rule does not insulate as well as masonry, there is greater energy consumption in the new buildings.

In the 1970s and 1980s some of the glassy-skyscraper structures began to zig and zag, with slanted tops, pyramidal bases, and other architectural variations from the basic box shape. Some were built with tops looking like cathedrals or Chippendale furniture. In 1982 the Century Development Corporation announced it would build a flashy 1,400 foot, eighty-two-story tower in Houston. The second tallest building in the world, this massive spire would be built of glass, metal, and marble laid out in black and white strips; the building was designed to rest on eight huge columns. Designed by architect Helmut Jahn, this modern adaptation of glass-box towers is designed to attract attention for its owners and developers. Such buildings are thus called "signature" buildings because of their uniqueness. A growing number of the new office buildings, Jane Holtz Kay suggests, look like "wacky sculpture"; although innovative and unique, these glassy zig-zag skyscrapers retain many of the same problems of the more common glass boxes still being built.[19]

In the 1950s British glass companies invented the thick float glass that made the massive glass buildings possible. A few companies make most of the glass used in high-rise construction. The shift to glass-box architecture reflected elitist, not democratic, decision making. One city analyst has commented that

> we have no figures to tell us how the urbanite reacts to the adamant geometry of the glass box, or how the bleakness of our main streets, studded with parking lots, hits small town and rural folk. Who can doubt, though, that our architecture of the slick, boring highrise, the empty plaza, the desolate shopping mall in the suburbs—all those structures that forbid human congress— contribute to the poverty of...public life.[20]

We do have a few opinion surveys on how urbanites react to the geometry of high-rise buildings. A survey of 300 University of Maryland students asked what they liked and disliked about tall buildings. A majority said they liked the views from the buildings; a significant percentage felt large buildings made efficient use of space. But the majority mentioned more features that they disliked: (1) waiting for elevators; (2) absence of greenery;

(3) threat of fire; and (4) impersonality. Many disliked the monotonous architecture and the difficulty of egress; they feared getting stuck in skyscraper elevators. Among those who lived near a tall building, one-third said it was annoying. When asked, "What do you think would improve tall buildings?" the major answers were greater fire safety, more greenery, and a height maximum of twelve stories.[21]

On the West Coast a survey of Bank of America employees found that a large proportion felt oppressed by the large buildings around them. What seemed to bother them were the scale, the closed-in feeling, and the lack of breathing space. Large buildings with repetitious elements, such as thousands of similar windows, are troubling to many urbanites; they are frequently viewed as giant "anthills" or cold "tombstones."[22]

Energy Questions.   Do large glassy office buildings, hotels, and apartment buildings squander energy unnecessarily? Environmental groups have begun to raise this question. In a time of recurring energy crises does it make sense to have buildings with windows that do not open? Even some savvy developers and their corporate tenants are becoming aware of the cost savings of structures built to conserve energy. For example, the new twenty-eight-story West Monroe office building in Chicago will save at least 30 percent in energy costs, compared with a higher-rise fifty-story building with the same amount of space in square feet; the reason is that it has less exterior wall area exposed to the elements and less glass as part of the walls. However, most office towers with energy-wasting plazas and central atriums are still seen by many business analysts as beautiful "signature" monuments that are "people oriented." What they have in mind is that people as *consumers* can sit and dine in the plazas or shop in the stores often located around the plazas—that is, they can engage in consumption activities profitable to the owners and their business tenants.[23]

Towering Infernos?   The movie *Towering Inferno* was a disaster film about people trapped at the top of a fire-consumed office tower. Moviegoers remember vividly the images of people screaming and dying because they are trapped in a tower built without adequate fire protection. Fire disasters are perhaps the most widely discussed problem of high-rise construction.

Before the early 1950s most high-rise buildings were constructed in ways that stalled or reduced the hazards of fire. Concrete floors, steam heat, no air conditioning ducts, windows that opened, hard plaster walls, dropped ceilings—these features produced buildings with few open air shafts and much solid, heat-absorbing material throughout. Modern buildings, however, have panel walls hung from floor slabs, insulating materials that reflect rather than absorb heat, windows that will not open, and multiple air shafts for heating and air conditioning. These features can make fires spread more easily. According to fire experts the new plastic materials increase the problem of toxic fumes in new buildings. Extreme heights make it difficult for fire fighters to combat fires, and the concentration of high-rise buildings makes it difficult for fire engines to get near because of traffic congestion.

The building industry has been concerned about films such as *Towering Inferno* and has tried to push forward an image of safety. Developer-owners and leasing companies vigorously argue that high-rise buildings are very safe because of the absence of fire trouble spots such as cooking facilities and the presence of alert security personnel. Yet, surprisingly, many developers and other building owners are fighting the implementation of new fire safety systems for towers, which they consider unnecessary and expensive.[24]

Some critics wonder whether today's cheaply built office buildings may be the central-city "slums" of tomorrow. Many buildings have a relatively short life expectancy; the average building, according to the federal Bureau of Standards, can be expected to last no more than forty years.

CRADLE TO GRAVE: MULTIPLE-USE DEVELOPMENTS

Visionaries portray the city of the future as a giant integrated physical structure housing people from cradle to grave. If this really is the city of the future, a scaled-down version already exists today in the urban multiple-use developments.

Called MXDs in the trade, these developments are so huge that they can shove aside other urban uses. In Houston, a giant MXD called Greenway Plaza encompasses 127 acres of central-city land. In its first two phases nearly 4 million square feet of office space were constructed. Greenway Plaza includes a thirty-two-story Conoco Tower, an eleven-story Union Carbide building, a multistory Dow Center Complex, a twenty-two-story Kellogg building, the Richmond and Buffalo towers, a chemical company building, a luxury hotel, high-rise apartment buildings, a huge parking garage, a heliport, and a major sports arena. Construction of Greenway Plaza began in the late 1960s and is projected to be finished in the mid-1980s, at a total cost of about $1 billion. As described in Chapter 1, preparation for this mammoth undertaking involved the acquisition and destruction or removal of several hundred single-family houses in four subdivisions.[25]

An MXD Defined.   There are many MXD developments in North America. According to the Urban Land Institute, these developments are "reshaping much of American life."[26] Developers and allied real estate actors see the MXDs not just as profit-making enterprises but as major examples of societal restructuring. An MXD is defined by the Urban Land Institute as a large-scale real estate project with (1) three or more different types of revenue-generating uses and (2) an integration of facilities in a land-intensive project with an overall coherent plan. The main uses in MXDs are office, retail, residential, and hotel or motel. A mid-1970s study found eighty-eight existing or planned multiple-purpose centers, fifty of which were in central business districts, thirty-one in central cities, and seven in suburbs. Most were in cities with populations over one million. Most MXDs had been built since 1964. By the early 1980s there were more than one hundred MXDs.[27]

The Scale.   Multiple-use centers are huge sets of buildings extending over a city block or more. These are different from other projects because they involve integrated building patterns and larger-scale organizational and financial power over a longer period of time, requirements that can only be met under the conditions of monopoly capitalism, that is, where very large development and lending corporations can put them together.[28]

The powerful actors include the developers who package and develop the MXDs, the large retail and service corporations that acquire or go into a joint venture with a developer, and the financial institutions, usually commercial banks and insurance companies. Among the major U.S. corporations operating as MXD developers or financiers are the following: Alcoa Properties; Metropolitan Life Insurance Co.; Prudential Insurance Co.; Travelers Insurance Co.; Hallmark Cards, Inc.; David Rockefeller Associates; Aetna Life and Casualty Company; Texas Eastern Transmission Corp.; Equitable Life Insurance Co.; John Hancock Mutual Life Insurance Co.; and Ford Motor Co. Even this abbreviated list includes some of the largest U.S. nonconstruction corporations.[29]

The enormous scale and cost of MXDs can be seen in three famous projects:

Place	Name	Size (million sq. ft.)	Estimated Cost in millions (1975)
Washington, D.C.	Watergate	1.8	$45
San Francisco	Embarcadero	3.9	$175
Houston	Galleria	4.6	$70

Watergate, of course, is a household word, an MXD that is now a part of the history of political corruption. These three projects are located in the largest cities, involve major U.S. or foreign corporations, and cost over $45 million each. Their scale rivals that of the pyramids of ancient Egypt.[30]

A Manhattan Disney World?   Rockefeller Center, constructed in Manhattan by the Rockefeller family, is the earliest and perhaps most famous major multiple-use urban development project. It has been described by one admiring writer as "a cathedral of the mid-twentieth century."[31] This multi-building complex dwarfs St. Patrick's Cathedral across from it; it clearly symbolizes the rise to prominence of oil, banking, and communications corporations in the United States and the decline of religious edifices as the high points of central cities.

This business and entertainment center was begun during the first years of the Great Depression and is apparently the largest privately owned multiple-purpose project yet to be completed. It was made possible by the fortune built by John D. Rockefeller, Jr. (1874-1960). Rockefeller himself controlled the development of the center by choosing the members of the Board of Rockefeller Center, Inc., and of the companies tied to it. By the late 1970s it consisted of twenty-one skyscrapers; it had two miles of underground passageways and planned services for its 200-plus tenants. Although Rockefeller Center is not an MXD by the strictest definition because it has only two of major land uses emphasized by the Urban Land Institute, it is similar in overall conception. The Center includes office buildings, landscaped plazas, theaters, an outdoor skating pond, and many restaurants.[32]

Mammoth projects such as Rockefeller Center inspire odd reactions from commentators. One author, apparently unaware of the irony in her statement, notes that the "influence of Rockefeller Center extends even to Walt Disney World, also designed under single-minded control. Like the Center, it has underground facilities, plants, an almost obsessive interest in cleanliness, and an up-to-date if not avant-garde standard of modern architecture."[33] The comment is ironic because critics of projects such as Rockefeller Center have argued that they embody the negative characteristics associated with a Disney World: a plastic, contrived, and artificial character. Rockefeller Center became the model for many other multiple-purpose developments.

The Rockefeller Center, Inc. (RCI) company has begun to participate in designing, developing, financing, and running similar large-scale projects across the United States. RCI became the owner and operator of the Wells

Fargo Building in downtown Los Angeles, a major project with Atlantic Richfield as a major tenant and codeveloper. The company has been involved in the Continental Center in New York City, the Irving Trust Operations Center in New York City and the Renaissance Center in Detroit.

Largest Urban Project in History?   Even Rockefeller Center will be smaller than one massive Houston MXD when that project is finally completed. About 1970 the oil-gas company Texas Eastern Transmission Corporation bought thirty-three square blocks on the older east side of downtown Houston. Once an expensive residential area, this had become a diverse area of commercial buildings, small hotels, apartment houses, and older homes. Called Houston Center, the new development project has been seen as remolding urban life. According to its own advertising, the center means "the creation of an entirely new city offering fresh approaches to work, recreation and residence. It may well be the prototype of the city of the future."[34]

The developers see themselves as building a new way of work and leisure life, not just a profitable project. They are building a new city for urbanites, without, of course, consulting those urbanites. The Houston Center developers have a twenty-year time frame for completing the project. They received permission from the city government to close some streets. Texas Eastern ran into a problem with its development schedule and sold half of its interest to the Canadian-based Cadillac Fairview corporation. Moreover, the developers gave 4.5 blocks to the city of Houston to build a convention center complex using public tax revenues; that seems useful for Houston Center's profitability. The buildings destroyed for this massive project included some older buildings, which could have been reused. They are being replaced with numerous high-rise buildings. When completed this will reputedly be the largest single private development project in urban history. It is interesting that Bernard Siegan has argued that zoning regulations would have made it more difficult to put together such a huge development project in any other American city. Packaging large blocks of land for large-scale development seems easier in Houston than in most other metropolitan areas.[35]

Money-making Machines.   MXDs can also be money-making machines; typically they permit above-average rents to be charged to their business tenants. They are viewed as commodities by their producers. One recent handbook portrays the MXD image as a new means of product differentiation; MXDs are viewed as being different enough to attract people away from other shopping areas.[36] A variety of national and multinational corporations have gotten involved in such developments for both short-term and long-term profits. Many see MXDs as good advertising for their companies, prestigious locations bringing public attention to themselves and encouraging consumers to come to their projects.[37]

Building the New Capitalist City.   Multiple-use projects are seen by developers, architects, and architectural critics as the wave of the future. They have been called the most "viable" form of new urban development. An MXD, planner Alan M. Vorhees claims, provides for "a variety of life styles. ... It tends to reduce energy requirements, particularly if it replaces vehicle trips with walk trips. ... It tends to break up the monotony of the urban environment." Advocates believe such mammoth developments "intensify the richness of living, enhance people's range of experience and create easy access to a nearly inexhaustible variety of activities."[38]

From this perspective MXD and large shopping centers are portrayed as moving city life from the streets into air-conditioned complexes where people can live, work, and even die inside one privately owned urban project—a business version of cradle-to-grave existence. Developers argue that multiple-use malls with entertainment, housing, and other nonretail facilities are easier to sell to communities. One producer noted that making an issue of the multiple-use approach helped to defeat a local ballot proposal to prevent the building of his business-shopping center. Oddly enough, MXDs are seen as a way to keep "central cities alive" and to make cities "viable organism[s]." They are said to represent "new thinking." Social prestige is emphasized.[39]

For example Houston's Galleria, with its many shops, hotel, office building, and theaters is often claimed to be *"the place"* to be seen in Houston. And it is also cited as a reorganizer of Houston's metropolitan growth, as providing a major "focal point" for urban development outside the downtown area. Many MXDs are touted as reversing much blight and decay, wherever they may in fact be located. Multiple-use developments such as the famous Watergate complex in Washington, D.C. have been viewed as bringing new recreational and residential life to areas that would otherwise be dead at night. Yet, it cannot be forgotten that much housing and many smaller businesses were destroyed to make the developments possible.

The large multiple-use developments tend to operate like new central business districts. They are somewhat similar to the castles of the Middle Ages and may well reflect some of the same concerns about crime and protection. Their builders see them as exclusive oases. Their luxury component is emphasized, and the class structure of MXDs is freely admitted. Upper-income and upper-middle-income people are the cultivated and preferred clients. No poor people need come by.

A recent study, *The Costs of Sprawl*, prepared for the federal government, defends these high-density developments. They are seen as less costly in terms of land consumption, air pollution, and energy consumption than lower-density residential developments. Advertising higher-density land use is done by developers to generate government and public interest in the MXDs. However, the same arguments are rejected when it comes to surburban development. In suburbia many developers and their allied governmental defenders see low-density sprawl as best.[40]

The Problems of Aging.   Place Ville-Marie, one of the first curtain-wall MXDs in North America, was considered a jewel in the crown of Bill Zeckendorf when he built the cross-shaped complex in Montreal in the early 1960s. With a large shopping area, a forty-one-story tower, several other buildings, and transportation ties to other buildings nearby Place Ville-Marie became the model for many multiple-use projects to follow in Canada and the United States. (It was later acquired by Trizec corporation.) Once Canada's premier office address, housing companies like the Royal Bank of Canada, Air Canada, numerous oil companies, and top law firms, the center was recently described by a real estate broker as a "twenty-five-year-old Chevy" which is becoming technologically obsolete. What the broker probably had in mind was the aging of Place Ville-Marie—its energy-inefficient architecture of single-glazed, floor-to-ceiling glass windows, its absence of sprinkler systems, and its lack of fashionability for many corporate clients.[41]

The significance of declining office complexes and MXDs like Place Ville-Marie can be seen in the attention being given to their aging problems. Place Ville-Marie recently was singled out by the *Wall Street Journal* in a major story entitled "Top Montreal Office Complex Encounters Trouble As It Ages." Some corporate investors have become worried about the potential early demise of these monumental development projects—projects that have consumed a large amount of investment capital.

NOTES

1. Quoted in Donald Appleyard and Lois Fishman, "High-Rise Buildings versus San Francisco: Measuring Visual and Symbolic Impacts," in *Human Response to Tall Buildings*, edited by Donald J. Conway (Stroudsburg, Penna.: Dowden, Hutchinson, and Ross, 1977), p. 82.

2. Ibid., p 81.

3. Cited in ibid., p. 83.

4. Larry Sawers, "Urban Form and the Mode of Production," *The Review of Radical Political Economics* 7 (Spring, 1975), pp. 65-66; Institute of Real Estate Management, *Managing the Office Building* (Chicago: National Association of Realtors, 1981), pp. 7-8.

5. Alexander Stuart, "Texan Gerald Hines Is Tall in the Skyline," *Fortune* 101 (January 28, 1980), p. 101; and Gerald D. Hines Interests news release, in author's files.

6. Stuart, "Texan Gerald Hines Is Tall in the Skyline," pp. 102-104.

7. "Office Space Review, 1981," *Buildings* 75 (January, 1981), pp. 52-65; "News," *Buildings* 75 (March, 1981), pp. 16-17; Stanford Hory, "San Francisco Bounces Back," *Buildings* 73 (July, 1979), p. 92; Peter Meyer, "Land Rush," *Harper's* 258 (January, 1979), pp. 45-60; "Office Spaces Goes Begging," *Newsweek*, October 11, 1982, p. 96.

8. "End of the Office Boom," *Business Week* (October 4, 1982), pp. 94-98.

9. The data on Houston came from a Houston planning department official; from data collected by the Houston Chamber of Commerce and Property Research and Development Consultants (published in "Buildings of 100,000 Square Feet or More," *Houston* 52 (February, 1981), pp. 35-37; and from Harris County Metropolitan Transit Authority, *Draft Environmental Impact Statement, Transitway Alternatives Analysis*, Houston, Tex., September, 1980, p. I-10.

10. Richard A. Walker and David B. Large, "The Economics of Energy Extravagance," *Ecology Law Quarterly* 4 (1975), pp. 963-985; James Lorimer, *The Developers* (Toronto: James Lorimer and Co., 1978), pp. 160, 170-171.

11. Institute of Real Estate Management, *Managing the Office Building*, p. 97.

12. "Leaving Nothing to Chance," *Financial World* 150 (February 1, 1981), p. 24. See also p. 25.

13. Ibid.

14. Institute of Real Estate Management, *Managing the Office Building*, pp. 287-288, 293-295.

15. This paragraph and the next draw on my interviews with Houston planning department and private research company officials; on "Prudential Subsidiary to Expand $2 Billion Houston Asset Base," *Houston Business Journal*, November 17, 1980, sec. 2, p. 2; and on "End of the Office Boom," *Business Week*, p. 98.

16. Sam Bass Warner, *The Urban Wilderness* (New York: Harper and Row, 1972), pp. 34-35.

17. Lorimer, *The Developers*, pp. 161, 184; Leonard Downie, *Mortgage on America* (New York: Praeger, 1974), p. 74.

18. Warner, *The Urban Wilderness*, p. 34; Henry Aubin, *City for Sale* (Toronto: James Lorimer and Co., 1977), p. 116.

19. Jane Holtz Kay, "Rubik's Cube in Steel," *Christian Science Monitor* (January 8, 1982), p. 15; "The Sky's the Limit," *Newsweek*, November 8, 1982, p. 67.

20. Quoted in Aubin, *City for Sale*, p. 95. See also pp. 116-118.

21. Gilda Moss Haber, "The Impact of Tall Buildings on Users and Neighbors," in *Human Response to Tall Buildings*, pp. 51-57.

22. Cited in Appleyard and Fishman, "High-Rise Buildings versus San Francisco," p. 81.

23. Institute of Real Estate Management, *Managing the Office Building*, pp. 14-15.

24. Neal D. Hougoton, "The Myth of the Towering Inferno," *Buildings* 75 (May, 1981), pp. 48-50.

25. Century Development Corporation, Greenway Plaza brochures and fact sheets in author's files; some data are drawn from an interview with a research official at the Rice Center research facility in Greenway Plaza, Houston, Tex., May, 1981.

26. Robert E. Witherspoon, Jon P. Abbett, and Robert M. Gladstone, *Mixed-Use Developments: New Ways of Land Use* (Washington, D.C.: Urban Land Institute, 1976), p. 3.

27. Ibid., pp. 6, 11, 17, 40-44.

28. Ibid., pp. 52-53, 84.

29. For a long list see ibid., pp. 179-191.

30. Ibid., pp. 91-153.

31. Carol Herselle Krinsky, *Rockefeller Center* (New York: Oxford University Press, 1978), p. 31.

32. Ibid., p. 15; Lillie A. Mikesell, "Rockefeller Center, Inc.," *Buildings* 75 (April, 1981), pp. 44-50.

33. Krinsky, *Rockefeller Center*, p. 7.

34. Quoted in Bernard H. Siegan, *Land Use without Zoning* (Lexington, Mass.: Lexington Books, 1972), p. 70.

35. Ibid., pp. 69-71.

36. Witherspoon, Abbett, and Gladstone, *Mixed-Use Developments*, p. 64.

37. Ibid., pp. 74-76.

38. Quoted in ibid., pp. 3, 5.

39. Ibid., pp. 4-5.

40. Council on Environmental Quality, Department of Housing and Urban Development, *The Costs of Sprawl: Environmental and Economic Costs of Alternative Residential Patterns* (Washington, D.C.: U.S. Government Printing Office, 1974).

41. Alan Freeman, "Top Montreal Office Complex Encounters Trouble as It Ages," *Wall Street Journal*, November 10, 1982, sec. 2, page 1.

5
BECKONING THE AFFLUENT BACK: REDEVELOPING CENTRAL CITIES

INTRODUCTION

Ernestine Turner, mother of eight, was evicted from her somewhat dilapidated row house in a changing area of Washington, D.C. Given forty-five days' notice, she was unable to find a new place that she could afford on her low monthly welfare check of $346. According to a Washington *Post* story, she collapsed with a nervous breakdown and was taken to the hospital. Ms. Turner reportedly said, "I've been to the mayor's office, the Department of Human Resources, and the public housing office. Everybody says there's nothing available for a family my size." Her landlord owned many houses in the area and was selling them to developers and other affluent individuals interested in redeveloping centrally located properties. Long ago abandoned by whites, central-city areas such as Ms. Turner's have received renewed attention from white land speculators and developers in the last two decades.[1]

Central cities have long been discussed in terms of their problems of decay, poverty, and fiscal crises. Numerous analysts have written that the central cities are "doomed," "physically obsolete," and even deserving of "extinction." Recently, however, new visions have been suggested, picturing central cities with new investment, rejuvenation of central-city neighborhoods, and a back-to-the-city movement of affluent whites (often called *gentrification*). In a *Harper's* article T. D. Allman argues that central-city revitalization is well underway and that cities are attracting new investment to projects such as office towers and rebuilt residential areas. Blake Fleetwood reviewed the New York situation: "Indeed, the evidence of the late 70s suggests that the New York of the 80s and 90s will no longer be a magnet for the poor and homeless, but a city primarily for the ambitious and educated — an urban elite." Horace Sutton, in the *Saturday Review,* has spoken eloquently on revitalization: "It is dusk, many have strayed far, but mother [the city] beckons and the wayfarers [middle-income people] are on the way back."[2]

THE SEESAWING OF INVESTMENT: UNEVEN URBAN DEVELOPMENT

The central city has been a profit center for American capitalism. The large central city has been the hub for economic, political, and cultural dominance by the ruling class. In addition, decline there can have a negative symbolism for a local business elite. Decline may be tolerated for a period; then new pressures often arise for revitalization.

Over the last two decades we have seen an urban renaissance in many U.S. cities. The new office towers, hotels, exclusive neighborhoods of historic homes, marinas, and specialty shops signal the return of some well-off people to many central cities. But this is the superficial face. Beneath is the long-term process of uneven investment. Cities under capitalism grow and decline as part of this process of uneven development, which in the first instance reflects the profit needs of industrial and real estate capitalists, not primarily the needs of urbanites taken as a whole. The spatial seesawing of capital, from central cities to suburbs, then from suburbs to central cities, is a key feature of our capitalistic system.

Some Examples.   There is a widespread myth of central-city development, which was well stated by Stanford professor Richard Muth in a 1978 interview.

> To make money and to survive, the private developer must convert less highly valued to more highly valued real estate, making everybody richer as a result. To paraphrase Adam Smith, the private developer in seeking his own interest promotes *society's* even though this was not part of his intention. ... In the procees, the city's housing stock will have been upgraded and the city's tax base increased. *All* of us consumers will benefit.[3]

But then there is the everyday reality. Many urban consumers, particularly those who are black, poor, or elderly, often do not benefit from the activities of powerful city re-builders.

Residential areas once populated by affluent whites were abandoned in past decades as they left for the suburbs. Later the same areas may be reclaimed by whites. An example of this seesawing can be seen in the Bunker Hill area near downtown Los Angeles. Once an area of mansions owned by doctors, lawyers, and merchants, by the 1920s and 1930s it had become populated by poorer whites and Chicanos. Well-off whites had moved to suburbs. This disinvestment by whites was followed in the 1960s by new investment, and new human costs for the poorer residents. In 1954 the city council voted to seek $33 million to redevelop the Bunker Hill area. The city officials had earlier rejected a plan for moderate- and low-income public housing in the area as "socialistic"; yet the preferred redevelopment plan itself included large federal subsidies and local tax benefits for the business interests that would profit from redevelopment.[4]

In the 1960s the houses were leveled, poor people were displaced, and huge buildings—a bank complex, oil company offices, a music center complex, luxury apartment towers—were erected. All together, 6,000 people had been pushed out to other neighborhoods. The Community Redevelopment Agency, as it does in most cities, worked hand in hand with corporate interests. In the redevelopment process banking and industrial corporations, developers, and landlords received the federal and local subsidies (a type of business "welfare"), not the local tenants.[5]

In San Francisco the Tenderloin area—home for 20,000 low-income and elderly citizens—has been invaded by the hotel industry. Three large hotels are being constructed there, bringing a new "touristification," which threatens this important residential area. In Atlantic City, New Jersey, casino hotels and specialty shops are displacing moderate-income and elderly residents. Real estate speculation has driven taxes so high that homeowners must sell out. Reportedly, landlords have forced black and Hispanic tenants out by reducing maintenance, then selling off to developers of resort projects. The casino building boom continues to have severe displacement effects, particularly on minorities, the poor, and the elderly.[6]

Institutionalized Racism?   Central-city reinvestment can also be seen as part of the dynamics of urban racial relations. Whether redevelopment is done by urban renewal, gentrification, or some other type of redevelopment, frequently the greatest impact has been on black and other nonwhite residential areas. More than three-quarters of those displaced by urban renewal programs have been nonwhite. Black, Chicano, and other nonwhite families have been forced out of one residential area after another so that white businesses and affluent families could convert the land for their uses. Since World War II a basic dynamic creating racial problems has been the movement of white midle-income families to the suburbs, leaving behind a substantially poorer, nonwhite population in the central cities. As we will demonstrate in the next three chapters, this suburban migration of whites has been linked to investment decisions of industrial corporations, banks, and developers and has been assisted by governmental subsidies for home mortgages and road building. In this process of uneven development much capital has flowed away from the basic needs of the central cities.

Yet in the latest phase of the cycle capital is flowing back into certain areas of the central city for construction of commercial and housing projects. Housing is being renovated to accommodate those white professional and managerial families that now prefer central cities. They "require" better housing and city services than the nonwhites and poor they are displacing. Norman Nager highlights the contrast here: "Serious attempts are being made to make the city attractive to these people. When whites moved out of the cities, deterioration was allowed to occur by the public as well as the private sectors."[7] Services and schools were allowed to deteriorate. Now the whites moving back demand a change. They want services and housing comparable in quality to what they, or their parents, had in the suburbs. The land occupied by nonwhites becomes a prime target for real estate speculation and development. The disinvestment-investment process has a racially discriminatory impact. This central-city seesawing may be rational from the points of view of profit-seeking white developers and the retail corporations and affluent homeowners they serve, but it is clearly irrational for those nonwhite urbanites whose lives are uprooted.

CENTRAL-CITY DEVELOPMENT: WHO DECIDES?

We have previously described numerous examples of downtown redevelopment projects, including the Rockefeller Center and the World Trade Center in New York, the Watergate complex in Washington, D.C., and the Bunker Hill project in Los Angeles. Many other examples of central-city projects are scattered across U.S. cities. In the 1970s the Hyatt Corporation moved to invest in refurbishing New York hotels; in Philadelphia and Kansas City major investors bought downtown hotels; in Detroit old hotels were refurbished, and a new $500 million Renaissance Center complex was built.

A massive shopping mall called Gallery at Market East was constructed in downtown Philadelphia's decaying retail sales area. A broad variety of these projects has been built in central-city areas.[8]

In some cities developers worked with other corporate and key government officials to build new convention centers. In central cities such as Baltimore, older retail and industrial buildings have been rehabilitated to provide space for chic shops and expensive restaurants to serve conventions and affluent white-collar workers. Some MXDs have been located in central cities. There has been a resurgence in the downtown areas of larger cities, such as New York, Chicago, and Philadelphia, of certain types of retail sales operations. Much of this development—the specialty shops, theaters, chic restaurants—is directed at the consumption interests of the affluent.

Yet even in redeveloped central cities development tends to be spotty and uneven. Robert Beauregard notes that "a new, vigorous and highly capitalized central core is surrounded by gentrified and affluent neighborhoods, declining industrial districts, and both stabilizing and deteriorating neighborhoods."[9] Urban redevelopment never revitalizes the entire central city.

A Good Business Climate?   In examining possible downtown projects executives of industrial and development corporations are again concerned about the "business climate." They are most likely to participate in downtown revitalization if they are given special tax breaks, if labor unions are restrained, if business leaders are central in the public planning groups, and if government officials cooperate with business leaders. The city re-builders put these conditions into a sanitized language, such as this: We are interested in situations where "the municipal administration treats labor and management evenly."[10] But the perspective remains the same. The basic concern is that labor organization be weak and wages be relatively low. The Urban Land Institute has been active in promoting downtown areas as good places for business development—accenting the well-developed transportation networks, the (unemployed) blue-collar work force, and the (new) pro-business attitude of central-city governments as attractive.[11]

Developers' organizations recommend political analyses of downtown projects in advance, so as to forestall or frustrate opposition from citizens' groups and stubborn government officials. They consider protests against development as "irrational," and they are increasingly aware of the need for persuasion campaigns to convince the public to go along with their ventures.

Behind the Scenes: The Power Structure. How does a typical central business district (CBD) project develop? A ULI handbook describes the process as follows:

> Individual businessmen, developers, or investors may be the first to recognize and pursue the opportunity for development of a project in the CBD. This fairly *random* operation of private market forces may be assisted by public or quasi-public groups seeking to stimulate downtown revitalization, perhaps to stabilize the local economy.[12]

Central-city development is here viewed as random, but in reality that process is coordinated and managed by developers, landowners, and executives of industrial corporations operating in concert with local and state government officials. Behind the scenes in every city business groups are pressing for growth and development.

On the one hand there is formal government power—the mayor, city council, zoning commission, and planning commission. On the other hand, is the invisible government of business organizations, policy groups, and blue-ribbon panels that greatly influence the governmental decisions.

In Los Angeles, for example, there has long been a powerful behind-the-scenes organization of business leaders that shapes both private and public action. At the heart of this group are local corporations such as the Los Angeles *Times*. Its owner, Otis Chandler, once said, "I think the *Times* is the only thing in Los Angeles that brings cohesion to the entire area. Even more than the mayor, the City Council, the Board of Supervisors. It is the only thing that tells you what is happening every day and what might happen. It is a tremendous force." Such newspapers are often central to a local power structure. Many are owned by local wealthy families or by large corporate chains tied into the national ruling class. They are heavily dependent on local advertising from department stores and other businesses, and for this reason newspaper corporations are aggressive defenders of growth.[13]

The *Times* executives and organization have been powerful in Los Angeles, but they share power with other corporate leaders whose unified efforts have reshaped the physical face of that city. In the 1970s a new downtown development group was formed, the Committee for Central City Planning (CCCP) Inc. The CCCP, made up of top executives from major downtown businesses, persuaded the city council to help pay for a study of downtown development. Approved by the city council in the mid-1970s, the new plan proposed business-oriented redevelopment that would be subsidized substantially by county taxes. The Los Angeles *Times* supported the plan, reportedly playing up its advantages in editorials.[14]

Since World War II leading businesspeople in many other cities have organized themselves to prepare central-area development plans: the Central Area Committee of Chicago, Civic Progress in St. Louis, the Allegheny Conference in Pittsburgh, the Civic Conference in Boston, the Greater Philadelphia Movement. These business elites meet privately and coordinate their activities with the press and sympathetic politicians. Edward Banfield and James Wilson have emphasized the image these individuals (mostly men) like to project:

> The new committees were different in that they consisted of a few "big men" whose only concern was with the central business district and who, far from regarding themselves as special interests, insisted that they served "the public interest," often at a considerable sacrifice of private business interests.[15]

Government Subsidies for Private Enterprise.   Ordinarily, where projects are not too risky and profits are likely to be large, developers may prefer to go ahead with little government involvement. If there is a "strong market" (in other words, high profits), the private sector wishes to minimize government involvement. Where risks are greater, however, even conservative executives in major private enterprises may seek out government assistance.

In unemployment-troubled Detroit, for example, General Motors expressed the desire to build a new Cadillac plant rather than rehabilitate an older one, so the city officials worked with GM to provide land east of downtown, cleared and provided at taxpayer expense—a project fraught with serious human costs. A New York *Times* story describes the scene:

> Ann and Andrew Giannini have, they say, everything they want: a home they enjoy, neighbors who watch over one another, stores within walking distance. ... But the Gianninis live in the path of a major project designed to preserve jobs for Detroit and to help revitalize the American automobile industry. ... Under present plans the site would be sold or leased to G.M. at prices comparable to those of open land in suburban or rural areas.[16]

One Detroit City Council member commented on the dilemma of city officials: "I think we are so desperate for jobs we will do anything. The multinational corporations are doing the economic planning for the world."[17] At stake is the destruction of Poletown, a large multiethnic neighborhood, at public expense to provide land for private use. The "new" land will come from bulldozing a stable, racially integrated, residential neighborhood with 3,500 people in 1,500 homes. Local citizens' groups proposed alternative sites for this much-needed job-creating auto plant, but as of 1982 GM had rejected alternatives.

Many corporate executives no longer are willing to put up all the front-end money; they prefer that government—which means the taxpayers —pay for clearing the land, provide cheap land for development, pay for market surveys and building analyses, and sometimes even provide no-interest or low-interest loans.[18]

One important federal subsidy for private development was provided by the 1977 Housing and Urban Development Act, which authorized Urban Development Action Grants (UDAG) to local governments in areas with specified poverty, housing, and unemployment problems. Governments are supposed to use the grants for services to encourage private investment in depressed areas. Instead, UDAGs have often been used for streets, utilities, and other services for various types of private residential, commercial, and industrial projects benefiting affluent urbanities.[19]

Governments are pressured to provide parking facilities, tax abatements, public services, zoning permissions, and even administrative assistance in finding federal grants and loans. Subsidies for the builders of downtown developments include zoning changes to permit development, tax abatements sharply reducing taxes (often for twenty-five years), cheap land provided by land clearance programs, and utilities. Taxpayers are expected to pay for projects whose profits are not publicly controlled, but rather are privately appropriated by the business elite. Developers do not mind seeking government handouts. Generally speaking, in selling their projects, they argue that the projects are a way of getting rid of urban blight and organizing urban growth, and they emphasize the tax revenues new projects will bring to city governments.[20]

As one developer's organization puts it, city governments "now recognize" that they must work more closely with private developers to rebuild central cities and that they must provide incentives for private developers to come into central-city projects. A number of states have passed laws easing downtown redevelopment by giving developers quicker access to the powers of eminent domain. Removing "blight" has been the usual rationalization for using this power. In recent years some state legislation has greatly expanded the definition of "blight" to make government clearance for private enterprise easier. Eminent domain can be used not just for public highways but also for private development projects. A Michigan law, the Downtown Development Authority Act, permits government authorities to demolish buildings and acquire property for private economic development. A city government can use its powers to condemn property and transfer it to a public development authority, which can in turn prepare it for private development projects. Other states, such as Ohio and Missouri, have passed similar legislation. One basic objective of these questionable arrangements is to pass the right of eminent domain from elected officials to public agencies run by nonelected officials largely for the benefit of private developers or to private developers themselves. These nonelected agencies are easier to shield from citizens' democratic input and control than are elected officials.[21]

Government officials have gone to great lengths to subsidize private enterprise. For example, for the Greenville Commons project in Greenville, S.C., private interests decided to build a hotel, office building, and retail facilities, if the city would build support facilities including a convention center, a parking garage, and a landscaped atrium. The city put out $7.5 million; business interests risked only $4 million for the hotel and office buildings. And in the Fountain Square project in Cincinnati, Ohio, the city government spent $18 million of the $84 million for that large project, including the costs of land clearance and packaging and a parking garage.[22]

GENTRIFICATION:
WHITES IN, BLACKS OUT

What Is Gentrification?   Often associated with the industrial and commercial development projects are residential development projects tied to a process called *gentrification*. Gentrification has seldom been carefully defined, but many share the view that it refers to a significant turnaround in the "decay" of central-city areas. What most have in mind is some type of housing renovation and an increased movement of middle- and upper-middle-income people into central-city areas, often pushing out poorer residents. Many central cities have had significant housing renovation. One Department of Housing and Urban Development survey estimated that housing renovation projects were taking place in a quarter of western cities, 43 percent of north-central cities, half of northeastern cities, and 60 percent of southern cities.[23]

The most likely areas for housing revitalization are in larger cities; in the Northeast and South; in neighborhoods near central business districts and on mass transit lines; in areas with housing built originally to the standards of upper-income families; and in neighborhoods with good facilities, such as libraries and hospitals.[24] Phillip Clay's study of 195 neighborhoods in thirty cities found many cases of gentrification. The majority of these gentrifying areas were neighborhoods with one- and two-family houses. In most, newly rehabilitated housing was priced well above the central city's average. Not surprisingly, they were near commercial, business, or governmental renewal or renovation projects.[25]

Residential gentrification is commonplace in "headquarters" cities. Corporate headquarters cities including New York, San Francisco, and Houston, are particularly well known for office skyscrapers, luxury apartments, and thousands of white-collar workers. Much housing revitalization has taken place in these cities; a key factor behind it is the existence of white-collar jobs in the central city. Corporate headquarters cities tend to be growth areas for professional and managerial jobs. The office area and residential area requirements of these cities are different from those of industrial-factory cities such as Jersey City, Pittsburgh, and Youngstown. Redevelopment varies greatly by region and city size. Predominantly manufacturing cities in the Midwest and Northeast have seen much less gentrification.[26]

A Typical Pattern.   Drawing on a study of gentrifying areas in Washington, D.C., Dennis Gale has suggested that housing change and neighborhood resettlement go through three stages.[27] We can elaborate on Gale's typology a bit.

1. *Stage One:* A few pioneering households move into a deteriorating area. Many are young professionals. Initial pioneers often supply their own funds, because banking institutions are reluctant to make loans. Because the number of newcomers is small, there is little displacement of indigenous residents.

2. *Stage Two:* After a year or two, some realtors, developers, and local media discover the area. Larger numbers of people become attracted to its accessibility and investment potential. They buy houses and renovate them. Financing is difficult to obtain. Newcomers tend to be young couples in professional, technical, and managerial occupations. Their numbers are greater; tensions with lower-income residents increase. Rents are raised; tenants are evicted to provide renovated housing for higher-income households. Some commercial establishments such as boutiques move into the area.

Local government begins to pay more attention to the quality of services. Developers and speculators begin to buy up property for resale.

3. *Stage Three:* Resettlement increases at a rapid rate. Indigenous residents are squeezed out of the neighborhood completely. Renovation is now a large-scale process. Older couples with children join the ranks; they are more likely to have moved from the suburbs. Developers and speculators are operating widely. Local government may help to advertise the area; more improvements are made in local services. Banking institutions become interested; financing is easier to secure for renovation.

We can flesh out this portrait a bit with two specific cases. The Capitol Hill area in Washington, D.C., began gentrification in the 1960s, and several other neighborhoods subsequently started the process. Gale's study found considerable gentrification in the Capitol Hill area. New homebuyers were mostly younger white couples and individuals without children. Virtually all were college graduates. There were no black couples. The neighborhood is a typical seesaw investment area. The Victorian houses, once occupied by affluent whites, were abandoned to poorer blacks in the 1950s and 1960s. In the late 1960s the area began to change. White professional families, preferring city life and excitement, moved in; builders and developers bought up and renovated the housing. This white immigration forced black families out; landlords sold houses to speculators and developers. Washington, D.C., has numerous neighborhoods that have undergone gentrification, with thousands of affluent white families involved; also involved have been thousands of poorer, disproportionately nonwhite families displaced in the process.[28]

One ironic example of gentrification can be glimpsed in San Francisco's Haight-Ashbury, a once vibrant counterculture community, which had declined into a drug-scarred ghetto by the early 1970s. Most of the gentrifiers were young professionals. They brought a new life-style to the area; head shops and crash pads were replaced with professional offices, boutiques, and restored town houses. Older counterculture residents, as well as poor and black families, were forced to move to other areas of the city. Yet these were the very people who worked hard in recent years to improve public services and who gave the area the diversity that attracted newcomers.[29]

Speculators and Developers.   Speculators and developers commonly play a critical role in the gentrification process. One study in Washington, D.C., found speculators combing "neighborhoods on foot and by telephone just ahead of the restoration movement, making attractive cash offers to owners."[30] If owners do not wish to sell, building inspectors may be called in by the potential buyers; they may order expensive repairs, forcing sale. For example, between 1972 and 1974 one-fifth of all recorded sales in Washington, D.C., involved two or more sales of the same property, a key sign of speculation. A National Urban Coalition report found significant speculative activity in the forty-four cities surveyed.[31]

Developers play an important role in gentrification, sometimes early, sometimes later. Gentrification can occur when developers buy buildings at a cheap price, get loans to rehabilitate them, and sell the renewed housing at a profit to higher-income households. A survey of thirty cities found developers to be important at a relatively early point in 40 percent of the gentrifying neighborhoods. They become more prevalent later. Many have the capital to choose an area and spur reinvestment changes in it with little or no participation by local residents in the decision making. In some cases developers are also speculators who buy up properties in a deteriorating area, waiting for land appreciation. They may or may not begin development later. Many of the early renovators have been smaller builders whose interest in seeing risky investments pay off in substantial profits was coupled with the courage to work in older central-city areas where larger development corporations were more reluctant to venture.[32]

Schur's New York research indicates that some real estate operators buy property in revitalizing areas and intentionally drive out existing tenants because the costs of repairs and maintenance exceed revenues from low rents in this housing. Those first displaced are often low-income and moderate-income renters in apartment buildings. A second stage of displacement pushes out the long-term homeowners, who are worried about accelerated deterioration of their neighborhoods.[33]

Much gentrification occurs only when financial institutions become willing to make loans to older neighborhoods formerly redlined. Decisions by finance capitalists may determine whether or not housing gentrification will occur on a large scale. Government officials have played their part in spurring development of gentrifying areas by providing improvements in services and advertising the neighborhoods.[34]

PAYING THE PRICE:
DISPLACEMENT

"Displacement" occurs when a household is forced to move by local housing or neighborhood conditions beyond its control that make the housing hazardous or too expensive. Urban displacement has been caused by a variety of factors, including gentrification, airport and highway construction, public urban renewal, and school construction. George Grier and Eunice Grier note three kinds of private displacement: housing gentrification displacement, abandoned area displacement, and enhanced competition displacement (when upper- and middle-income families compete against moderate-income families, the poor, and the elderly for the same housing). Enhanced-competition displacement is caused by the tight housing market for renters in many cities. Competition-related displacement, including condominium conversions by developers,* is probably the largest-scale form of displacement in central cities.[35]

Displacement from all causes is serious. A 1979 *Displacement Report* commissioned by Congress explored the impact of gentrification and other housing-related causes of urban displacement. It estimated that at least 370,000 households were displaced in metropolitan areas each year. The private sector accounted for more than 83 percent of the displacement in all regions.[36]

Condomiums and Displacement.   In addition to gentrification, much central-city growth has involved the conversion by developers of apartments for rent to condominiums as well as construction of new condominiums. By the late 1970s many potential homebuyers, faced with too-high prices for single-family homes, turned to moving in with relatives, competing for the limited pool of apartments, or buying condominiums. Urban office workers are among those buying condominiums.

Some new condominium buildings are being constructed, and older apartment buildings have been converted by developers from rental units into condominiums for sale. Often only a few improvements are made before these older apartments are sold. There were few condominium units before 1970. The number of apartments built as condominiums increased to 1.3 million by 1975 and to more than 3 million in the early 1980s. Condominium construction exceeded detached housing construction in many areas. Moreover, just under half a million existing apartment units have been converted to condominiums between 1970 and 1980; more than a million more are expected to be converted by the mid-1980s. Most have been in larger cities, thus concentrating the impact on metropolitan tenants. Federal housing authorities have estimated that half of U.S. families may live in condominiums by the year 2000.[37]

*Condominiums typically are apartments or town houses that are bought rather than rented.

Condominium conversions can be similar to gentrification in displacement effects. A Denver study found that in the 1973-1978 period 5,500 apartments and multifamily structures there were converted to condominiums, and a significant number of low- and moderate-income households were thereby displaced.[38]

In Philadelphia an apartment building worth only $25 million was sold to a condominium development corporation for $50 million. That firm converted the rental apartments, with little renovation, into condominiums for sale. Reportedly a typical rental charge was about $560 per month before conversion, but after conversion the total payment (for mortgage and interest, taxes, fees) was $1,200 per month. New households also paid several thousand dollars in down payments on the units. Most existing households would have to leave such a building because they could not afford the sharply higher cost. Profits from one owner's conversions in Chicago have been estimated at 44 percent for one complex and nearly 100 percent for another. Because of this high level of profitability banks were eager to finance conversions at high interest rates.[39]

There can be a severe negative impact on tenants when an apartment building is converted to condominiums. Peter Drier and John Atlas report that 50 percent to 75 percent of existing tenants cannot afford condo-converted apartments, because monthly costs often double after conversion. Even with discounts some condo-converters provide to existing tenants, the cost for households skyrockets. In most cases low-income and low-middle-income families will never again be able to afford housing in such apartment buildings, forcing them to look elsewhere, often for less than adequate accommodations. At the same time, the new condo-conversion corporations and affluent investors who frequently buy up condominiums as tax shelters, can make significant profits. But problems abound. "Buy or move" letters have spurred tenants to form protest organizations across the nation. Pressure by tenants' groups on legislatures and city councils has resulted in modest laws to protect tenants from "condomania" in a dozen cities and nearly twenty states. Major repairs and maintenance costs loom for those who have bought the converted apartments. In spite of developers' claims that condo-conversions improve the housing stock, in reality conversions do not increase the number of units available, but only accelerate rising housing costs.[40]

Much controversy has arisen over the impact of conversions, to the point that a special federal report on the topic was released. Yet it played down the impact of conversions on displaced renters; federal housing authorities have thus defended the condominium trend, thus reflecting the owners', not the tenants', perspective.[41]

Gentrification Displacement. The extent of gentrification-related displacement is difficult to estimate precisely. Grier and Grier conclude that displacement by the private renewal processes affects a relatively small number of families. Yet an estimate by Cushing Dolbeare, a national housing consultant, has put the number displaced by gentrification at approximately 100,000 per year.[42]

Some social scientists, such as John Kasarda, see "displacement" as a "loaded term." Kasarda argues that "from the standpoint of the city, the movement represents neighborhood upgrading and urban reinvestment." He criticizes those who worry so much about the poor that they do not see the advantages of gentrification and argues that from the standpoint of the city as a whole gentrification represents good revitalization.[43]

But this is mythology, for certain social classes benefit much more than others from gentrification and condo-fication. Urbanites as a whole do not benefit. Among those who benefit are profit-seeking speculators and developers and the new affluent immigrants. The greatest sufferers are those with low to moderate incomes, who are pushed aside. Housing gentrification does bring some higher-income people into the core areas of central cities, but it also brings problems of social justice. The displacement it causes is producing political conflict in cities, with tenants' groups fighting the damaging activities of speculators and developers. Gentrification creates, as Clay puts it, "little gilded islands" and forces low- and moderate-income families into competition for a declining number of areas they can afford.[44]

The National Urban Coalition found displacement of low- and moderate-income families in two-thirds of the gentrification neighborhoods it examined. And a recent study of displacement in Portland, Oregon, found that about 3,000 families were forced to move involuntarily each year, with 40 percent displaced by rehabilitation in central-city areas. Most of the displaced were renters between the ages of twenty-five and thirty-five, and 40 percent had incomes below $7,500. The displacers, on the other hand, tended to have higher incomes.[45]

Those displaced tend to move to nearby poverty areas, to move several times, and to pay higher rents in their new housing. Some of those displaced by private redevelopment are the same families displaced in previous decades by public urban renewal projects. Under housing capitalism, the private housing market does not have to provide moderate-rent housing elsewhere for those displaced. Moreover, a move has been found to be high on the list of causes of major stress for people of any age or income level, but a relatively sudden forced move for the aged or poor can be even more severe.[46]

Abandonment Displacement.   Many U.S. cities have some areas that look like the bombed-out cities of Europe after World War II, where half the houses are boarded up with plywood or stand with all windows broken out. Steps hang down, gutters are in disrepair. Fires break out periodically. Nearby families struggle, living in dilapidated and deteriorating houses owned by absentee landlords. When they must leave, their houses become further additions to the rows of abandoned central-city housing. The famous South Bronx in New York City is similar to areas in Brooklyn, Seattle, St. Louis, and Los Angeles.[47]

     This large-scale abandonment of central-city housing is usually seen as the fault of tenants, who allegedly destroy the buildings. But large-scale abandonment is really just part of the disinvestment process central to urban real estate capitalism. Some abandonment is the result of homeowners or small landlords getting in over their heads, but most results from ownership by a series of landlords who, one after another, let the property run down. This is *conscious* activity by absentee landlords seeking to make a quick profit. Buildings are bought with a small down payment and a big mortgage; tenants are charged rents, but maintenance is not provided. Often utility bills are not paid by the investor-landlord, who gets depreciation deductions that reduce taxes. He or she soon sells the property to another profit-seeking investor, and so on, until the last one abandons the used-up property. A story in the Washington *Post* described a fifty-two-unit apartment complex abandoned by a landlord who owed the city $140,000 in unpaid utility bills and back taxes. These "disinvestment" profit makers walk away from their used-up investments, leaving city officials and urban taxpayers to pick up the pieces. Or sometimes arsonists are hired to destroy the buildings for insurance, a criminal process that has taken many tenants' lives in cities across the nation.[48]

NOTES

    1. Joseph D. Whitaker, "Convalescence of an Area Causes Pain for the Poor,"Washington *Post*, May 29, 1977, p. A8.

2. T. D. Allman, "The Urban Crisis leaves Town," *Harpers* 257, December, 1978, pp. 41-56; Blake Fleetwood, "The New Elite and Urban Renaissance," *New York Times Magazine*, January 14, 1979, p. 17; Horace Sutton, "America Falls in Love with Its Cities—Again," *Saturday Review*, August, 1978, pp. 16-21.

3. Richard Muth, in the San Francisco *Chronicle*, January 30, 1978, as quoted in Chester W. Hartman, Dennis Keating, and Richard LeGates, *Displacement: How to Fight It* (Berkeley, Calif.: National Housing Law Project, 1982), p. 27.

4. Robert Gottlieb and Irene Wolt, *Thinking Big: The Story of the Los Angeles Times* (New York: G. P. Putnam's Sons, 1977), pp. 260-268, 365, 530-531.

5. Ibid., pp. 530-531.

6. Hartman, Keating, and LeGates, *Displacement*, p. 6.

7. Norman Nager, "Continuities of Urban Policy on the Poor," in *Back to the City*, edited by Shirley B. Laska and Daphine Spain (New York: Pergamon Press, 1980), p. 240.

8. Daniel Machalaba, "Philadelphia's 'Gallery' Tests a City's Ability to Lure Back Shoppers," *Wall Street Journal*, March 30, 1978, p. 1; Margaret Yao, "Return to Boosterism," *Wall Street Journal*, July 11, 1979, pp. 44-45.

9. Robert A. Beauregard, "The Redevelopment of the Advanced Capitalist City," Paper presented to Conference on New Perspectives on Urban Political Economy, Washington, D.C., American University, May, 1981, p. 17.

10. Urban Land Institute, *Downtown Development Handbook* (Washington, D.C.: Urban Land Institute, 1980), p. 15.

11. Urban Land Institute, *Industrial Development Handbook* (Washington, D.C.: Urban Land Institute, 1975), p. 227.

12. Urban Land Institute, *Downtown Development Handbook*, p. 39. Italics added. See also pp. 59, 93-98.

13. Gottlieb and Wolt, *Thinking Big*, pp. 524-526.

14. Ibid., pp. 532-534.

15. Edward Banfield and James Q. Wilson, *City Politics* (Cambridge: Harvard University Press and MIT Press, 1963), p. 267. See also G. William Domhoff, *Who Really Rules?* (New Brunswick, N.J.: Transaction Books, 1978), pp. 172-174.

16. The *New York Times* story (September 15, 1980) is quoted in Hartman, Keating, and LeGates, *Displacement*, p. 100.

17. Ibid.

18. Urban Land Institute, *Downtown Development Handbook*, p. 50.

19. Ibid., pp. 93, 172-173; Robert M. Byrne, Douglas R. Porter, and Elizabeth D. Baker, "Urban Development Action Grants," *Urban Land*, June, 1980, pp. 3-10.

20. Robert E. Witherspoon, Jon P. Abbett, and Robert M. Gladstone, *Mixed-Use Developments: New Ways of Land Use* (Washington, D.C.: Urban Land Institute, 1976), pp. 14-15, 86-100.

21. Urban Land Institute, *Downtown Development Handbook*, pp. 16, 170-172.

22. Ibid., pp. 53-63.

23. J. Thomas Black, "Private-Market Housing Renovation in Central Cities: An Urban Land Institute Survey," in *Back to the City*, pp. 3-13; the HUD study is cited in "Back to City Moves Displace the Poor," *New York Times*, October 14, 1979, p. 51.

24. Biliana Cicin-Sain, "The Costs and Benefits of Neighborhood Revitalization," in *Urban Revitalization, Urban Affairs Annual Review*, edited by D. B. Rosenthal, vol. 18 (Beverly Hills, Calif.: Sage Publications, 1980), pp. 52-53.

25. Phillip L. Clay, *Neighborhood Renewal* (Lexington, Mass.: Lexington Books, 1979), pp. 18-25.

26. David Perry and Alfred Watkins, "The Urban Renaissance for Business," *Nation*,

March 1, 1980, pp. 236-238; Franz Shurmann and Sandy Close, "The Emergence of Global City USA: New Affluence and a New Kind of Misery," *Progressive*, January, 1979, pp. 27-29; S. Gregory Lipton, "Evidence of Central-City Renewal," *Journal of the American Institute of Planners* 43 (April, 1977), p. 138.

27. Dennis E. Gale, "Neighborhood Resettlement: Washington, D.C.," in *Back to the City*, pp. 106-109.

28. Ibid., pp. 96-97; Dennis E. Gale, *The Back-to-the-City Movement Revisited: A Survey of Recent Homebuyers in the Capitol Hill Neighborhood of Washington, D.C.* (Washington, D.C.: Department of Urban and Regional Planning, George Washington University, 1977), pp. 2, 13-14.

29. Marilyn Chase, "The Haight-Ashbury Turns into a Bastion of the Middle Class," *Wall Street Journal*, July 24, 1978, p. 1.

30. Carol Richards and Jonathan Rowe, "Restoring a City: Who Pays the Price?" *Working Papers for a New Society* 4 (Winter, 1977), pp. 196-197.

31. National Urban Coalition, *Displacement: City Neighborhoods in Transition* (Washington, D.C., 1978).

32. Clay, *Neighborhood Renewal*, pp. 26-27.

33. R. Schur, testimony presented before the U.S. Senate, Committee on Banking, Housing, and Urban Affairs, July 7, 1977, as summarized in Cicin-Sain. "The Costs and Benefits of Neighborhood Revitalization," pp. 70-71.

34. Clay, *Neighborhood Renewal*, pp. 27-30; Robert M. Byrne, Douglas R. Porter, and Elizabeth D. Baker, "Urban Development Action Grants," *Urban Land*, June, 1980, pp. 3-10.

35. George Grier and Eunice Grier, *Urban Displacement: A Reconnaissance* (Washington, D.C.: U.S. Department of Housing and Urban Development, March, 1978), pp. 8-9, 21-22.

36. Office of Policy Development and Research, Department of Housing and Urban Development, *Displacement Report* (Washington, D.C.: U.S. Government Printing Office, 1979), p. 23.

37. Peter Drier and John Atlas, "Condo Mania," *Progressive*, March, 1981, pp. 19-21.

38. Marty Flahive and Steven Gordon, *Residential Displacement in Denver: a Research Report* (Denver: Joint Administration-City Council Committee on Housing, May, 1979).

39. CBS News, "60 Minutes," March 29, 1981; Drier and Atlas, "Condo Mania," p. 20; Robert Sheridan, "Condo Conversions," *Buildings* 75 (September, 1979), p. 67.

40. Drier and Atlas, "Condo Mania," pp. 20-22.

41. Cf. Office of Policy Development and Research, Department of Housing and Urban Development, *The Conversion of Rental Housing to Condominiums and Cooperatives* (Washington, D.C.: U.S. Government Printing Office, 1980).

42. Grier and Grier, *Urban Displacement*, p. iii; Cushing Dolbeare quoted in "Fixing Up Big-City Neighborhoods; Who Loses Out," *U.S. News and World Report*, February 19, 1979, p. 73.

43. John D. Kasarda, "The Implications of Contemporary Redistribution Trends for National Urban Policy," *Social Science Quarterly* 61 (December, 1980), p. 394.

44. Clay, *Neighborhood Renewal*, p. 31.

45. National Urban Coalition, *Displacement*, pp. 3-7.

46. Cicin-Sain, "The Costs and Benefits of Neighborhood Revitalization," pp. 69-72; Flahive and Gordon, *Residential Replacement in Denver*, Appendix 4.

47. Brian D. Boyer, *Cities Destroyed for Cash* (Chicago: Follett Publishing Co., 1973), p. 3.

48. Hartman, Keating, and LeGates, *Displacement*, p. 62.

6
"RITES OF WAY": AUTOS, HIGHWAYS, AND CITY DECENTRALIZATION

Jamaica Plain is a blue-collar neighborhood southeast of downtown Boston. In 1970 its Lamartine Street had a diverse population of blacks, Puerto Ricans, and white Catholics. A colorful neighborhood, it was a residential area typical of older American cities. Yet the business and political powers that be, those who decide on massive highway systems and where they go, picked Lamartine Street as the right-of-way for a section of Boston's Interstate 95 highway.

> To find out what Lamartine Street was like, you have to look on the odd-numbered side of the street, because that's not part of the rite-of-way. It ranges from well kept two- and three-story houses to somewhat shabby three-deckers. ...Some houses on the even-numbered side also remain. Number 260, for example, is a yellow house with brown trim and a neat garden. Its occupants are an elderly couple. Their home is not needed for the highway. But they have seen and heard the bulldozers and the earth movers rip up their neighbors' homes and leave a flat dirt wasteland all the way to Number 226, a vacant space two blocks long and a block from the street to the railroad tracks.[1]

People pushed aside for highways. People, particularly the poor, the non-whites, the ordinary working people making sacrifices. People protesting the destruction of their homes. In many parts of the country one finds Lamartine Streets bulldozed to prepare acreage for ribbons of asphalt and concrete. These ribbons connect central cities to suburbs, permitting the movement of workers and real estate investments from one part of the city to another. We have already looked at office tower and other development projects in central cities. In the next few chapters we will look at development projects farther out—the industrial parks, shopping centers, and the omnipresent suburbs. Essential to this decentralization has been the extension of an auto-centered transportation system substantially paid for by ordinary taxpayers. With and without citizen consent, corporate capitalists, industrialists and developers, and allied political officials have made key decisions heavily shaping the type of transportation upon which all Americans now depend.

KILLING OFF MASS TRANSIT

The combustion-engine (automobile, truck, bus) industry is today at the heart of the urban transportation system in the United States. Automobile and auto-related industries provide a large proportion, perhaps one-sixth, of all jobs, although this proportion may be decreasing with recent stagnation and decline in the auto industry. An estimated one-quarter to one-half of most central-city and many suburban areas is used for the movement, storage, selling, and parking of automobiles, trucks, and buses. The growth in the number of automobiles and trucks has required expansion and development of highways and freeways and greatly facilitated the bulging suburbanization around today's cities.

Early Mass Transit.   In the 1880-1940 period many American cities had significant mass transit systems. By 1890 electric trolleys were in general use. Electric trolley routes, elevated railroads, and subways facilitated the first urban expansion. Indeed, some investor-owned transit companies extended their lines beyond existing urban areas in an attempt to profit from the land speculation that usually followed such extension. Transit companies were a significant early force in urban sprawl. The suburban sprawl of Los Angeles, for example, got its initial push from the expansion of transit lines.

The reorganization of mass transit that took place in the early 1900s did not result just from improved technology. Rather, capitalist entrepreneurs and corporations seeking greater profits reorganized and consolidated transit systems. Mergers of old firms and assembly of new companies were commonplace, and there was much speculation in traction company stock. Sometimes the capitalists involved in the transit companies were too eager for profits; their financial schemes and manipulations created serious problems. "These actions in turn," Charles Cheape notes, "drained funds, discouraged additional investment, and contributed significantly to the collapse and reorganization of many transit systems shortly after World War I and again in the 1930s."[2] Milking the mass transit companies for profits helped force them into marginal operation or bankruptcy, making it more difficult for them to compete with automobiles. Moreover, in numerous cases the extraordinary profits of these transit entrepreneurs, together with their ties to political corruption at local and state levels, created a negative public image —which in turn made the public less enthusiastic about tax-supported subsidies and fare hikes for the troubled systems.

As profits declined public authorities in cities such as Boston and New York were forced to take over the transit lines from private companies, because city governments felt citizen pressure to continue to provide cheap mass transportation. There has long been popular demand for publicly owned transit that is reliable, convenient, and reasonably inexpensive. Ironically, one consequence of the so-called progressive political reform movement in cities in the first decades of the twentieth century was that control of public mass transit systems was often placed in the hands of regulatory commissions, many of whose members were committed to the interests of corporate America rather than to the welfare of the general public. Ultimately, this meant that even government investments moved away from heavy support of public transit to disproportionate, if not exclusive, support of automobile and truck transportation systems.[3]

Killing Off Mass Transit. This movement of government money to auto-related transportation highway needs took place in the same period that some corporate action was taken to destroy electric transit systems and replace them with highway systems. A bus or trolley car can replace several dozen automobiles; a subway or rapid transit rail car can replace many cars; a railroad train between cities can replace hundreds of cars. Eliminating much of this rail competition has been important to the growth of the auto industry.

According to Snell, the process had three stages. First, General Motors (GM) helped Greyhound corporation displace long-distance passenger transportation from railroads to buses. Then GM and other auto-related companies bought up and dismantled numerous local electric transit systems, replacing them with GM-built buses. The diesel buses were expensive public transit: "The diesel bus, as engineered by GM, has a shorter life expectancy, higher operating costs, and lower overall productivity than electric buses. GM has thus made the bus economically noncompetitive with the car also."[4]

According to Snell's research, in the 1930s GM created a holding company through which it and other auto-related companies channeled money to buy up electric transit systems in forty-five cities from New York to Los Angeles. In the late 1940s GM was convicted in a Chicago federal court of having conspired to destroy electric transit and to convert trolley systems to diesel buses, whose production GM monopolized. The fine, however, was a modest $5,000. In spite of this conviction, GM continued to play a role in converting electric transit systems to diesel buses. Between 1936 and 1955 the number of operating trolley cars in the United States dropped from about 40,000 to 5,000. General Motors, replying to Snell in a lengthy report of its own, has argued that the electric transit systems were already in trouble when it began intervening in a big way. Some transit systems were declining already, and some had begun to convert partially to buses before GM's vigorous action. So from the GM viewpoint, the corporation's direct intervention only accelerated the process. Perhaps even more important in destroying mass transit was the new and aggressive multi-million-dollar marketing and advertising of automobiles and trucks by General Motors and other automobile companies.[5]

Automobile companies were not the only powerful actors involved in killing off numerous mass transit systems. Bankers and certain public officials also played a role. Glenn Yago notes that "after World War II, banks sold bankrupt and obsolete transit systems throughout the country at prices that bore no relation to the systems' real values."[6] And financial institutions controlled the bond issues that financed new equipment for the transit systems remaining. New purchases were made by public officials, but maintenance was often neglected. Street and highway construction was usually considered a higher priority. In this manner, public officials have also cooperated with the auto industry in eliminating mass transit systems.

Over the last several decades mass transit subsidies have been small compared with highway subsidies. This extreme imbalance has spurred the decline of taxpayer-supported mass transit. Yago has demonstrated systematic disinvestment in mass transit systems by government officials as they increasingly supported auto and truck transportation systems. This decline affects low- and moderate-income people the most. Less public transit since World War II has meant increased commuting time in large cities where people are dependent on the automobile, which is especially troublesome for blue-collar workers; it also has increased consumer expenditures for automobiles and gasoline. Auto expansion inhibits public transit because growing street congestion slows down buses and trolleys, further reducing their ridership. As a result, maintenance of public transit is cut, again chasing away riders who dislike poorly maintained equipment. And fares are increased. Riders who can go to automobiles do so. And the cycle continues. The impact of the initial governmental disinvestment in public transit snowballs over time.[7]

Mass transit has been allowed to die by the powers that be. Consumer desires were only partly responsible for this. Consumers did discover the freedom of movement of autos, and even with excellent mass transit systems many might prefer the auto for at least some types of travel, such as that between cities. But consumers make their choices from the alternatives available. With no real transportation alternative to the automobile in most urban areas, consumers have turned to it as a necessity.[8]

THE AUTOMOBILE: BOON OR SCOURGE?

Owners of the first automobiles were primarily capitalists, small and large, and some self-employed professionals, such as physicians. By 1915 two auto markets developed: the elite market, with its expensive automobiles; and a market of Model T type cars for ordinary workers with decent-paying, full-time jobs. In the United States the number of autos increased from 10.5 million in 1921 to 26.5 million in 1929.

Gradually the automobile industry became a monopoly. In the 1908-1924 period there were at least one-hundred auto companies, but this number had declined to three major companies by the 1970s. General Motors, Ford, and Chrysler make most of the cars produced in the United States. Historically the U.S. auto industry has kept out new competitors by its high-cost styling, exclusive dealerships, and administered prices. Ford and Chrysler can follow General Motors's price decisions. And, until recessions in the 1970s and 1980s, automobile companies have been very profitable enterprises. In recent years the Big Three U.S. auto manufacturers have faced stiff competition from foreign companies, in part because of past management decisions not to invest in making what top executives had long regarded as less profitable smaller cars. Now top executives are seeking government and union subsidies and concessions to improve their profitability.[9]

Automobiles have taken up a large share of consumer income. It is estimated that the average motorist pays out five to seven times the initial cost of an automobile if he or she keeps it for ten years or so, for gasoline, insurance, and other expenses. There are, in addition, the costly health and environmental hazards of automobiles. Tens of thousands of Americans are killed each year by cars and trucks. Hundreds of thousands more are injured. Air pollution generated by cars and trucks damages the lungs of millions. Congested city traffic makes it difficult and frustrating to get around; commuting times increase sharply, particularly compared with European cities. Many consumers are becoming aware of the high human costs of their freedom of "choice" in owning and operating automobiles.

Many who analyze the current problems in the American transportation system see "technology" as the cause: "the city dweller, especially in recent times, has been a victim of the technological changes that have been wrought in transportation systems."[10] Conventional explanations for auto-centered urban transportation patterns focus on the needs of a market system and on shifts in transportation technologies. The rise of cars and trucks is assumed to have been inevitable, to have shaped cities and suburban migration naturally. Coupled with this view is an emphasis on consumer preferences; consumers have always demanded automobiles. An example of this consumerist bias can be seen in Ralph Gakenheimer's statement that "in the postwar years, the pent-up demand for automobile travel was resulting in the very rapid increase of car ownership."[11] This perspective ignores the issue of whether consumers really demand energy-inefficient cars that self-destruct from built-in obsolescence in just a few years. It also neglects the critical role of auto companies in killing off or starving mass transit. Consumers cannot choose mass transit if powerful elites have previously decided to get rid of it. Important too are the roles of advertising, product design, and mass marketing in shaping consumer tastes for autos with annual model changes and poor energy efficiency.

Aggressive advertising has played a key role in wedding Americans to the automobile. During the mid-1920s General Motors pioneered in developing new marketing and advertising techniques, including installment buying, annual model changes, and widespread advertising. Product designers and advertisers for auto companies worked together to sell a broad array of "necessary" options they decided to put into cars. Thus a 1940 Chevrolet ad emphasizes a powerful engine and size: "It measures a thrilling fifteen feet plus—181 inches from front of grille to rear of body— and it's 'every inch the king' of lowest-priced cars."[12] A 1965 Pontiac GTO ad shows a car covered with tiger rug. The caption says: "Purrs if you're nice. Snarls when you prod it. Trophy V-8, standard in Pontiac GTO. 389 cubic inches. 335 horsepower. 431 1b-ft of torque. ... Then prowl in a Wide-Track a while. You'll know who's a tiger."[13] A 1968 Dodge 440 Magnum ad shows a blond woman posed provocatively next to the car on a beach, with the caption: "Mother warned me...that there would be men like you driving cars like that. Do you really think you can get to me with that long, low, tough machine you just rolled up in?"[14]

Billions of dollars have been spent by auto companies on advertising that emphasizes style and snobbery, sex, speed, and size. Annual model changes, however cosmetic and trivial, are sold as necessary for the intelligent car buyer. Product designers incorporate unnecessary features that can enhance profitability. And, as these ads clearly show, the pressure is hard sell. There is a definite suggestion that one cannot be intelligent, comfortable, a ladies' man, or a macho-male without an automobile. If consumers are indeed "kings" and "queens," why have so many billions of dollars been spent to convince them to buy the cars that are available?[15]

BUILDING ROADS AND HIGHWAYS:
A MODERN CRUSADE

Government subsidies have been critical to the process by which automobile transportation substantially replaced railroad and mass transit transportation. This can clearly be seen in the development of massive intracity and intercity road and highway complexes in the United States, particularly the Interstate Highway System. Over the last six decades the federal government has emphasized highways in its subsidies for ground transportation.

The Interstate System. In the 1950s a major escalation of the public commitment was made. Military defense needs constituted the rationale President Dwight Eisenhower used in defending his mid-1950s proposal for a $50 billion intercontinental highway network. He even appointed a member of the military elite, former General Lucius D. Clay, to head a committee to report on the nation's highway and transportation needs. The committee included a top construction company president, the head of a major bank, the head of an auto-related corporation, and the head of a truck drivers' union—not exactly an objective review panel. Most who testified before the panel were organized groups of auto-related companies, oil companies, other large corporations, and government highway officials. Not surprisingly, the report recommended a greatly expanded highway system to meet military and civil defense needs, as well as the needs of an expanding economy.[16]

Soon Congress had before it a number of bills designed to expand government subsidies for highway building. Testifying before Congress on the highway bills in the mid-1950s, Robert Moses, a prominent New York official, said that "I still have not found anybody who can tell me how you are going to keep on turning out all of these cars without decent, first-class, modern highways for them to run on, in particular on the routes that connect the big cities and their suburbs, and run through the cities, because that is what we have to do today."[17] Moses, who was responsible for proposing and supervising extensive highway systems himself, is candid. Not only does he explicitly link the production of autos to expanded highway systems, but he also emphasizes the role of these road systems in organizing and shaping land development in cities and suburbs. Private-sector capitalists and government officials developed a major public relations campaign to generate public support for a tax-funded national system of highways; most newspapers across the country supported the proposals. In 1956 a law was passed setting up a Highway Trust Fund collected from gasoline taxes to build an interstate highway system. This transportation system was funded by taxpayers, some of whom would seldom or never use it. In effect the federal government provides a huge subsidy for the auto-related industries in the form of gasoline taxes collected for this trust fund; other types of surface passenger transportation have in recent decades received relatively small government subsidies.

The highway industry exerts its dominance through coalitions of corporate capitalists and state and federal highway officials. The highway construction and auto lobbies have dominated the Federal Highway Administration as well as state highway departments. Government officials, elected and unelected, usually see eye to eye with the lobbies and thus defend an auto-centered civilization.

Their implicit (and sometimes explicit) national goals are usually two cars in every garage, a gasoline station on every corner, and cities devoted overwhelmingly to streets, parking lots, and maintenance facilities for the auto.

Progress is measured in terms of car ownership and highway and street mileage. If the cities seem choked and under strain the solution is to improve and expand car-carrying capabilities.[18]

In 1963 the *Asphalt Institute Quarterly* strongly supported a statement by then Secretary of Commerce Hodges, who said that traffic problems would be solved by providing better roads for cars, not by restricting the number or caliber of cars. "We shout a 'Hear, hear!' and let's construct those better roads out of asphalt so they will cost less to build and thus be easy on taxes—at the same time providing more roads for more cars to travel more miles and use more petroleum products."[19] It must have seemed a bit odd to Americans living in the oil-crisis world of the 1970s and 1980s that prominent U.S. leaders had been calling for more auto travel and expanded oil consumption just a few years earlier.

One major lobbying force for expanded highway programs has been the American Road Builders Association, including highway construction corporations, materials suppliers, engineering companies, and investment corporations. The association worked vigorously for expanding highway construction and citizen protests over various highway construction projects. One association official wrote that local business leaders should actively massage public opinion.

The truth is, however, that the local people are not entirely aware of their best interests. They do not know for sure what the new highway will mean to them. That is why those who oppose a proposal usually appear in large numbers and talk longer and louder than do those who favor the project. And that is precisely why a softening-up or pre-selling public relations campaign must be waged in those communities before the public hearing is held.[20]

This association has periodically helped to organize massive public relations campaigns on behalf of expanded highway construction. Highways are defended as critical to industrial and residential growth; freeways open up new areas for developers, make suburbanization possible, and increase land values. Many other auto-related organizations, such as the National Asphalt Pavement Association, the Truck Trailer Manufacturing Association, the American Petroleum Institute, the National Automobile Dealers Association, and the Rubber Manufacturers Association, have been important in lobbying for an extensive highway system.[21]

Key members of Congress have been lobbied by auto-related interests. Corporate officials frequently move into the executive branch or Congress, and vice versa; campaign contributions and intensive lobbying help shape government action on behalf of business. Recent government policies have supported billions of dollars in subsidies to save a troubled auto industry. Yago notes that "increased highway construction, bus purchases, and rail disinvestment are the emerging lynchpins of national transportation policy."[22]

These government policies will, as in the past, contribute to the pressures for expanding the spatial form of American cities. Attempts to direct significantly more federal money to mass transit over the last decade or so have generally failed because of the auto-oil-highway bias built into government policies.

The Cost and Impact. This government-subsidized highway system has exacted a heavy price from the American people — and it is now escalating. At the cost of billions of dollars an interstate highway system has been constructed, one of the largest public works projects in U.S. history. Today this expensive system is deteriorating rapidly in many areas. Officially, one-tenth of it is in poor condition, full of potholes and deteriorating bridges.

A major reason is that usage has been much greater than expected. Both auto traffic and truck traffic have grown at rates double or triple original projections. Particularly harmful is the truck traffic, because one overweight truck can do damage comparable to that of thousands of automobiles. A number of analysts have noted that many trucks are operated at illegally high weights to increase profitability; it is often cheaper to pay fines than to run with less weight. The highway system was not built to withstand this punishment. Maintenance and replacement costs to keep it in shape have been estimated at $3 billion a year, but in the late 1970s only a few hundred million dollars were being made available for this purpose. The growing maintenance costs for these highways mean that new taxes will be required. The Highway Trust Fund no longer provides enough revenue; even *conservative* politicians have recommended more than doubling the federal gasoline tax in order to repair highways.

The U.S. highway system represents a giant and continuing governmental subsidy not only for auto and truck corporations but also for other industrial corporations. These corporations often do not pay a fair share of the total cost, and much of what they do pay is passed on to consumers. The ordinary worker and consumer through his or her taxes heavily supports this expensive, inefficient, and wasteful transportation system. Highways are thus a general tax on the public, generation after generation. Gains in salary may be offset in part by taxes paid for maintaining highway systems. The recurring fiscal crises at the local government level are also partially fueled by large huge expenditures for street and highway construction and maintenance. The tremendous commitment to the interstate and other highway systems means that little money is left over to support more efficient mass transit and rail systems.[23]

Automobile manufacturing, moreover, accounts for a large proportion of the basic resources, such as oil and iron ore, consumed in the United States. Freeway construction has destroyed many urban neighborhoods and further segregated, often intentionally, black and white communities in many cities. And street construction, by reducing taxable land, decreases the tax base of central cities, while it increases auto congestion.

New freeways are built. Soon they too become filled with cars. This overflow is in turn used to justify even more freeways. And the vicious cycle continues. Part of the reasoning behind the tremendous increase in highway expenditures after World War II was the idea that traffic congestion and the absence of parking were causing central-city decline. Yet the vigorous road construction undertaken created more of the same problems. In many cities the expensive highway system does not work at the very hours—rush hours —when it is supposed to work. Rush hour congestion brings traffic nearly to a halt. In many cases the average speed on traffic arteries was higher in horse-and-buggy days.[24]

Extension of the Interstate Highway System into urban areas was not an original goal. Rather, cities were to be bypassed. Yet by the 1960s federally funded expressways around, within, and through cities had become an important part of the growing system. With government providing most of the money, business and local government leaders eagerly sought these new highways. Interstate highways in and around cities are primarily used by commuters and other local transporation, not for the interstate travel that was the system's original purpose. As a result, these highways have played a role in facilitating decentralization of industry and suburban development.

Cracks in the Road: The "Infrastructure Crisis."   Recently the mass media have discovered the rapid deterioration of the nation's roads, highways, and bridges. Numerous articles have been written on the "crisis." In addition to 8,000 miles of Interstate highways, thousands of miles of other roads are in severe disrepair. Many roads are being used well beyond their expected lifetimes. Some 1980s' estimates of the cost of repairs and reconstruction on the roads go as high as $600 billion. Moreover, an estimated 200,000 bridges—40 percent of all bridges—need to be replaced and repaired at a cost of tens of billions of dollars. Analysts from the media and industry are calling on local, state, and federal governments to pay for costly repairs and reconstruction. This will be difficult in times of government retrenchment.

This infrastructure crisis signals that the American "love affair" with the automobile has had an extraordinary long-term cost, which was not seriously considered in the beginning. And this cost may be more than our troubled economic system can bear. The alternative system of mass transit would probably have been much less costly in the long run.

Highway Superbuilder: New York City's Robert Moses.   Just one strangely curved mile of the Cross-Bronx Expressway was at issue. Local neighborhood groups, mostly low-middle-income Jewish residents, in one area of the Bronx protested that the proposed route for the expressway would destroy more than 1,530 apartments officially admitted. They knew that far more than the official figure of 5,000 people would be displaced by that one mile of concrete. What puzzled neighborhood leaders and their advisory engineers was that an alternative route along an existing city avenue would have made a straighter expressway and would have consumed only a few small buildings. Instead, city officials proposed to destroy the homes of thousands. As a result, neighborhood groups aggressively protested the threatened loss of homes, neighborhoods, shopping, parks, and schools. They were angered by the dry, bureaucratic letters, which arrived in December 1952, giving them ninety days to move before the city tore their homes down. The neighborhood groups went to meetings. They were abused, ignored, and stonewalled. They slowed the political process down. But they lost the battle. Together with business leaders and politicians, the powerful New York bureaucrat Robert Moses had imposed his own will on the people. The expressway was built with its strange curve. And, according to Robert Caro, no one is sure today why it was built that way—perhaps only to show ordinary people that they have so little power to shape transportation systems.[25]

Until 1945 most superhighways had been built around or between cities, not within them. But that year Moses, head of a powerful public agency in New York, was planning to build a hundred miles of expressways in the city, more superhighway mileage for this one city than existed in the world in that year. Moses eventually built 700 miles of expressways and roads in and around New York City. Thousands of houses, apartment buildings, and businesses were destroyed. Caro sums up the impact.

> Even for the "easiest" of these monster roads, those traversing relatively "open" areas of the city, there were always private homes, small apartment houses— and whole factories—which had to be picked up and moved bodily to new locations. For most of these roads, Moses had to hack paths through jungles of tenements and apartment houses, to slash aqueducts in two and push sewers aside, to lift railroads in the air or shove them underground.[26]

By the time he was through Moses had built $2 billion worth of highways and roads in New York City. He built virtually all of the city's major expressways and many major bridges. More than 250,000 people had been displaced in the process. Neighborhoods, schools, and parks had been destroyed to provide room for more automobiles, without much democratic input into the critical decisions.

Autos and the Physical Layout of Cities.   In many cities, sprawl and congestion go hand in hand. There is a tendency for those who can afford it to shift their use of automobiles, and the location of their residences, as new freeways and other highways are developed. They can move to farther-out suburbs, where housing can be cheaper. At first, home-to-work trips take less time than before, even over greater distances, because of the new highways. But then traffic is attracted to the new roads, congestion increases, and travel time usually increases again. Shifts to the automobile because of the early advantages of a freeway affect mass transit lines, which may become unprofitable and die out, even though motorists later experience severe freeway congestion and desire mass transit. At that point, however, building mass transit is a very expensive undertaking.[27]

Because it is spread out, much of suburbia is not easily serviced by mass transit. Commuters need cars even to get to mass transit stations. Developers are still building subdivisions that require automobiles for access. Builders of office buildings construct huge garages for employees to park their cars in; some office towers have many floors of parking. Shopping centers, particularly larger regional centers, reserve most of their acreage for cars, which are often the only means of access to them. Most new suburban subdivisions and shopping developments are automobile dependent.[28]

Low-density urban sprawl is very costly; it costs about twice as much in terms of land, street, and utility costs as high-density development. Moreover, maintenance and energy consumption costs are higher in low-density developments. Much urban architecture has been shaped, directly and indirectly, by automobile transportation. There are many drive-in and drive-through establishments—banks, liquor stores, even churches. High-rise parking garages and home garages dot the urban landscape. Central cities, especially in the South and West, are very auto oriented. Indeed, most downtown areas of central cities are "places to drive through, or to drive into in the morning and out of in the afternoon. Their architecture is that of a way station, not of a place to live."[29] The automobile has accelerated the extreme specialization of land use in urban areas.

The scale of American cities has been greatly affected by the automobile. Cars require a lot of space. As Delbert Taebel and John Cornehls put it, "The space required to house, feed, and tend the car is larger than human, and its speed creates drastic alterations in our perception of distance."[30] Cars require a lot of space. Auto-related land use consumes large proportions of city and suburban land. One study found that 59 percent of downtown Los Angeles was devoted to streets, parking, and similar uses. For most other major cities the proportions were 40 percent to 55 percent; the highest proportions tend to be in the larger Sunbelt cities. Automobiles have remade the built form of cities because of their requirements for streets, parking lots, garages, repair facilities, and new and used car businesses.[31]

This auto-centered built form shapes and interrupts social life at home as well as in downtown business areas. Residential streets are commonly 50 feet or less wide; but freeways can cut 300-foot-wide swaths of urban landscape. Residential streets with heavy traffic have been found to have much less social life than light-traffic streets. Streets busy with automobiles make it difficult for urbanites to visit with neighbors in front yards, for children to play outside, and for neighboring to extend across the streets.[32]

One of the serious problems in this auto-centered society is that many millions of people have no automobiles; in the mid-1970s the figure was 35 million people over the age of sixteen for the entire United States. The low-income family, the handicapped, elderly households, the poorer minority family—these are the Americans who depend most heavily on public transportation. One Chicago study found that three-quarters of bus riders could not have made their trips by car; many of these riders were poor, elderly, and minorities. Minority workers tend to commute longer distances to work than white workers, and they depend more heavily on public transportation than do whites. Many of the automobiles people in poorer groups do own are older, often unsafe, or unreliable. Indeed, several government commission reports have found that the lack of good public transportation was an important factor in the ghetto riots of the 1960s and in the major 1980 riot in Miami.[33]

RENEWING MASS TRANSIT

Alternatives to Automobiles. Why do many Americans continue to "prefer" the automobile? Some say it is a fundamental human preference for freedom of movement. Others argue that this preference is "attributable to the fact that alternatives to the car are virtually nonexistent; that some very powerful economic interest groups have labored hard and long to keep it that way; and that the structural characteristics of the nation's economy work to prevent the kind of changes needed to develop viable transit alternatives."[34]

A number of organizations have studied American attitudes on the automobile. Even a 1968 study financed by highway-building interests found that the general public favored improved public transit as well as highway systems. One question asked in this survey was "The auto pollutes air, creates traffic, demolishes property, and kills people. Is the contribution the auto makes to our way of life worth this?"[35] Fifteen percent said no, and 85 percent said yes. This would seem to confirm the argument that consumers prefer, and have in fact demanded, heavy reliance on auto transportation. Yet in this same survey fully *half* of those who said *yes* said the auto was worth all this damage because it was the only type of transportation available to most people. One has to wonder whether the availability of more efficient types of surface transportation might well alter the apparently favorable attitudes Americans express toward automobiles. Our economy is not in fact a free market where consumer needs and desires are met by the best products that can be made to meet those needs. Rather, the American transportation industry has long been controlled by a small number of corporations interested primarily in providing automobiles and similar vehicles. The alternatives allowed are riding bicycles or walking in most cities, or, perhaps, riding diesel buses.

Expanded mass transit is an obvious alternative to automobiles. The importance of mass transit has long been recognized in many European countries, where pressures from the public have kept rail transit systems as major parts of urban and national transportation systems. Organized citizen movements in Europe have defined public transportation as a political rather than a technical issue. Even governments in capitalistic countries such as Great Britain and France have recognized that they do not have the economic resources to rebuild cities to fit the automobile alone.[36]

Automobiles are probably the least efficient method of transportation for trips to work in larger cities. Public rail transit can carry ten times the passengers as a single lane of freeway, on a per-hour basis. But in spite of this, there is a crisis in public transportation. This crisis is closely tied to the way capitalism is structured. It is hard to get investors interested in putting their surplus capital into constructing mass transit. Capital moves away from mass transit even when transit systems show modest profits. Capitalists will shift their investments when a given sector becomes less profitable than some other arena of investment. Until the early 1960s virtually all bus systems in the United States were profitable. As had happened earlier with electric rail transit, private enterprise decided to move money away from these less profitable mass transit bus systems, accelerating their decline. Moreover, in the United States public transportation is paid for in regressive ways, such as with sales taxes, increased fares, or bonds backed by property taxes, in contrast to Europe, where more progressive forms of tax support have been used.[37]

The dominance of government transportation policy by auto, truck, oil, and construction company officials has led to an antirail, antielectric bias in planning for future needs. The United States does not now have the sophisticated electrical transit capabilities it once had. The few local government authorities that have added new electrical transit and subway systems, or repaired old ones, have usually had to go to Europe for the know-how, the engineers, the equipment, and the parts.

Nonetheless, support for greatly improved mass transit does exist in the United States. Public opinion surveys indicate widespread support for using tax money to improve and expand public transportation. There have been numerous public protests over transit reductions in cities such as New York and Boston. Recent reorganizations of public transit systems—in New York, Massachusetts, and other areas—have typically demonstrated a concern with reducing services and raising fares, over the protests of many local transit riders.[38]

Some Corporate Rethinking of Mass Transit.   In the 1970s and 1980s some corporate leaders outside the auto industry have come around to support for publicly financed mass transit. The Bay Area Rapid Transit District (BARTD), a rail system, is one example. This system has been strongly supported by corporations with administrative offices in densely populated San Francisco. However, the new system there was from the beginning designed to meet the needs of the business community. For San Francisco to be a centralized administrative, banking, and insurance center, it requires a convenient transportation system for thousands of people. The system is seen as helping San Francisco become another Manhattan. It was presented to citizens as a solution for transportation problems such as congestion. Yet Stephen Zwerling suggests that the planners and business promoters of BARTD saw it primarily in terms of its economic benefits for the business community, as "a tool by which the future growth of the region could be shaped."[39] The new rail lines were seen as a permanent feature of the urban landscape; and they permitted profitable real estate development along the lines.

Some working developers have also become much more interested in mass transit in recent years. An Urban Land Institute report notes that "many people (i.e., developers) feel the private automobile cannot remain the primary mode of travel for the work trip."[40] Many developers now prefer project locations with both good highway service and, if possible, mass transit service, because of rising fuel costs. Even in the Sunbelt some corporations have become increasingly interested in public transportation for clients and workers. An example is Houston's proposed mass transit system and the extensive van-pooling arrangements provided by its larger employers. Nonetheless, there is little support for direct business taxes to pay for this reinvigorated public transportation.

Some business officials complain that individual employees are too tied to automobiles and thus that it is difficult to get large numbers of them interested again in mass transit to places of employment, such as the industrial parks. This clearly illustrates one of the basic contradictions of modern capitalism. Consumers have to be carefully sold a product; later their socialization into a certain pattern of consumption can be a problem for top decision makers when the new conditions of profit making requires a rapid change.

NOTES

1. Alan Lupo, Frank Colcord, and Edmund P. Fowler, *Rites of Way* (Boston: Little, Brown and Co., 1971), p. 9.

2. Charles W. Cheape, *Moving the Masses* (Cambridge: Harvard University Press, 1980), p. 215. See also p. 216.

3. Glenn Yago, "The Coming Crisis of U.S. Transportation," Paper presented to Conference on New Perspectives on Urban Political Economy, American University, Washington, D.C., May, 1981, p. 9.

4. Bradford C. Snell, "American Ground Transport," in *The Urban Scene*, edited by Joe R. Feagin (New York: Random House, 1979), pp. 239-266; Larry Sawers, "American Ground Transport Reconsidered," *The Review of Radical Political Economics* 11 (Fall, 1979), pp. 66-69.

5. Delbert A. Taebel and John V. Cornehls, *The Political Economy of Urban Transportation* (Port Washington, N.Y.: Kennikat Press, 1977), p. 72.

6. Yago, "The Coming Crisis of U.S. Transportation," p. 10.

7. Ibid., pp. 6-7.

8. Helen Leavitt, *Superhighway-Superhoax* (Garden City, N.Y.: Doubleday, 1970), p. 9.

9. Taebel and Cornehls, *The Political Economy of Urban Transportation*, pp. 55-60.

10. Ibid., p. 17.

11. Ralph Gakenheimer, *Transportation Planning as a Response to Controversy* (Cambridge: MIT Press, 1976), p. 11.

12. The ad is reproduced in Robert Atwan, Donald McQuade, and John W. Wright, *Edsels, Luckies, and Frigidaires: Advertising and the American Way* (New York: Dell Publishing Co., 1979), p. 171.

13. Ibid., p. 183.

14. Ibid., p. 347.

15. For a discussion of autos and the ethic of individualism, see Manuel Castells, *City, Class and Power* (London: Macmillan Press Ltd., 1978), p. 31.

16. Leavitt, *Superhighway-Superhoax*, pp. 34-36.

17. Quoted in ibid., p. 40.

18. Taebel and Cornehls, *The Political Economy of Urban Transportation*, p. 5. See also pp. 4-7.

19. Quoted in Robert Goodman, *After the Planners* (New York: Simon and Schuster, 1971), p. 69.

20. Quoted in Leavitt, *Superhighway-Superhoax*, p. 116.

21. Ibid., pp. 153-155.

22. Yago, "The Coming Crisis of U.S. Transportation," p. 35.

23. Ibid., pp. 8, 24-25.

24. Yale Rabin, "Federal Urban Transportation Policy and the Highway Planning Process in Metropolitan Areas," *Annals of the American Academy of Political and Social Science* 451 (September, 1980), p. 24; Leavitt, *Superhighway-Superhoax*, pp. 7-8, 13.

25. Robert A. Caro, *The Power Broker* (New York: Alfred A. Knopf, 1974), pp. 837-879.

26. Ibid., p. 843.

27. Cf. Leavitt, *Superhighway-Superhoax*, pp. 260-265.

28. Henry Aubin, *City for Sale* (Toronto: James Lorimer and Co., 1977), pp. 348-349.

29. Taebel and Cornehls, *The Political Economy of Urban Transportation*, p. 121.

30. Ibid., p. 116.

31. John B. Rae, *The Road and Car in American Life* (Cambridge: MIT Press, 1971), p. 220.

32. Donald Appleyard, *Livable Streets* (Berkeley and Los Angeles: University of California Press, 1981), passim.

33. Taebel and Cornehls, *The Political Economy of Urban Transportation*, pp. 98-111.

34. Ibid., p. 60.

35. Cited in Leavitt, *Superhighway-Superhoax*, p. 186.

36. Peter J. Hovell, William H. Jones, and Alan J. Moran, *The Management of Urban Public Transport* (Lexington, Mass.: Lexington Books, 1975), pp. 6-10.

37. Leavitt, *Superhighway-Superhoax*, pp. 13-14; Richard A. Walker and David B. Large, "The Economics of Energy Extravagance," *Ecology Law Quarterly* 4 (1975), p. 974.

38. Yago, "The Coming Crisis of U.S. Transportation," pp. 13, 29-32. He cites the surveys.

39. Stephen Zwerling, *Mass Transit and the Politics of Technology* (New York: Praeger, 1974), p. 30. See also pp. 31-33.

40. Urban Land Institute, *Industrial Development Handbook* (Washington, D.C.: Urban Land Institute, 1975), p. 221. See also p. 203.

7

THE "MALLING" OF AMERICA: SHOPPING CENTERS AND INDUSTRIAL PARKS

INTRODUCTION

In the late 1970s the Massachusetts Court of Appeals granted a temporary injunction stopping construction of a new seventy-store mall in Hadley, one of several towns clustered together in central Massachusetts. The mall was being built by the Pyramid corporation on farmland near this town of 3,800 and would bfing thousands of cars daily onto the town's streets. Pyramid's representatives in public meetings argued that the new mall would be landscaped with a running brook and trees inside to create a "rural atmosphere." The mall would house numerous fast-food restaurants, dozens of other stores (mostly national chains), and several large department stores. Supporters argued that the mall would bring jobs and prosperity with no significant negative side effects.[1]

Many local people saw the project differently. They protested. One local activist explained: "Our town's selectmen and planning board told us there was nothing we could do to stop the mall. But we talked, we organized, we hired a lawyer, we held meetings, we raised funds, we went to court."[2] Local citizens' groups argued that the mall would have many social costs for the people and towns in the area.[3]

Organized citizens took this case to town meetings and argued against the facility. But they had to contend with city officials who wanted "growth" and "progress." They had to contend with fatalism. Many residents felt that

122

the "big boys" would get their way, that projects like this were inevitable. The Pyramid corporation did have the best lawyers and consultants money could buy. Pyramid conducted, according to an analysis by Jay Neugeboren, an aggressive campaign to win over local politicians and citizens. They took senior citizens' groups to dinner, made a contribution to the Little League, and offered to give land to the town for road expansion. And they succeeded. The mall was built. However, one major result was increased opposition to development; subsequent projects were stopped.

According to Neugeboren, the mall and allied development had many social costs. There were traffic snarls on roads near the shopping center; there were more accidents. Crime increased. The town dump's capacity was pressed, and $300,000 in repairs on the sewage treatment plant became necessary. Most ironic of all was the destruction of local downtown businesses by the mall.

> Business in the downtowns of Amherst and Northampton was, according to published admissions, off by about 30 percent. Privately, the figures were worse. Merchants at the other two malls in Hadley privately conceded losing business, and Pyramid was already planning to expand: to add six new theatres, 500 new parking spaces, a new supermarket, a drugstore and more.[4]

The citizens of this small urban area had fought what has been called the "malling of America," and in the short run they had lost. As this Hadley struggle indicates, large-scale urban development projects are not confined to central-city areas. They can also be found in suburbia and outlying smaller cities.

Two major types of projects that increasingly symbolize the decentralized urban geography of modern capitalism are shopping centers and industrial parks. Together with suburban residential developments, these projects are viewed by many observers as remaking the social fabric within which we live out our lives. Thus just under half of all retail trade now takes place in shopping centers. Commercial and industrial decentralization have been critical factors behind residential developments in suburbia and in smaller cities beyond the fringes of metropolitan areas.

MODERN SHOPPING CENTERS

Nothing seems to characterize the changing character of capitalist cities as does the large shopping center dominated by a handful of the largest retailing chains and sitting astride a government-funded highway surrounded by acres of autos parked on an asphalt carpet. Many see these centers of retail capitalism as the new village squares in which the community life of America is now centered. Others are not so sure, suggesting that these centers are signs of decline.

Piped-in Music and Chain Stores.   A shopping center has been described by developers as an integrated set of buildings providing space for retail stores, which is owned and managed as a unit and has its own parking facilities. These centers dominate the shopping of many consumers; they account for about half of annual retail sales in the general merchandise and clothing categories. There are three major types of shopping centers: (1) neighborhood centers providing essential items for purchase in a few stores, including a supermarket; (2) community centers with specialty department stores and a supermarket, serving a broader range of consumer needs and a larger area; and (3) regional shopping centers, with a large leasing area, centering around one or more large full-line department stores. Superregional shopping malls are very large centers with three to six major department stores, located in major growth centers, often along suburban highways. Shopping centers both require and generate residential and commercial growth around them.[5]

Piped-in music, plastic flowers in nice rows, electronic games, junk-food restaurants, chain stores specializing in clothing and greeting cards, a long air-conditioned mall anchored at the ends by department stores—this is the modern shopping center, the landmark on many a suburban highway. Often a few miles away is a decaying downtown area with empty or boarded-up retail stores, now defunct small businesses with old family names, and graffiti—a ghost town since the regional shopping center has been built. Some say that the birth and the death are not connected; others argue that shopping centers destroy downtown areas.

An example of a regional shopping mall is Paramus Park in the New Jersey suburbs near New York City. Completed in the mid-1970s, it has 276,000 square feet on sixty acres of land, three-quarters of which is parking and landscaped area. There are more than one-hundred mall tenants, including two major department stores. By the mid-1970s retail sales had reached $60 million. The Paramus Park mall was only one of two dozen shopping centers owned and managed by one major development corporation, the Rouse Company, in the late 1970s. Connecticut General Life Insurance Company was a key financial partner in the project, again illustrating the role of insurance companies in financing large-scale projects. Yet the prosperity of malls such as this one contrasts with the decay in the once-bustling downtown areas of nearby New Jersey cities.[6]

The Mall Developers.   In building and operating the larger shopping centers, several groups of powerful actors are involved: developers, financial institutions, national chain stores, and smaller business tenants. Developers typically locate the malls, sign up tenants, and secure the loans. They view shopping centers as a response to consumers; a recent handbook says that "the shopping center exists in response to a consumer demand for retail goods and services."[7] Of course, other shopping arrangements meet consumer demand, such as small businesses in downtown areas, but these developers usually do not highlight that fact.

The character of retail merchandising capitalism has indeed changed over the last few decades. There were only a few large integrated shopping centers and malls before 1945; those that did exist often served rich communities, such as the River Oaks area in Houston. Neighborhood centers increased rapidly after World War II, but not until the 1950s were the first large regional shopping malls focused on major department stores were constructed. One of the first large enclosed malls was built in a suburb of Minneapolis in the mid-1950s. Thousands have been built since then; an association, the International Council of Shopping Centers, has been formed, signaling the importance of shopping center developers in postwar cities. In the mid-1970s the *Shopping Center Directory* listed nearly 19,000 shopping centers in the United States and more than 1,200 in Canada. The number had increased to 22,700 by 1982. Nine in ten of these centers and malls are less than two decades old.[8]

By the early 1980s shopping centers were not quite the "hot" investment opportunities they once were, for there were relatively few large metropolitan areas without numerous regional malls in key places. It was becoming more difficult to find a profitable place to locate a larger mall. In many areas there has been a trend to building smaller shopping centers and to introducing centers in towns and small- to medium-sized cities. Still, the president of the International Council of Shopping Centers has predicted a bright future for shopping center profits, particularly in neighborhood and community centers and large regional centers in growing Sunbelt areas.[9]

The "Science" of Location.   The business of locating, building, and operating shopping centers is sometimes called a "science." Many developers pick locations years in advance along actual or projected highways. Shopping center developments require careful decisions about location, to assure enough affluent consumers within easy driving distance. Developer analyses look at the income of people in the retail trade area to be served, competition from other shopping centers, site location, local government regulations, and land costs. There are "scientific" formulas: according to developer lore an average person will drive 1.5 miles for necessities such as food, 3-5 miles for other necessary items where a range of selection is not important, and 8-10 miles when range of selection is important.[10]

Because of the concern for automobile accessibility, regional malls tend to be located near freeways and interstate highways. Smaller centers are linked to nearby residential developments. If they wish, developers involved in nearby subdivisions can have a captive audience for their own neighborhood shopping centers. Developers of centers have a strong interest in the development of the surrounding areas. One developers' handbook recommends that shopping center owners should own adjacent land to expand into, such as a reserve of land zoned residential nearby that can later be rezoned when the developer needs it.[11]

Even the positions of shops within malls are worked out in terms of suitability of location, compatibility with nearby shops, and crafty merchandising. Retail shops are located to maximize the seduction of consumers. The large "anchoring" department stores are usually located at a distance from one another to maximize the forced exposure of consumers to small stores in between. A number of technical terms are used: gross leasable area, parking index, convenience goods, and impulse goods. The last two terms refer to types of products presented to customers. Rules dictate how to arrange centers to manipulate customer expenditures. One handbook suggests that "impulse goods have an indefinite trade area and are placed so as to get them into the customer flow created by other businesses or within a store where people are passing by on their way to find a definitely sought-for item."[12] In other words, items people do *not* seek or need are put where people see them on their way to items they do seek. Not surprisingly, considerable attention is given by the developers of, and commercial tenants in, larger shopping centers to product promotions and advertising campaigns. "Creative" promotions and advertising are the way to secure greater profits, according to the comments of the president of the International Council of Shopping Centers, Neil R. Wood, who in 1981 was also the head of Cadillac Fairview Corporation, Ltd.[13]

Money Machines: Rents and Profits.   Developers, lenders, and chain stores alike profit from shopping malls. Large department store chains such as Sears and Montgomery Ward earn a large proportion of their profits from their stores in shopping centers. In the 1970s Montgomery Ward reported that 70 percent of its profits came from stores in shopping centers. Large retail corporations have the power to dictate construction and leasing conditions to shopping center developers, such as lower rents for themselves. For consumers, moreover, chain-store retailing in shopping centers means less variety in some items, more standardization, and the same goods and services in every center across the country. This often can mean higher prices.[14]

In many cases the developer-owner manages the shopping center; in other cases a management company is hired. Management includes rent collection, security, and sales promotion. Centers have been profitable for many of the reasons associated with other developments. Annual return on investment in many U.S. and Canadian shopping centers has ranged from 15 percent to 100 percent. Profits come both from rents and from selling the centers later on. Income from sale is usually taxed at capital gains rates, less than half ordinary tax rates. A typical smaller (100,000 square foot, nineteen-store) shopping center can bring the owner a profit of 60 percent to 70 percent of the cash investment in the project once it is sold. Indeed, the *Shopping Center Development Guide* views shopping centers as "money machines."[15]

Developer-owners can make a substantial profit on the regular rents from tenants. Rents can involve a percentage of total sales, so that the owner of the shopping center not only gets a normal per-square-foot rent but also a percentage of the profits (called overage rent) of profitable stores. Overage rent has made many shopping centers very profitable; it is, to quote a real estate journal, "a major reason why well conceived and carefully planned regional shopping centers have emerged as secure and profitable investments for long-term lenders and equity interest." Complex property depreciation arrangements are also used by developer-owners to reduce taxes due on income. According to the *Shopping Center Development Guide*, the income from centers can be "tax sheltered by depreciation reserve."[16]

Creative Financing.   Lenders, the omnipresent banks and insurance companies, can make substantial profits from shopping center financing. As with other projects, finance capital can exert control not only over the mortgage loans themselves but also over construction and day-to-day operation. If the majority of stores are local businesses, lenders will lend perhaps only half as much as when most of the renters are large-chain stores. Some lenders have required three-quarters of malls to be occupied by national retail chains, rather than independent businesses. Many lenders have become more cautious about making loans for shopping centers, particularly in suburban areas where a number have already been built. There are now more joint ventures by developers and lenders and more participation by financial institutions in actual ownership as a condition for making the loans. In recent years foreign capital—Dutch, Mexican, West German, and Middle Eastern—has been used for shopping center development in the United States and in Canada.[17]

More Government Subsidies.   Local governments usually provide many services that make shopping malls possible. Part or all of the cost of sewerage, water, gas, and electric utility services for shopping centers may be covered out of local government bonds and funds. The Urban Land Institute has noted that "enlightened municipal planning bodies tend to look favorably on planned developments, such as shopping centers."[18] Government officials are seen as "enlightened" if they meet the service needs of development. Developers have pressed for government-subsidized utility and other service districts for projects such as shopping centers. Yet the same real estate actors usually resent government agencies becoming involved in such problems as pollution, architecture, and traffic.

Because suburban sites for shopping centers have become harder to find some developers have begun looking more carefully at building in central-city locations and at redeveloping older shopping centers. Downtown development has become more viable because of the return of population and employment in some downtown areas, as well as renewed government assistance to such development.

PEOPLE WHO HATE MALLS: PROTESTING AND DEFENDING DEVELOPMENT

Protests.   Malls have a negative effect, some argue, on everyone involved, other than the developers and retailers. Not surprisingly, then, a few citizens' groups have protested, even slowed, mall development. Antimall protests in a number of North American cities have led to government regulations and commissions to study the problems created by shopping centers. For example, cities in Ontario, Canada, have seen citizen struggles over mall development, with several shopping centers being delayed or vetoed by governmental officials under citizen pressure. Recently in Fredericton, New Brunswick, after a long battle a regional shopping mall was rejected by city officials and local voters. Moreover, the province of Prince Edward Island established a freeze on shopping center development, followed by an in-depth public study of such centers. The Newfoundland Independent Business Association, formed in 1980, pressed governments for a freeze on mall development until new controls could be put in place. Interestingly, these *local* business leaders made the radical demand that half the ownership of new malls be local, that half of all retail spaces be reserved for local businesses, that local businesses be charged the same rent per square foot as national chains, and even that national chains be specially taxed on mall profits. Remarkably, these demands came from conservative businesspeople in the towns and cities. As one local merchant put it, without these controls, "you have the Marxist idea [being fulfilled]: the big boys squeeze out the little fellows, the rich get richer."[19]

The Developers' Defense.   Shopping center developers have a different view. They and associated politicians argue that center projects improve the local tax base and increase employment, that whole communities benefit, that development means tax revenues and general prosperity. Whether far out in suburbia, or in closer older residential suburbs, centers are defended by developers in this way.

A major controversy has developed in Denver, Colorado, over the rebuilding and redevelopment of the older Cherry Creek Shopping Center just a few miles from downtown in a famous older residential-shopping area. A top executive of the owner-developer argued that there would be a tremendous benefit to the city in the form of sharply increased tax revenues from the center, which would "more than pay for all of the traffic improvements and other services needed to handle the increased density." His explicit statement was that "this is our neighborhood too" and that we "intend to preserve and protect it," a common view among powerful real estate actors.[20]

The Cherry Creek Shopping Center was originally built in the mid-1950s. The 600-acre Cherry Creek area includes not only a shopping center but also a large number of boutique shops and a small but exclusive residential section. One of the nation's largest shopping center developers was brought in by the owner of the mall there to rebuild it into a huge multiple-use project with a regional mall, office buildings, a luxury hotel, and parking garages for thousands of cars. However, thirteen citizens' and downtown business groups protested this redevelopment. A University of Colorado study revealed that downtown businesses would lose millions in annual sales and their growth rate would decline substantially. Downtown business groups became concerned about this decline. Neighborhood groups expressed concern with the traffic problems an enlarged center would create and worried about destruction of the unique architecture and character of the area. Some were also concerned that taxpayer-assigned costs would exceed new tax revenues.

In the long run new development may or not bring increased tax revenues; in any event, some taxes may be lost because some older stores are abandoned as local businesses go bankrupt. Some of the new tax revenues are paid by the developers and new businesses; they can pass these tax costs along to their local consumers by higher retail prices, lower wages, or both. Increased business taxes mean that the general public pays for the new development in one way or another, a point developers do not mention in their public defense. It would doubtless be cheaper for local citizens if governments would increase taxes directly—the taxes then could be lower, because no expenditures for the broker services of developers would be paid.

In addition, the business growth coalition argument that shopping center development brings new jobs is problematic. New construction jobs are short term, and some are filled by outsiders. Moreover, jobs are lost in the local businesses forced into bankruptcy by the new retail developments. New retail jobs in a shopping center may mean a complementary decline in jobs in older (in other words, downtown) local stores. Introducing new retail centers usually means, according to one study, that "once the new mall becomes firmly established, the number of retail jobs in the city will not be higher than the number there would be had the mall never been built."[21] Construction of shopping malls may bring increases in taxes and short-run employment, but these advantages can be offset by major costs for taxpayers and workers.

A developers' handbook candidly admits that "new shopping centers do not create new buying power; rather, they attract customers from existing districts or capture a portion of new purchasing power in a growing area."[22] Shopping center producers seek territorial monopolies. For decades diversified downtown shopping areas in cities have been destroyed by suburban shopping centers. Many shopping centers have been developed with the explicit intention of drawing business away from these older facilities. In this fashion the commercial geography of cities has been reshaped.

Many cities are "over-stored" in terms of shopping center retail space. For example, in Atlanta, Georgia, between 1964 and 1977 the general population increased 73 percent, but the amount of shopping center space went up a remarkable 439 percent. Developers compete with one another to attract regional and national stores to their malls, even if that means killing off older shopping centers and local businesses. Developers and chain stores may even be willing to take some losses for a few years if they can drive out competitors and gain substantial monopoly control over local shopping markets in the long run.

Even the increase of store bankruptcies within shopping centers in the early 1980s did not dampen the trend toward shopping center dominance of retail trade. Whereas the majority of centers saw at least one of their member stores go bankrupt in the early 1980s, still an estimated three-fifths of all new retail store square footage was being provided in shopping malls.[23]

Few Americans know how shopping center economics works or have given much thought to the spread of these shopping malls. Small-business people in downtown areas typically know little about the process of suburban mall development, except that it costs them business. In addition, large shopping centers have increased the dominance of large corporations in the retail markets because smaller businesses cannot compete in the more or less closed (to them) mall settings as they can in downtown areas. A major consequence of shopping mall expansion is the centralization of shopping in a decreasing number of areas and the concentration of control of shopping centers in the hands of top executives in a few corporations. Fewer companies, as the years pass, control shopping in America.[24] The mayor of Ithaca, New York, who had a major mall built near his house, recently told the citizens of Amherst, Massachusetts: "You've been raped. It's naive to think you can co-exist with those people out there. They are big national Triple A retailers. The mall people work 24 hours a day to eat you alive."[25]

Shopping in large centers and malls across the United States probably means higher prices for consumers over the long run, because the developer-owners get their slice of the pie. The retail businesses will often pass along some or all of the developers' added charges to their customers. In addition, malls owned by outside developers channel profits away from communities into outside investments that do not benefit local consumers.

Environmental Problems?   Shopping centers depend heavily on cars and trucks. Two-thirds to three-quarters of a typical center's acreage is reserved for parking. Large centers use huge amounts of land; acres of trees may be destroyed and water runoff problems thereby created. The energy crisis has made the construction and operation of malls with large open spaces to heat and cool much more expensive. Today many developers are worried about the threat of citizen intervention in shopping center development and about the imposition of environmental rules and traffic regulations.

Across the nation the architecture of shopping centers is standardized, what some critics have called an architecture of "upside-down ice cube trays on a carpet of macadam."[26] Internal and external mall architecture is linked to the central concern for maximizing profit. Stark exteriors encourage people to gather inside rather than outside. The interior is designed to attract and seduce customers: It lacks outside windows and includes planned variations in the lighting, greenery, and physical layouts of products to increase impulse buying.[27]

MODERN VILLAGE SQUARES: A DEBATE

Replacing Candy Stores of Our Youth?   Some see shopping malls as the new village squares, as combination community and social centers. Philip Brous, president of a large retail chain-store company, sees the modern enclosed shopping center as replacing

> the candy store of our youth as the place for young people to go to congregate ...young people like to go there and particularly to show up on Saturday and Sunday. They also like to go there all summer long when school is out. ... In suburbia, there are no downtowns. The youngsters (whom Bloomingdale's calls "the Saturday generation") gravitate toward the enclosed shopping mall. They like nothing better than to arrive early on a Saturday morning and do some shopping, have lunch in one of the fast-food places, do some more shopping or meet friends, and then possibly go to the movies or to an ice skating rink if the mall has one.[28]

In the shopping centers you can eat, drink, shop, play, and even sleep or exercise. And, of course, this Saturday generation should spend money at retail chain stores, the point of it all. The future of centers is viewed as tied to their becoming part of community life. Fearful of community protest against development, handbooks encourage shopping center developers to introduce public uses into their projects, such as libraries and day-care facilities. Mass media commentators have discussed the new social life the centers supposedly provide. According to a 1979 *Business Week* article, malls are becoming "modern village squares."[29] Some conventional social scientists agree about the virtues; one says malls have become "Main Street, Fifth

Avenue and the community social and entertainment center—all wrapped in one." He further notes the malls' year-round "springlike climate; clean pedestrian arcades...excellent security."[30]

Whether shopping malls become new centers of social life like the old community store, the malt shop, or downtown area yet remains to be seen. There are few systematic studies of the actual social life of malls. Some observers find little real social life in malls, in part because owners look with displeasure on groups of people having fun or meeting in malls without their permission. Teenagers are often discouraged from gathering in them. Often, only "desirable" community groups have access. A few observers' reports do indicate that some have become social centers, at least for adults. The Rimrock Mall in Billings, Montana, a regional mall, has reportedly displaced the downtown area as a central gathering place for ranchers and other people coming to town on nights and weekends.[31]

Advocates for shopping centers hope they are providing a new community, but their idea of community may be distinctly commodified. Many new centers not only include retail stores, but also entertainment features such as skating rinks and movie theaters. The idea is to reshape urban social life in a profit-oriented setting. Shopping centers are viewed as concentrating more citizens' time under the auspices of property and retail capitalists who can profit from this concentration.

Private Property: Enter at Your Own Risk?   A sign at one downtown office plaza says this: PRIVATE PROPERTY. CROSS AT THE RISK OF THE USER AND BY REVOCABLE PERMISSION ONLY. Shopping centers, malls, and MXDs can never really replace the older centers of urban social life, because unlike downtown and real village squares, shopping malls are private property. Owners can prohibit malls from being used for purposes with which they do not agree. Centers are not public places. Community groups may be excluded or have to pay rental fees; signs are posted indicating that the management controls the malls. Political candidates, leafleting, and campaigning can be excluded.[32]

In the late 1960s five young people went to a shopping center in Portland, Oregon, and passed out antiwar leaflets to those passing by. They were peacefully exercising First Amendment rights of free speech. The center management prohibited the distribution of leaflets. A federal judge ruled for free speech for the young people, arguing that the mall with its fifty acres of stores, professional offices, auditorium, and parking areas was "open to the general public" and was a public place because the mall management encouraged use of the facilities by groups such as the Salvation Army and The American Legion. The Court of Appeals upheld the rights of the young leafleters; but in 1972 the U.S. Supreme Court in a five-to-four decision ruled in favor of the *property rights* of the owner. Shopping malls have the right to ban freedom of speech if they believe that to be in their interest. The Supreme Court, especially the appointees of Richard M. Nixon, supported property rights over First Amendment rights.[33]

One shopping center advertising manager candidly expressed the owners' perspective: "We don't try to duplicate the downtown community. ... We don't do anything unrelated to our main purpose, which is merchandising."[34]

A dominant concern of center owners is with security. "Security" in their language refers not only to medical emergencies and criminals but also to community groups that "may create problems—picket lines, political rallies, panhandlers, noisy youth, vagrants, and street people," to quote a handbook.[35] This handbook goes on to say that owners and managers must weigh the rights of assembly and free speech against property and profit rights, with the latter doubtless being atop priority. In major ways center owners can contribute to changing patterns of urban life by prohibiting their shopping areas from being places in a community for many types of social and political contacts.

Pacifying the Community.   Numerous communities have protested the construction of shopping malls. As a result, organizations of developers have sometimes sought to deal with local communities in a sophisticated way. One developers' organization framed it this way: "Community attitudes are demanding. They are apt to be fraught with political intrigue and occasional bad judgment. ... Because he is asking for a change, the developer must be able to overcome people's natural preference to keep things as they are."[36]

Ordinary people, local residents, are here seen as conservative; it is the developers who bring progressive changes to suburban areas. The National Association of Home Builders has published a *Shopping Center Development Guide* to assist developers in putting together shopping center projects. This guide recommends that developers map out a campaign to pacify the surrounding community. For example, it suggests that developers seek to share their large parking areas with a church, library, or other community facility to "make important allies."[37]

MOVING INDUSTRY OUT OF CITIES:
INDUSTRIAL PARKS

Suburban shopping centers are one anchor of real estate capitalism outside central cities. Another major anchor is the industrial (or office) park. By the 1950s two-thirds of new industrial development in metropolitan regions was taking place in suburban and other outlying areas. Developers, bankers, and construction firms collaborated with industrial corporations in building plant, warehouse, and office facilities in such locations.

Planned Parks. The U.S. Department of Commerce has defined a "planned industrial district" (industrial park) as a "tract of land which is subdivided and developed according to a comprehensive plan for the use of a community of industries, with streets, railroad tracks, and utilities installed before sites are sold to prospective occupants."[38] In effect, an industrial park is a packaged arrangement with its own zoning controls and regulations. Many industrial plants and distribution facilities are now located in industrial parks. In Louisville, Kentucky, to take one example, most newer factories are in such parks; many of these plants have been moved out from the central business district in recent decades.[39]

Most facilities in parks are for manufacturing plants, warehouses, and commercial distribution. Many parks have included lighter industry, as well as office towers, shopping centers, and occasionally, recreational facilities. For example, the Los Angeles Industrial Center is a 549-acre industrial park with light manufacturing, research, warehousing, distribution, and commercial facilities. Its developer later added a motel and a bank and has even provided some space for police and fire stations. One study of industrial parks in the 1970s found that there were 700 major parks at that time, averaging about 300 acres each. There were at least 1,000 industrial parks of all sizes.[40]

Development of industrial parks is similar to development of residential suburbs. Developers provide the land packaging, the roads and services, the government permits, and often the landscaping and building design. Space is leased out to commercial and manufacturing companies; the companies that locate in the industrial park may not own the land but pay a leasing fee to the owner.

The developer's job is to pull together the financing for a business park.

135

Developers put up the start-up money for projects and secure longer-term financing from finance capital institutions. As with shopping centers and central-city development, major sources of financing for parks have been insurance companies, banks, real estate investment trusts, and foreign investors.[41]

Substantial profits can be made from major urban development projects such as industrial parks. For example, a 1977 report by Cadillac Fairview on a 132-acre industrial park in Los Angeles noted that the company had spent $2-$3.5 million per year in cash investment in 1976-1977. By 1980 it expected to have its total investment back plus a profit of nearly $10 million. According to James Lorimer's study, overall return on its investment would actually be 75 percent per year over five years.[42]

Profiting from Park Location.   Industrial park developers have specific requirements in selecting locations. One company that assists in development has listed the following requirements for larger parks:

1. Select cities of one million or more people, with economic growth potential
2. Select large sites near expressway systems
3. Analyze population growth and composition in the area
4. Analyze industrial growth in the area, especially type of industries
5. Analyze community attitudes toward industry
6. Make sure gas, water, sewer, electric, and other facilities will be available at low rates.[43]

Here we see the concern of industrial and development corporations with highway access; publicly subsidized highway systems are important to profitable operations. Real estate actors emphasize cheap government services and favorable community attitudes.

Assembly-line manufacturing has contributed to the suburbanization of industry by requiring greater horizontal space for its layout. This creates a need for cheaper land on the urban fringe. Most industrial parks have longer buildings with fewer stories because their land costs are cheaper. Of course, other ways of organizing work, such as worker-controlled team assembly, might decrease the demand for horizontal space as well as reduce worker alienation. Larry Sawers suggests that in a more worker-oriented society "where a major goal of the primary decision makers is to reduce work alienation and involve the worker in his/her job, assembly lines make no sense."[44]

Conventional locational analysis emphasizes the lower costs attached to decentralized locations, including lower labor costs and less unionization.

A survey of top corporate officials in the New York area found those who relocated their corporate headquarters from city to suburbs believed operating expenses were lower, housing was better for employees, quality of life was better, and commuting was easier. Yet the moves to the suburbs reportedly hurt lower-paid employees because they could not afford housing near the relocated headquarters, nor was commuting from central-city areas easy for them. Although this survey referred to corporate headquarters, not just industrial plants, its findings do suggest that executives see suburban locations as cheaper and "nicer" for their facilities and themselves as well-off individuals.[45]

Moreover, a study of Elk Grove Village in the Chicago area, a huge industrial park with many companies, found that the corporate executives liked the suburban location of the park because of its beauty and nearness to *their* homes. Inner-city blue-collar workers, white and black, are often required to commute to industrial parks, while office workers commute not only within suburbs but also from suburbs to central-city office towers. This two-way flow increases traffic congestion on highways in many metropolitan areas. How much time workers waste in cars is thus determined in part by new development decisions.[46]

Between 1960 and the early 1980s a thousand or so industrial parks of varying sizes were built along suburban and other outlying freeways. A study of 157 industrial parks in the New York-New Jersey metropolitan area found most were near an interchange of a limited-access highway. Since corporations have moved out of central cities and away from railroads, the suburban locations mean a heavier dependence on trucks, automobiles, and highways. Highway systems have developed hand in hand with industrial parks. Here again the needs of corporations and the actions of government correspond. Developers begin to acquire sites near projected highways years before the first roads are built. And many industrial park developers have lobbied for the expansion of highways at public expense.[47]

Government Subsidies. Local governments have been eager to secure industrial parks for their areas; they provide the local services and tax concessions that make suburban parks possible. Industrial park location may affect a local community's basic services in ways the community did not adequately anticipate. Providing new water and sewerage facilities and adequate streets may mean a sharp increase in expenditures by local governments, and this in turn can mean an increase in taxes. Some industries have pressured local officials to supply cheap or free land for industrial parks, and many officials have been only too happy to comply.[48]

CONCLUSION:
NEW PLACES TO SHOP AND WORK

When corporate America decentralized its shopping facilities and its industrial complexes, together with many office parks, it determined the shopping places and the work places for millions of Americans. Only a few decades back, most Americans worked in central cities. Today increasing numbers work in the shopping centers, industrial parks, office parks, and similar developments outside central cities. No democratic vote was taken in this process of relocating jobs; ordinary Americans were not consulted. Yet it is they who must move. Moreover, the explosion of suburban residential developments relates directly to this decentralization of commerce and industry. We will now turn to these suburbs.

NOTES

1. Jay Neugeboren, "Mall Mania," *Mother Jones* 4 (May, 1979), pp. 21-24.
2. Ibid., p. 21.
3. Ibid., pp. 22-23.
4. Ibid., p. 31.
5. Urban Land Institute, *Shopping Center Development Handbook* (Washington, D.C.: Urban Land Institute, 1977), pp. 5-11. (Cited hereafter as Urban Land Institute, *Shopping Center*.)
6. Ibid., pp. 207-217.
7. Ibid., p. 249.
8. Ibid., pp. 12-17; Leonard Downie, *Mortgage on America* (New York: Praeger, 1974), pp. 102-104.
9. "Convention '80: On the Treshold," *Buildings* 74 (July, 1980), pp. 60-61.
10. Urban Land Institute, *Shopping Center*, pp. 25-26.
11. Curtis T. Bell, *Shopping Center Development Guide* (Washington, D.C.: National Association of Homebuilders, National Housing Center, n.d.), mimeographed, pp. 50-56.
12. Urban Land Institute, *Shopping Center*, p. 3. See also pp. 71-72.
13. "Bright Future for Mature Industry," *Buildings* 75 (January, 1981), pp. 46-47.
14. Downie, *Mortgage on America*, p. 102.
15. James Lorimer, *The Developers* (Toronto: James Lorimer and Co., 1978), p. 215; Bell, *Shopping Center Development Guide*, pp. 56-57.
16. Bell, *Shopping Center Development Guide*, p. 8; Edward J. Minskoff, "Mortgaging-Out the Regional Mall," *Real Estate Review* 7 (Fall, 1977), pp. 38-40.
17. Bell, *Shopping Center Development Guide*, pp. 17-18; Lorimer, *The Developers*, p. 200; Urban Land Institute, *Shopping Center*, pp. 256-257.
18. Urban Land Institute, *Shopping Center*, p. 46.
19. Graeme Lang, "Shopping Centres: The Case Study of Corner Brook," in *After the*

Developers, edited by James Lorimer and Carolyn MacGregor (Toronto: James Lorimer and Co., 1981), pp. 58-59.

20. The Cherry Creek story is reported in John Simms, "Creative Gambler Marches On, *Colorado Business*, June 15, 1981, pp. 12-13; and Jeff Smith, "Cherry Shopping Center to Cost Downtown," *Denver Business World*, June 7, 1982, pp. 13-14.

21. Lang, "Shopping Centres," p. 57. See also pp. 52-58.

22. Urban Land Institute, *Shopping Center*, p. 25.

23. Lang, "Shopping Centres," p. 55; "A Liferaft for Malls when a Tenant Sinks," *Business Week*, August 30, 1982, p. 30.

24. Langs, "Shopping Centres," pp. 46-47.

25. Quoted in Neugeboren, "Mall Mania," pp. 23-24.

26. Quoted in ibid., p. 31.

27. William Applebaum and S. O. Kaylin, *Case Studies in Shopping Center Development* (New York: International Council on Shopping Centers, 1974), pp. 38-40, 70-71.

28. Philip Brous, "The Chain Store Looks at the Future," in *Shopping Centers: U.S.A.*, edited by G. Sternlieb and J. W. Hughes (New Brunswick, N.J.: Center for Urban Policy Research, Rutgers University, 1981), p. 247.

29. "A Spurt in Shopping Centers," *Business Week*, January 15, 1979, p. 92.

30. John D. Kasarda, "The Implications of Contemporary Redistribution Trends for National Urban Policy," *Social Science Quarterly* 61 (December, 1980), p. 386.

31. Urban Land Institute, *Shopping Center*, p. 263.

32. William H. Whyte, *The Social Life of Small Urban Spaces* (Washington, D.C.: Conversation Foundation, 1980), pp. 65-69.

33. "Shopping Centers: Property Rights versus Free Speech," *New York Times*, July 9, 1972, p. 53.

34. Quoted in Downie, *Mortgage on America*, p. 103.

35. Urban Land Institute, *Downtown Development Handbook* (Washington, D.C.: Urban Land Institute, 1980), p. 131.

36. Urban Land Institute, *Shopping Center*, pp. 53-54.

37. Bell, *Shopping Center Development Guide*, p. 6; see also "News," *Buildings* 73 (September, 1979), p. 30.

38. Quoted in Urban Land Institute, *Industrial Development Handbook* (Washington, D.C.: Urban Land Institute, 1975), p. 4.

39. Urban Land Institute, *Downtown Development Handbook*, p. 10.

40. Urban Land Institute, *Industrial Development Handbook*, pp. 30-33.

41. Ibid., p. 159.

42. Lorimer, *The Developers*, p. 153.

43. R. John Griefen, "Creating an Industrial Park," *Lawyer's Title News*, May-June 1972 (Richmond, Virginia, Lawyers Title Insurance Corporation), as cited in Urban Land Institute, *Industrial Development Handbook*, pp. 76-77.

44. Larry Sawers, "Urban Form and the Mode of Production," *The Review of Radical Political Economics* 7 (Spring, 1975), p. 57.

45. See the President's Commission for a National Agenda for the Eighties, Panel on Policies and Prospects, *Urban America in the Eighties: Perspectives and Prospects* (Washington, D.C.: U.S. Government Printing Office, 1980), p. 24; "Corporate Location Is Largely a Matter of Priorities," *Buildings* 75 (February, 1981), pp. 68-69.

46. Lorimer, *The Developers*, p. 150.

47. Urban Land Institute, *Industrial Development Handbook*, pp. 78-81.

48. See Lorimer, *The Developers*, pp. 154-155.

8
TICKY-TACKY HOUSES: SUBURBAN RESIDENTIAL DEVELOPMENT

INTRODUCTION

Suburbs—no other areas of our cities have received so much attention. Much-maligned suburbanites have been the butts of countless jokes and the centerpieces of many a fiction article in popular magazines. Supposedly the suburbs are breeding new types of Americans—lonely, bored, carbon copies of one another as they conform with similar ticky-tacky houses, yards, and life-styles. Authors such as John Keats have fostered a distinctive image of suburbia: "For literally nothing down...you too can find a box of your own in one of the fresh-air slums we're building around the edges of American cities."[1] Other writers have also emphasized conformity, mental illness, family chaos, and adultery in suburbia, as in John Conway's *Love in Suburbia: They Spiced Their Lives with Other Men's Wives*.

Critics of this suburban image have pointed to its many flaws. Researchers have found that suburbanites are much like other residents of cities. They have no more psychological or family problems than their peers elsewhere in the city. Nor is crabgrass conformity limited to the suburbs. Although suburbanites do tend to be white, white collar, and middle- to upper-income, even this homogenized character of the suburbs is being challenged by the growing number of minority and blue-collar people who live there. The flaws in the fictional portrait of suburban life and life-style have been thoroughly examined elsewhere and will not be repeated here.[2]

However, even the critics of the suburban myth have missed an essential point. All the hoopla about sex and family life, about conformity, has suggested that it is the consumers, the residents of suburbia who alone have produced the great decentralization waves in our cities. Implicit is the suggestion that suburbs are the spontaneous result of the housing demands of consumers expressed through a rational market system. Suburbs appear as unplanned accretions to the body urban. What is missing here is the *producers* who in fact plan, build, and if necessary destroy residential areas in a never-ending quest for profit. Developers are responsible for farmers' fields being rapidly converted into large subdivisions of single-family homes. Many developments are indeed large, such as Lakewood Village near Los Angeles, with its sixteen square miles and 100,000 people.

THE DEVELOPERS

Portrait of a Master Developer: William J. Levitt.   No individual has had more influence on suburban development than the powerful developer William J. Levitt, as we have already noted in Chapter 1. Builder of at least 140,000 houses in subdivisions across the nation and around the globe, Levitt has been the model for other suburban builders. By the 1950s two-thirds of local industrial development and three-quarters of local residential development in metropolitan areas was taking place in suburban areas. Large residential developments were characteristic of this vigorous postwar expansion. By the 1950s developer-builders such as Levitt and Sons were producing large-scale housing developments with standardized housing. On Long Island, for example, Levitt and Sons built large subdivisions, not only houses but also roads and utilities. One area, called Levittown, has 18,000 houses. Earlier in the 1930s, the firm built several small subdivisions on Long Island, but these were priced for upper-middle-income families. During World War II it built military housing and pioneered in the mass production process that was its trademark in the postwar period.[3]

After the war Levitt and Sons further developed prefabrication and assembly techniques that enabled the firm to build identical houses at the rate of 150 per week. Levitt pulled together in one corporation the various aspects of the house manufacturing and marketing process, from controlling the source of nails and lumber to marketing the finished house. Levitt and Sons arranged the structure and design of the houses to fit its own assembly-line construction techniques and their production goal. The firm had a working arrangement with key federal agencies administering housing loan programs (FHA, VA), which provided insured loans for the thousands of houses being built. Indeed, without these loan guarantee programs the Levittowns and similar subdivisions would not have been built, because bankers have not been willing to risk loans to middle-income Americans without the federal government protecting this ostensibly "private" enterprise.

Levittowns were built on Long Island, New York, near Philadelphia, and in New Jersey. The Pennsylvania Levittown was begun in 1951 and included a master plan with 17,000 homes, schools, playgrounds, and a huge regional shopping center. As we noted in Chapter 1, William Levitt was not greatly concerned about building communities, but sought to build "showpieces."[4] Profitability was the basic standard in designing the Levittowns; community-oriented designs and features were for the most part accepted only when they enhanced profit.

Building in Earnest.   Subdivision development had begun after World War I. A few real estate developers bought land on the edges of expanding cities and divided it into lots and blocks. But for several decades builders and their suburbs were relatively small scale. By 1938 there were 70,000 or so homebuilders, averaging three to four homes per year. There were few developer-builders operating on a larger scale in integrated operations and few large subdivisions. There were exceptions, a few scattered attempts at larger planned subdivisions, but areas such as River Oaks in Houston were usually built for wealthy families. At the end of World War II there was a severe housing shortage. The typical builder of houses was still a small local firm without the ability to undertake large-scale development. This soon changed. Studies by S.J. Maisel and J.P. Herzog for the San Francisco area revealed that by 1949 half of all the new houses were being built by medium-sized and larger builders, who at the time made up only 2 percent of all builders. The national pattern was similar. By the 1960s large builders were constructing from two-thirds to three-quarters of all new housing units in the United States.[5]

Suburbanization has been tied to the spread of industry outside the cities; decentralization of industry creates a related demand for housing nearby. The previously discussed government report *Urban America in the Eighties* acknowledges that the migration of jobs to suburbs did in fact precede the migration of people. It recognizes that population increases in the suburbs have been attracted by new businesses there. In a 1981 interview William Levitt underscored the close ties between industrial decentralization and suburban development. "But you can't build if you don't have an economic base. So you have to build and work in conjunction with industry, so that industry moves into the area, people move into it, and land is bought at a respectably low price." Once suburbanizaton takes off, it attracts more capital and workers to the new locations, often to the point of costly exaggeration of the suburban trend.[6]

The larger developer-builders such as Levitt are different from smaller firms. They can buy materials in bulk directly from manufacturers, develop specialized work forces, do real estate research analyses, and make more systematic use of government assistance programs. New land development, site packaging, and prefabrication construction techniques were pioneered by larger developers. Larger subdivision developers often landscape and decorate their models to get buyers to identify their houses with "home," that is, a warm human environment in which to reside. Developers and builders sell trees, flowers, and warm places by the fireplace, not just plain houses. Larger developers have typically had higher volumes and higher profits than smaller builders.[7]

Developers Shaping Suburbs.   Suburban developers have fundamentally altered the pattern of city expansion. The older pattern was for city governments to expand roads and services gradually into rural land on the edges of cities. Now developers' actions force government action. Large developers package large amounts of land, plan the suburbs, seek financing, and build large numbers of houses or sell lots to smaller builders and homeowners to build in the subdivisions. Large developments have required large and cheap areas of land—which are most easily found on city fringes. Developers in the United States and Canada, beginning in the 1950s, have bought up great amounts of land for future urban development. In some cases this land monopoly has enabled a handful of developers to provide most of the desirable new lots available for housing construction in suburban areas.

Developers who own the land along transportation routes, the freeways and the highways, shape the character of much suburban development. The availability of auto and truck transportation, and the interest of businesses in moving to locations in suburban industrial areas, has spurred the development of suburbs strung out along highway routes. As a result, the postwar suburban developers have for the most part assumed that people had autos; suburbs have been designed with much area reserved for automobiles. Until quite recently, most houses have been detached single-family homes with larger lots because the space was available.[8]

Concentration in Homebuilding.   By the 1970s some multinational companies such as Boise Cascade, Alcoa, and Penn Central were involved directly in building large amounts of housing. Other corporations, such as banking institutions, Oil of California and major insurance companies, were making loans for many types of suburban projects. Some large developer-builders have been acquired by even larger multinational corporations. In the late 1960s Levitt and Sons (then the second largest builder) was bought by the International Telephone and Telegraph Corporation.

Large homebuilding corporations are today a major factor in residential housing. They are frequently touted as providing lower-cost housing because of volume purchase of materials and the special mortgage arrangements buyers can make through their mortgage subsidiaries. As one recent builders' journal puts it, "to live up to these prospects, the large builders will have to grow even larger."[9] Large homebuilding corporations have commonly expanded by absorbing smaller profitable local builders. Concentration seems to be increasing in the housing industry. In 1980 there were 459 companies in the U.S. housing market with revenues above $15 million. That year four large builders, U.S. Home, Ryan Homes, Ryland, and Pulte, sold 32,000 housing units. U.S. Home sold 15,821 homes in 1980, about $1 billion in revenue; altogether it has developed 271 single-family-home subdivisions in 121 cities in eighteen states. This one company delivered just under 3 percent of all new houses for sale in the United States; and according to its 1980 annual report, U.S. Home was contemplating buying up some of the other large building companies to increase control of the residential market. In the early 1980s U.S. Home was becoming a multinational corporation; it sold a large block of its stock to a French company, Maisons PHENIX, with whom it had a joint venture in Florida; and it had begun to explore the development of housing in Mexico.[10]

Larger Than Life: Developers of PUDs.   New suburban developments today are often "larger than life." They are supersuburbs, which go by such names as "new towns" and "planned unit developments" (PUDs). One of the largest in the nation is called The Woodlands, a $5 billion development project on the edge of the Houston metropolis (see Chapter 3). Built by Woodlands Development Corporation, a subsidiary of George Mitchell's oil company, by 1981 this PUD currently housed 13,000 residents and 200 businesses.[11]

Public relations brochures for Woodlands speak of it as follows: "The hometown idea is refreshingly simple. You'll sense it during your first visit here." But his view of this "hometown" is broader and more idealistic than that of most major urban developers. Mitchell himself speaks of lower- and moderate-income housing as being a part of The Woodlands.[12] The Woodlands represents Mitchell's vision of how current urban problems are to be solved. Mitchell's vision of a satellite city where the poor and the rich mingle in one planned suburban development will probably not be fulfilled. The profit logic of modern capitalism is such that low- and moderate-income housing, in other than modest amounts, are practically beyond the pale, for they generate less profit. Mitchell's oil capital will probably create another upper-middle-income residential suburb of Houston, but one with its own careful (private) planning, and with industrial parks, shopping centers, and recreational facilities.

A significant feature of these large-scale PUDs in many cities across the nation is the role of government subsidies. For example, federal government loan guarantees have been provided for $50 million in loans for The Woodlands project. The government provides essential start-up support for developments, which generate privately appropriated profits. In 1970 a "new communities" bill was passed by Congress, and the Department of Housing and Urban Development (HUD) opened a new agency that provided loan guarantees to help developers get loans to build the "new towns," as well as direct federal grants for planning and subsidies for loans. Hundreds of millions of dollars in loan guarantees have been provided by HUD to new town developers. Not surprisingly, some conventional suburban developments have been promoted as new towns to get federal and local government assistance.

Planned unit developments have been described in dramatic terms: "a city in the country—ecology in action" (Westlake, California) and "the next America" (Columbia, Maryland). But they are usually only expensive suburbs with a bit more green space and the same suburban problems of race and income segregation and traffic congestion. Substantial federal subsidies—taxpayers' dollars—have supported most new town projects. An example of a new town is Westlake, California, a 12,000-acre development. American-Hawaiian Steamship Company and Prudential Insurance are the unlikely co-owners. The development relies in part on a number of smaller builders, has shopping areas, and provides narrow greenbelt strips in some of its subdivisions. It seems to be a relatively high-priced suburb of Los Angeles, which most ordinary working people cannot afford. Gulf, Exxon, Goodyear Tire and Rubber, Prudential, and other corporations known for products other than housing have periodically gotten involved in new town subdivisions.[13]

In the early 1980s two development companies were putting up Fox Valley Villages, a 4,000-plus acre development thirty-five miles from Chicago's central business district. The community has various types of low-density and high-density housing, its own shopping mall, corporate offices, some light industry, schools, and recreational facilities. A closer-in planned community is Montebello, a suburb of Denver, with similar multiple-use arrangements of housing, schools, shopping, and recreational areas. This 3,000-acre project was also being developed by the same corporations as Fox Valley Villages. Both of these developments signal longer-term planning by developers seeking to organize "how people will not only live, but work and play."[14]

Exceptionally large developments are frequently justified in terms of their presumed efficiency, diversity in terms of income, and protection of environment; smaller-scale development is sometimes criticized as chaotic, disorganized, and ugly by those who prefer these larger developments, which are thus defended as being much "better" for people living in urban areas. Those who make this argument tend to represent or reflect the interests of larger-scale developers.

In fact, according to Richard Walker and Michael Heiman, existing data do not generally support these contentions about large-scale development. For example, houses in these larger developments tend to be at least as expensive as those elsewhere, and very little housing in the new towns and similar large suburban developments is provided for low- and moderate-income families. Generally speaking, the cost savings of such development seem to go into higher profits, not provision of lower-cost housing. Efficiency of scale, if it exists, becomes superprofits. Moreover, the new towns and other large PUDs usually do not save transportation costs, because commuting distances are usually at least as great as those from conventional suburbs. And, with a few exceptions, the large PUDs are no more racially and class integrated than other suburban developments. Many have at least as serious environmental problems as conventional suburbs. Indeed, some of these large planned developments have become infamous for their environmental and racial segregation problems.[15]

CONSUMERS AND PRODUCERS

Consumers as Housing "Monarchs."   Whether they live in suburbia or in central cities, typical families spend the largest share of their income on housing and related expenditures. Low-income families spend 30 percent to 50 percent of their incomes on rent, even though they occupy much of the worst housing available. In one analysis, for both renters and "homeowners" (people who often share ownership with a mortgage lender), about one-quarter of housing expenses went for taxes, one-quarter for utilities and overhead, and half to payments (including profits) to the lender or landlord.[16] Housing is a major need for families.

Conventional city planning and social science analyses tend to view suburban residential sprawl as unplanned and haphazard. Suburban development is seen as an explosion on the urban scene—the result of unknown or "invisible" hands. Suddenly farmland becomes large suburbs. A related image sees disorganized suburban development as the result of consumer preferences. The traditional view is that "suburban development prevailed because the public demanded it, directed government to provide incentives for suburban production and consumption, and fuelled a revolution in the residential construction industry."[17] Here again is the idea of consumer sovereignty.

Developers and allied powerful actors in the housing sphere publicly suggest that the choices of consumers are the primary cause of their development actions. If they see housing and other problems in cities and suburbs, they tend to view them in terms of consumers' demands, rising consumer incomes, and consumer mobility. They may cite government policies and a variety of broad social forces as being responsible. Edward Eichler, a prominent builder-developer, and his coauthor Marshall Kaplan, have put it this way: "The owner, trader, or developer of land has not shaped America; rather, his behavior has been a response to such forces as national policies, changes in technology, social and cultural factors, shifts in income distribution, or rises in total income." They argue that land developers are pawns who respond to technological, consumer, and government forces. They further argue that it is snobbish of city planners and academic critics to complain of the ticky-tacky little houses chosen by ordinary consumers and that urban planners do not care about the housing that middle-income America desires. The implication is that large developer-builders do care.[18]

"Suburban sprawl" is a phrase that has become controversial among some social scientists. Conventional social scientists have suggested that the term is too critical in tone, that the spreading out of residential subdivisions reflects the desires of consumers for detached single-family homes with some green space. They see attempts to provide housing at higher densities (for example, apartments) as being rejected by most households.

Surveys of Americans are cited to indicate that 70 percent to 80 percent do in fact express a strong preference for owning a single-family home. Other surveys show that most Americans, wherever they now live, prefer living in small towns, rural areas, and suburbs to living in larger central cities. Thus, this argument goes, urban planners and other professionals should not force ordinary people to accept someone else's housing values.[19]

Many urban analysts also see the suburbanization of cities more or less in terms of technological determinism. Parker Frisbie argues that "deconcentration of population and industry occurred as new technology led to assembly-line techniques (and thus increased single story space requirements), as improvements in intramural transportation allowed easy accessability to all parts of the city."[20] In such analyses, however, the decisions by top business executives that determine whether, when, and how technological innovations are used are typically neglected.

How Is Suburbia Really Made?   These traditional views assume that ordinary consumers "were free to choose among several residential alternatives, that their choices reflected real preferences and that their preferences were the independent factor in suburbanization."[21] Suburbs do offer escape from the city and, sometimes, better housing for the money. Many families seek the privacy a detached single-family home provides, and more of these are being built in the suburban fringe than elsewhere.

But what is missing in the conventional consumer-as-monarch view is a clear understanding of the organizational and institutional *framework* within which consumer decisions about housing and suburbs are made. Too little attention is focused on the capitalistic producers of housing and their interests and goals. Barry Checkoway suggests that the major decisions were in fact made "by large operators and powerful economic institutions supported by federal government programs and that ordinary consumers had little real choice in the basic pattern that resulted."[22]

Suburbanization has been shaped in fundamental ways by the profit-oriented decisions of the real estate industry. This quest for profit both creates and exaggerates the trend toward suburbanization. Since the 1920s suburbs have gradually come to be seen in the eyes of many capitalistic investors as safer investments than housing in central cities, where utilities and housing are older, if not decaying, and where the population mix includes poor people who cannot pay much for housing. Moreover, when middle-income people in older central-city areas cannot get financing to improve their housing because banks will not make loans to them, they may move to the suburbs, accelerating decentralization. When small-scale landlords cannot get the financing they need, or when they try to squeeze out the most profit they can, rental housing in central areas deteriorates. But in the suburbs housing financing is usually easier to get. Taxes may be lower, at least in the beginning, and basic services are newer. Suburbia is more than the result of the American consumers' dream; it is the combined result of investor-produced options and consumer choices.[23]

Together with their allies, developers make most of the critical decisions. Those shopping for houses are given choices predetermined in large part. New houses in most subdivisions so look alike that there often seems to be one master architect who draws up the basic plans used by developers and builders across the country. Jeffrey Shrank argues that few attempt "to offer a well-made product, honestly presented and clearly explained." Aggressive advertising of the product often signals a certain deception involved. Developments are called names such as Briarwood, Normandy Village, Westwood Heights, Timberlake Estates, Riverview, Woodlake, and so forth. Most such names bear little or no relationship to the actual physical settings; and subdivision names are similar all over the country. People need to be convinced. "Most builders," Schrank notes, "work on the McDonald's principle—like a hamburger, housing is standardized and customers need to be convinced that the standard house is what they want."[24] Standardized housing is sold under dream labels. The homeowner may get to make trivial choices, such as colors of appliances and wallpaper, but the real choices as to location, lot size, and house design have already been made. In most subdivisions houses are built for anonymous buyers. Real needs are ignored, and illusions are presented. Consumers who, lacking alternatives, choose this type of housing are as a result said to be "freely" exercising their ability to choose in a market system.

Suburban areas are the housing ideal not because they provide the best type of housing and living spaces for Americans but rather because they are the best available option the producers have provided for Americans. There are certainly major alternatives to existing patterns of suburban housing, such as extensive closer-in developments of row houses and livable apartments, which have not, at least until recently, been pushed by developers.[25]

Profits in Suburban Development.   Housing prices include not only the costs of labor and materials, but also the profits of builders, developers, and other key real estate actors. One Canadian study of a suburb with $63,000 houses found that large land developers were making $20,000 on every house lot sold *beyond* the normal profit from building and selling the house. In such areas the sharp price increases in suburban housing have come more from the high profits made from lot prices than from rising construction costs. One study found the profit from home lot sales was 100 percent to 200 percent of total cost, often adding $10,000-$25,000 to the total cost of the house. Developer expenses were but a small part of the selling price of the lots.[26]

Where large developers control a lot of land, small builders can have trouble getting lots. And such action hastens the decline in the number of smaller builders and developers. Moreover, in depressed housing markets large developers usually do not sharply reduce house prices. They may reduce the amount of construction they are involved in, but they can generally keep house prices near the same level.

Inflation.   Sharp inflation in housing costs has been a serious problem in the United States, although recent decades are certainly not the first to experience it. In the first year after World War II, the price of homes went up 15 percent to 18 percent. Business and government leaders have done a poor job of explaining the lack of housing, as well as the housing inflation, in the United States. Optimism is the milk of the real estate industry. This comment was made during a 1980 housing recession: "Community living in the next decade probably won't be much different from what we have known during the past ten years. People will continue to buy homes... and everyone will continue to expect the high standard of living to which we've all become accustomed in this country."[27] There are many problems with this statement. In the early 1980s housing construction slumped to an all-time low. Moreover, many moderate-income Americans were not—and are not—accustomed to a high standard of living.

In the 1950s an optimistic history of the National Association of Real Estate Boards (now the National Association of Realtors) said that "for the first time in our history we have a situation in which the average young family, even the average newly married pair, can afford to own its own home."[28] This was an exaggeration at the time. Today it is far off the mark. Although in 1970 about half of American families could technically afford the $22,500 required for the average medium-priced home in the United States, by 1981-1982 only 15 percent could afford the medium-priced $60,000-plus home. The proportion of family income going for housing has been increasing sharply in the last decade. According to a survey by a Chicago title insurance company, by the early 1980s homebuyers were spending an average of one-third of their income on mortgage payments because of ever-rising home prices and interest rates. Just a few years earlier, homebuyers had been averaging 26 percent of their incomes for mortgage payments. By 1980 the median household income of homebuyers was up to $30,000, substantially higher than the median income of all U.S. households at the time. A large proportion of homes, estimated at three quarters, were being bought through financial arrangements other than the usual first mortgage.[29]

What are the causes of this situation? Why is owning a home such an expensive undertaking? The National Association of Homebuilders (NAHB) sees rising housing costs substantially in terms of government regulation. However, even the research discussed in a recent NAHB bibliography suggests that governmental regulation adds only a *small* amount to home costs— and that the main causes of housing inflation are rising land costs, financing costs, and the cost of building materials. One builders' survey has noted that minimum lot size regulations (for example, 6,000 square feet) are the major government regulations that affect developers' and builders' costs. Yet this particular type of regulation is widely supported by families that live in the suburbs; it is not an arbitrary regulation imposed by distant government officials. In some areas the cost of land for a single-family house is even approaching the construction cost of that house; rising land costs seem to be a great part of housing inflation. This situation is already forcing a reduction in minimum lot size requirements in many areas. Labor costs make up an estimated one-fifth of the total cost of new housing; this fact means that rising wages, and union wage contracts, ordinarily cannot be responsible for the lion's share of inflation in costs, in spite of the widespread business emphasis on their role as a dominant factor in housing inflation.[30]

Loans and Interest Rates.   A major reason for the growing cost of suburban and other residential housing is the high interest rate charged by financial institutions to individual homeowners, builders, and developers, as well as the new loan arrangements lenders have put together to increase or maintain their profitability.

Loans to developers, builders, and apartment owners have gotten much more expensive since 1970. By the early 1980s the standard commercial or apartment mortgage was becoming rarer. Lenders now want to share with developers the equity and long-term gains from projects and are no longer content with fixed interest rates. Lenders have replaced longer-term loans with short-term loans and adjustable interest-rate loans. Lenders thus pass along the costs of interest-rate inflation to developers, who usually shift these costs to their tenants or homebuyers. The way real estate is financed has changed dramatically in recent years as the so-called institutional investors (finance capitalists) have taken over a significant portion of the profits formerly reserved for developers.[31]

Homebuyers face finance capitalists as well. Suburbanization has been sustained by what *Business Week* has termed a "mountain of debt." Residential housing has traditionally been bought with the aid of a 70 percent to 90 percent loan, which is paid back over twenty to thirty years. In the last few years interest rates have risen well above ten percent. For the first years of the loan the house occupant's monthly payments are mostly interest paid to the lender; and over twenty to thirty years several times the original amount of the loan is paid back. The mortgage lending industry is dominated by commercial banks, mortgage companies, savings banks, and savings and loan associations, with some participation by insurance companies and retirement trust funds. Many savings and loan associations started out as mutual savings associations in which ordinary working people deposited their money and became shareholders with votes. Today, however, these associations are run by top executives just like private commercial banks. As one government-funded study put it, most savings and loans are "what amount to personal or family fiefdoms, or joint ventures controlled by small groups."[32]

The standard twenty- to thirty-year loan to homeowners, at a fixed interest rate, was becoming rarer by the early 1980s. New arrangements have been developed to enable homebuyers to finance the increasingly expensive single-family home. For example, in the early 1980s Ryan Homes tried a reduced-interest-rate loan that requires the homeowner to give Ryan Homes one-third of the appreciation in value when the house is eventually sold. Many types of new financial arrangements are being tried by lenders, including mortgage loans with variable interest rates. Most entail great risks for homebuyers, because the arrangements assume *rising real incomes*. If a family should not get the expected wage and salary increases in the future, or if an illness should occur, they may well lose their homes.[33] Some observers foresee many mortgage foreclosures in the future.

Selling single-family homes without selling the land is another idea that has spread in recent years. One strategy is to sell the house but lease the land to the homebuyer. The lease on the land may be for ninety-nine years, allowing the house buyer to purchase it at any time. This reduces the down payment and spreads out profits over time for developers. A number of housing projects have been set up so that the developer sells the house to another investor, perhaps an insurance company, which then leases the land back to the homebuyer. One problem with this device is that after fifteen years the land leasing fee often goes up sharply, which may make it difficult for the original buyer to stay in the home or even to sell it. This sort of housing deal assumes the homebuyer can purchase the land from the investor (at an ever-growing price) later on. In addition, seeking to assist homebuyers, some local governments have floated bonds to provide home financing to middle-income families at reduced interest rates.[34]

Profiting from Land Speculation.   So far the suburban migration has involved more than 50 million people. The area currently used for urban and suburban purposes in the United States is over 10 million acres, although twice as much land is withdrawn from other uses because of the leap-frogging that characterizes much suburban growth. Such idled land, one land use report notes, is "ripening for active urban use."[35] By A.D. 2000, perhaps 40 million more acres of land will be withdrawn from other uses for urban development, mostly for suburban growth. Marion Clawson has estimated that as of 1970 the rise in land prices each year, for land moved from rural to suburban use, was about $14 billion. With inflation since then the land annually removed from rural to suburban use is worth far more.[36]

Rising land prices lend themselves to extreme speculation. Suburban speculators, including development companies, operate as a critical group of capitalists who fill the ownership gap between agricultural and urban land. Pressures at the urban fringe eventually force most agricultural users to sell out, sometimes directly to those wishing to develop the land and sometimes to speculators willing to hold the land for price rises. In the fringes land will often go through the hands of a series of speculators before it becomes a housing subdivision or industrial site. A number of studies have illustrated the profits made by developers and speculators buying up such farmland.

In areas such as California land operators have bought out farmers by offering thousands more an acre than the farmers paid for the land. Such sales push up the property taxes on surrounding farmlands not yet sold.

Tax pressures, coupled with the common water runoff and pollution problems of new development, eventually force the most obstinate farmer to sell out. As a result, in many areas residential land prices have risen 200 percent to 400 percent faster than the price of housing. In some cities, such as Los Angeles, the price of residential land went up at the rate of 40 percent a year in the 1970s, a rise aggravated by speculative activity.[37]

Land speculation is regarded in the conventional business literature as a positive bridging force—a brokerage operation between the farmer and the suburban developers and the builders. But this speculation has negative effects. Illegal and unethical activity is, according to one researcher, to be found among speculators, allied developers, and their financiers. Leonard Downie notes that some "land speculators push farmers off their land and employ deceit and bribery to rezone and subdivide it. Developers knowingly throw up shoddy housing. Bank and savings and loan officials ignore conflict-of-interest regulations and make 'insider' mortgage loans to themselves, relatives, and friends." Moreover, Bruce Lindeman argues that real estate speculation and land banking *restrict* the supply of available land, forcing prices above what they would have been without speculative activity. Higher-than-necessary prices come in part from expensive, highly leveraged, financial arrangements that land speculators get into, as well as from competition in the speculative process itself.[38]

GOVERNMENTS AND HOUSING

Governments have cooperated with and subsidized the development industry. Many development costs are paid for by the general taxpayer; governments have provided the roads, sewers, and water lines required for suburbs. Right after World War I both the real estate industry and the federal government pressed for growth in home construction. The Labor Department actually put up "own your home" posters from Maine to California with captions such as: "Own a Home for Your Children's Sake," "Thrift Puts Savings into a Home," and "Construction Now for a Greater and Still Happier America." This clarion call for homeownership has been renewed each decade since.

In 1930 the president of the National Association of Real Estate Boards (NAREB) spoke out strongly for the development of more homes for middle America. He noted that since 1915 the cost of owning a home had doubled, and this had put a home out of reach of most people. American presidents have also extolled the virtues of homeownership. Since Herbert Hoover, every president has pressed the idea of homeownership as a key to being a *good citizen.* In a time of impending crisis Hoover articulately pressed this idea that homeowners were loyal citizens. Franklin Roosevelt's support for homeownership reflected his bias against multifamily dwellings; he felt every family should have its own detached home on its own piece of turf. And after World War II a large-scale government propaganda campaign on behalf of homeownership began again.[39]

Government Financial Assistance. Government officials not only have cooperated in extolling the virtues of homeownership but also have provided the financial assistance business leaders wanted. As early as 1913 the path-breaking Federal Reserve Act stabilized banking and commercial credit, but did nothing for expanding or protecting home loans. Direct financing for urban residential housing did not expand much until 1916, when nationally chartered banks were finally permitted to make some housing loans. Yet the limited appeal of these loans could be seen in their terms: one-year loans of 50 percent of property value. Real estate leaders sought government intervention to protect home loans. A Senate investigation led by New York Senator William Calder, a Brooklyn builder and finance capitalist, looked into the shortage of mortgage money. The NAREB supported a Calder bill to create homebuilding loan banks. At the 1920 NAREB convention emphasis was placed on tax law changes to encourage homebuilding and homebuying. NAREB recommended to Congress that interest paid on mortgages be exempt from federal income taxes. In this case the idea for tax concessions did *not* come from the consumers, but from the builders and real estate agents concerned with having more consumers to buy their products.[40]

In the 1930s home construction declined sharply; nearly a third of the unemployed were from construction-related industries. By 1931 real estate leaders were pressing President Hoover to set up a central mortgage bank to save the homebuilding industry. That conservative president put together a Conference on Home Building and Home Ownership, which called for the *government* to invest money in public housing, to be built by private enterprise, and for government agencies to provide money for privately owned banking corporations. By 1932 there were 5,000 bankrupt banks, and 7,000 other banks were in trouble, and it was not long before new government support for private banks was actually provided. The Federal Home Loan Bank Act, passed in 1932, set up the Federal Home Loan Bank Board (FHLBB)—with savings and loan associations constituting most of the membership. The FHLBB was a backup source of credit for savings and loan associations, which were to become the most important home mortgage lenders after World War II. This board acts as a bank for its member banks, making loans to them and accepting deposits from them, helping to maintain their profits. Funds for this lending come from selling FHLLB securities and notes to investors. Whenever the real estate lending industry has faced serious recessions, such as the severe problems of the early 1980s for savings and loan associations, government programs have been provided to shore up and subsidize the industry.[41]

In the mid-1930s a conference of real estate people and bankers helped work out a plan for the federal government to create an agency to insure the loans of private lenders. Industry executives suggested that borrowers pay an insurance fee with their monthly payments to the lenders. Created by the 1934 National Housing Act, the Federal Housing Administration (FHA) was the requested agency; it provided insurance making possible long-term loans with lower monthly payments. Ceilings and standards for its mortgages, for the loan insurance, and for determination of qualified buyers helped to stabilize the U.S. mortgage market. FHA-insured mortgages could cover up to 90 percent of the cost of a house. The idea behind industry demand for government intervention was to increase the loan money available by protecting lenders; and this program did encourage developers and builders to expand their operations. FHA protects *lenders*, not homeowners, from going bankrupt. This government intervention permits risk-free loans by lenders and helps shore up private profit making in the housing finance industry. The expansion of government into housing support programs in the 1930s was done to encourage ailing private enterprise.[42]

Nathaniel Keith notes that the "clientele of FHA was primarily the large commercial banks, mortgage banks, insurance companies, building material suppliers, and private builders."[43] The FHA and Veteran's (VA) programs have also stimulated an expansion of control over the entire industry by the larger financial institutions, those that can most easily meet government standards for making loans. Large lenders have directly or indirectly controlled the FHA system. Certainly homebuyers and tenants benefit; but the main thrust has been to protect the interests of lenders first, then to see how the needs of homebuyers can be met within the framework of that profitability. One result was that financial institutions often became citywide, providing mortgages for suburban development and at the same time restricting loans for rehabilitation in central-city areas. It is not a coincidence that the emergence of large-scale, citywide financial institutions making mortgage loans has paralleled the dramatic rise in suburban residential construction and the decline in low-cost housing construction in central-city areas.[44]

Government and Suburban Expansion.   After World War II much new housing was channeled by real estate industry groups and by federal agencies to the suburbs. At the same time, many central-city apartments were destroyed by urban renewal programs. Many middle-income couples were given no real housing choice but suburban housing. Charles Abrams notes that the homebuilding industry and the government could have decided to spur new housing development either in central cities or in suburban fringes. In his view development in central-city areas would have required some government involvement in the packaging of land. But it was easier at the time to facilitate development on undeveloped land on the suburban fringe.[45]

Homeownership, and mortgage indebtedness, have been vigorously advertised by homebuilding associations, chambers of commerce, and developers. Large builders have been historically favored by federal government housing programs; they received credit more quickly and easily in the early period. Moreover, FHA manuals discouraged development in central cities, particularly in the low- and moderate-income — and nonwhite — areas of the cities. Checkoway suggests that the suburban expansion was the result of government effort "to stimulate production in the housing field and in the national economy."[46]

Other Financial Subsidies.   Since the 1930s the federal government has provided many subsidies for building and banking interests. In the late 1930s the Federal National Mortgage Association (FNMA; "Fannie Mae") was created as a secondary market for FHA and VA loans. It was to stabilize the mortgage industry by buying up mortgages in times of recession in homebuilding and then selling them when times got better. In this way it could increase or decrease loan money available. This nationwide secondary market makes it possible for lenders to sell the mortgages they hold so to get funds for profitable new investment. The FNMA was created with federal funds and instructed to buy mortgages. It gets additional funds by issuing interest-bearing "discount" notes bought up by investors. The FNMA issued its own stock in the 1950s and 1960s, and now it is a government-sponsored private agency. In 1954 FNMA was rechartered as a reserve bank for all mortgages. Between 1938 and 1963 FNMA bought more than a million mortgages for $12.5 billion. Periodically, in recent decades FNMA has been called on to boost the home mortgage industry. In the early 1980s, for example, FNMA introduced new types of mortgage loans that reduced the initial loan payments for homebuyers, thus making it easier for more families to qualify for home loans. FNMA buys such mortgages from frontline lenders, and in this way makes more money available for home loans. Other government-sponsored corporations, such as the Federal Home Loan Mortgage Corporation ("Freddie Mac"), have done the same.[47]

Because of government intervention lenders can get mortgage money to loan when they need it. Abrams notes that "in short, the government now not only makes it possible for builders to embark on risky ventures with little or no cash but it underwrites risks in the mortgage business and provides liquidity to the lending institutions when they no longer want the paper."[48] Because of industry pressure the federal government has assumed many of the risks for private companies operating in the housing arena. Abrams views government intervention in the 1930s as a program primarily to bail out lenders and only secondarily to help homeowners. In the mid-1930s the federal government helped restore profitability to both the banking and homebuilding industries. New Deal housing programs were aimed at developers, builders, and the mortgage industry and thus helped rebuild an ailing industry.

Protecting developers and lenders from risks may seem un-American from a conservative free enterprise point of view, but private developers and lenders have been strong supporters of this government interference in the economy. A number of developers and builder organizations have played an important role in federal legislation. Publicly owned and built housing has been seen as "socialistic," but various business organizations (NAREB, U.S. Chamber of Commerce, American Bankers Association) have lobbied for intervention programs supporting suburban housing programs. Many high officials in government housing agencies have come from the home-building industry.

New Bankruptcies?   Savings and loan associations have been central to the financing of home mortgages in the United States. Yet in 1982 they were in such serious financial condition that the U.S. League of Savings Associations and the National Association of Mutual Savings Banks asked the federal government to bail out the thrift associations with a rescue plan costing billions of dollars. The savings and loan associations were in trouble because by law they must put most of their loans into long-term fixed-interest-rate mortgages. High inflation over the 1970s placed them in the position of paying higher interest to attract savings than they were getting on their own mortgages. Many older mortgages were below 9 percent, whereas thrift institutions were offering much more than that to get new deposits. The number of savings and loan banks in financial trouble increased sharply by the early 1980s. As a result, the supervising federal agency (FSLIC) forced the weak ones to merge with stronger savings and loan banks. Many observers have questioned whether these thrift institutions will be able to continue to play their central role in financing residential housing. If they do survive, more federal bailouts will probably be required. And if they decline, one must wonder where potential homeowners will go for loans.

Tax Subsidies for Housing.   The idea of income tax advantages for homeowners goes back to the Civil War emergency tax act, when mortgage interest and property taxes were made permissible deductions from certain types of taxes. This definition became part of federal income tax laws in the twentieth century. But the homeowner deductions did not become important until the 1950s, when tax rates were higher than before and tax advantages of housing deductions increased significantly. Indeed, income tax deductions for interest and property taxes helped to spur the subsequent boom in residential housing. As Downie puts it, these deductions are an "indirect subsidy" for builders and developers, because more people can buy homes if a large portion of their monthly payment is tax deductible. Without the mortgage tax deductions, even more Americans would be renters.[49]

It is interesting that federal government expenditures for assisted-housing payments for the last fifty years—from public housing in the 1930s to today's various HUD housing assistance programs—totaled less than the cost of housing-related tax deductions for the year 1980 alone. Government gives away more in homeowner tax deductions than it spends in all its direct housing programs. Tax losses from homeowner deductions have to be made up by other taxes, so these deductions can be regarded as "tax benefits" or "tax expenditures." Rolf Goetze has demonstrated that, of the $30.5 billion in direct and indirect tax subsidies that U.S. homeowners received in 1979, 64 percent ($19.6 billion) was in the form of deductions on their income tax forms. Subsidies for poor and moderate-income homeowners came to only $9.2 billion, much less than those for more affluent homeowners. In addition, tax benefits disproportionately benefit higher-income families with more expensive homes. In 1980 $5.4 billion went to families with incomes under $10,000; those with over $50,000 got $7.5 billion. About 60 percent of the benefits go to the top 10 percent of families, a group composed of capitalists, managers, and top professionals.[50]

The lion's share of homeowner deductions does not go to middle-income families, as is commonly believed, but to higher-income families. All higher-income families who own homes can get this deduction. In contrast, only one low-income household in ten that qualifies for direct federal housing assistance can actually get it, because so little money is appropriated for housing assistance. Cushing Dolbeare notes that

> The pattern of housing assistance provided by the federal government is so inequitable that, were we to start fresh with a clean slate in designing housing assistance programs, and propose a pattern of entitlements, benefits, and assistance that is equivalent to what is now in place today, not only would it fail to pass Congress, but it is doubtful anyone could be found who would introduce it.[51]

Tax subsidies for affluent and rich families spur housing inflation by bidding up the cost of housing and the cost of money from lending associations. Much suburban housing and more expensive housing in central cities are sought for investment purposes by affluent Americans not intending to live there. An array of tax advantages is part of the pressure directed toward conversion of existing apartments into more profitable condominium housing.[52]

SUBURBS AS UNNATURAL DISASTERS: THE NEGATIVE SIDE

Orange County: A Disaster Area?   In Orange County, California, famous as the home of Disneyland, the last few decades have seen much agricultural and coastal land transformed by residential million-dollar developers and construction companies into acres of houses and asphalt. Tomato fields and citrus groves have *will build to suit* and *land available* signs posted.

Subdivisions once planned for a few thousand people are now expected to be developed for a hundred thousand. Yet the developed area of northern Orange County has been described by the U.S. Army Corps of Engineers as the "worst flood hazard west of the Mississippi." An analysis by Wesley Marx highlighted the problem: "To look at a zoning map in Orange County today is to look at a guide to multiple disaster. Find a floodplain, an unstable hillside, or a fault zone, and chances are you will also find a building, an entire city, or at the very least a 'land available' sign."[53]

This area is a large floodplain for the Santa Ana River; normally a dry riverbed, the Santa Ana flooded in 1969, fueled by rainstorms. Seven people died, and there was $85 million in flood damage. An earlier flood took twenty-eight lives. Yet developers continue to put up subdivisions in the serious flood hazard areas, which according to Marx are artfully advertised as "Southern California's Fairest Valley! Beautiful! Busy! Bustling! Brimming!" More than a million people now live in this floodplain.[54]

California law requires that natural hazards be reported to homebuyers in new subdivisions. However, one study found that these reports often contained too-technical language, played up hazards the development did not face, or commented that hazards such as flooding are so far-reaching as to be beyond the reports' scope. Apparently, many land developers regard laws regulating building in floodplains and similar land-use reforms as too radical. One advocate of such regulations reports that such controls have even been characterized as "Communistic."[55]

Such hazards are not confined to California. A 1978 civil engineering report for the National Association of Homebuilders found that builders in Denver were constructing houses on land with serious soil problems. Swelling clay soils have cracked foundations and undermined houses in the metropolitan Denver area. Because of the housing boom there construction has expanded onto land once considered unsafe. In recent years a controversy has grown over this construction.[56]

Construction Quality.   Other critiques of suburbia have focused on the quality of construction, on energy and environmental problems, and on traffic congestion. Numerous suburban subdivisions have been poorly constructed. Many have housing that is not built to last. Residents in suburbs across the nation have complained about cracked foundations, water seepage into homes, leaning walls, leaky plumbing, and unbuilt (but promised) recreational and community facilities. Natural environments (trees, water) are sometimes destroyed in the too-quick seeking of profit from suburban development. Suburban growth also consumes large quantities of valuable farmland.

Rising energy costs have made suburbs more expensive to sustain. Recent suburban housing construction is not nearly as energy efficient as it could be. A modest additional cost—for more insulation, double-pane windows, and so forth—could slash most utility bills in half. And this added cost would be paid back to house buyers within a few years. Suburban office buildings also are not nearly as energy efficient as they could be.[57]

Sprawl? Numerous suburban critics have pointed to the "sprawl," the hedgehopping pattern of scattered residential development. According to Downie, real estate leaders in Los Angeles admit that sprawl development there was heavily shaped by the quest for private profit, that the sprawl pattern there was an easy way to profit from the

> California land rush: Buy a tract of vacant land, wait a short time for the population and roads to move toward it, subdivide it into lots for cheaply built single-family homes, and sell them to builders at prices that total several times the land's original cost—then take your profit and buy another, larger tract of land farther out to begin the process all over again.[58]

This drive toward profit accounts for the sprawling suburban and freeway system in many other cities as well.

Recently some analysts have taken issue with the sprawl arguments. Thus the *Urban America in the Eighties* report argues that suburbanites require less expensive packages of government services than do those in central cities and concludes that this fact indicates people are willing to do without the services. This is a wrongheaded argument—we are talking about different class fractions; lower-income people in central cities require more of certain types of services, such as unemployment aid, than do affluent suburbanites.[59]

The *Urban America* report argues that the physical landscape of older cities is technologically obsolete, that the new polycentered (sprawl) landscape better fits in with modern technologies. The report asserts that low density residential sprawl increases energy consumption by only 3 percent compared with higher-density construction. According to the report suburbia even reduces the exposure of people to pollution, because people are spread out more and thus per capita exposure to pollution is less than it otherwise would be. And suburban industrialization is seen as reducing commuter time, air pollution, and traffic congestion. Moreover, suburbanization, via the trickle-down process, has allegedly brought better housing to the central-city poor. In effect, the *Urban America* report is a thoroughgoing defense of what suburban developers have created over the last several decades. Yet the report largely ignores the many problems associated with suburbanization that we have noted in this chapter.[60]

Wasted Investment?   Capital spent on suburbanization, others argue, means valuable resources wasted, because there are more important social needs. A major problem in this era of late capitalism is finding new markets and new investment opportunities so that the mass of capital can be made productive and profitable. Suburbanization after World War II was a critical outlet for capital investment in housing, shopping centers, and credit arrangements.[61] Suburbanization has been an expensive capital-absorbing expansion. One estimate is that all goods and services directly or indirectly tied to this suburban phenomenon could be as much as half the total gross national product. In part, crises in capital accumulation have been resolved by pumping surplus capital into the built environment of suburbia. Research by J. Ullman and his associates has concluded that more concentrated urbanization would not have absorbed as much capital, in part because many consumer products (particularly autos) would not have been as necessary.[62]

Much suburbanization is part of the exaggerated consumerism of U.S. society. According to urban sociologist Manuel Castells, very "important was the role of the single-family house in the suburbs as the perfect design for maximizing capitalist consumption. Every household has to be self-sufficient, from the refrigerator to the T.V."[63] The automobile and yard-care equipment are items that row housing or apartment housing arrangements do not require in as massive quantities.

THE MYTH OF HOMEOWNERSHIP

National Variation.   Before World War II, most Americans were tenants; they did not own their own homes. Fifty-six percent were tenants in 1940; 45 percent in 1950; and 34 percent in 1974. A majority, though perhaps declining percentage, of Americans are now homeowners, with a significant proportion locating in the suburbs. Is there something in human nature that makes people want to own single-family homes? The answer seems to be

"no." If we look at industrialized countries in Europe we find a wide variation in homeownership views.

In exhaustive research on housing patterns in the urbanized industrial
countries, Jim Kemeny has demonstrated the tremendous variation in housing preferences. Homeownership rates ranged from less than 35 percent in
the very prosperous (capitalistic) countries of Sweden, West Germany,
Switzerland, and the Netherlands to highs of 63 percent in the United
States and 69 percent in Australia. Clearly, there is not a universal human
propensity for homeownership, not even in capitalistic countries. Countries
with a high standard of living have both low *and* high rates of homeownership. In the low-homeownership countries renting is commonplace
and quite respectable, from public housing authorities, private rent-at-cost
associations, and private landlords. There are also complex cooperative
(joint) housing arrangements, which combine certain features of owning and
renting.[64]

Homeownership is sustained by a variety of myths asserting its superi-
ority over other types of housing tenure. Defenders assert that homeownership "satisfies a deep and natural desire."[65] Various studies have shown the
financial advantages of owning a home in the United States. But what they
really measure is the structural bias built into the U.S. housing system,
which favors homeownership over other types of housing arrangements.
That is, homeowners receive *huge governmental subsidies* in the United
States. And private landlords can make high profits from their rental
apartments. Kemeny demonstrates that, without the huge governmental tax
subsidies for homeowners and private landlords, an efficient (public or
private) rent-at-cost housing system would cost households *less* than the
present system of homeownership. He also notes that homeownership locks
owners into long-term indebtedness, favors the well-off over poor and moderate-income households, and increases the costs of job and residential
mobility. The housing preferences of the general public are largely the
consequence of the housing tenure systems available, *not* the cause of the
systems. Kemeny sums up:

> It is hardly surprising, for example, that in a society where private land-
> lords make super-profits, where access to cost-renting is stigmatized and se-
> verely restricted, and where homeownership is heavily subsidized there is
> likely to be a very strong preference for home-ownership.[66]

Existing governmental subsidies and private economic arrangements substantially determine the dominant housing tenure system—and thus the housing preferences—of many individuals and families.

Homeownership helps keep working people wedded to the established social order. J.A. Agnew argues that homeownership is a key part of the contemporary capitalistic ethic of possessive individualism and helps it flourish. That ethic frustrates attempts to build a social consciousness for cooperative housing ventures. Homeownership has long been an important mark of social status in the United States; renters have been given a relatively low status. Working-class homeowners are divided from working-class renters. Moreover, homeowners themselves have different mortgage burdens, with some owing lenders a lot of money and others owing little or nothing at all. This situation reduces the possibility of solidarity among people with different housing situations.[67]

The Inevitable Trend to Higher-Density Living? We have previously noted how inflation in housing costs has excluded many American families, particularly younger families just starting, from owning a home. So the housing picture is changing radically. Families buying homes are paying larger percentages of their incomes for housing; and the average square footage in new single-family homes is declining. Some families are buying smaller homes; others are buying into converted apartments sold as condominiums and other multifamily housing. Even housing developers are turning to multifamily housing projects. Town houses are becoming part of housing areas where such higher-density housing was once banned. In some areas in Orange County, California, land sells for $300,000-$400,000 an acre, making it necessary to put a dozen or more condominiums on an acre of land. Several companies have switched to developing areas of attached row housing because of high land costs. One builder in Chicago recently said that "most builders in Chicago have given up on reasonably priced single-family houses and are building condos and townhouses." Smaller housing units will probably be the rule in the future.[68]

Apartments and Development. Apartment renting has been a major alternative to buying a single-family home. The rising cost of detached single-family homes is likely to increase the number of households that spend most of their lives renting. In New York City most families are not home-owners; most now pay rent to someone else. In other urban centers renters are a majority of the households. Vacancy rates are declining. By 1981 the rental vacancy rate in the United States was the lowest in peacetime history, at 4.8 percent. The Northeast had the lowest regional rate, 3.6 percent. One reason for this is the decline in rental housing built. In 1980, to take a recent example, construction starts (and completions) were the lowest since 1945; and major metropolitan areas in the Sunbelt—Houston, Dallas, and Fort Worth—accounted for more than a quarter of all those starts. Financing was a key problem. For the most part Sunbelt cities were the cities in the early 1980s with large numbers of multifamily units being built. New York and Chicago had some construction, but most cities had relatively small amounts of new apartment housing being constructed. More-over, the size of apartment units has decreased, and the amenities have been reduced, in response to higher construction costs and interest rates.[69]

The real estate industry blames the shortage of multifamily units on high interest rates, high construction costs, and government regulations such as rent control and zoning laws. Many in the apartment business are calling on governments to provide more subsidies for them to develop units for moderate-income families.[70]

In central cities or in suburbs apartments are less expensive alterna-tives to detached single-family housing. Yet apartment complexes can be profitable for developers. Land that is shifted from low-density (old houses, lots) to high-density use (apartments) can be sold at an above-average profit. Developers may buy land zoned for low-rise housing relatively cheap-ly, then they get the land rezoned for high-rise buildings. A variety of tactics have been used to secure land for high-rise developments. One study reports that some developer representatives posed as homeowners and put motorcycle gangs in a few developer-owned houses to drive out nearby home-owners; some even used arson. In some cases the buildings go up and the developers make their profits and move on to other projects, leaving tenants and nearby residents to cope with the long-term problems high-rise buildings bring.[71]

The development and operation of apartment buildings can be very profitable, because of special tax advantages provided by governments. Apartment buildings produce annual operating profits and long-term profits from inflation in the buildings' worth. Apartment buildings have been an investor's haven. Wealthy individuals and companies from around the nation and the globe have been putting money into Sunbelt apartment buildings.

If an individual buys a building for $500,000 he (less often she) will pay perhaps 10 percent down, and the rest will be covered by a mortgage from a bank or insurance company. Interest, taxes, and maintenance are tax deductible. When the building is later sold, the gain is taxed at less than half as much as income from salaries and wages. Investment corporations can pull together a number of apartment buildings into a portfolio and then sell an interest in the portfolio to several wealthy investors. Tax breaks are the incentive.[72]

A large proportion of the apartments and rental houses in a specific urban area is often owned by a small group. One study of ownership in Cambridge, Massachusetts, found that 6 percent of the city's households owned 70 percent of all housing units. The study found close connections among the local banks, which made most of Cambridge's real estate loans, local government officials, and property owners and developers. This incestuous network led to the promotion of luxury apartments and commercial development by the city government rather than to the needs and interests —effective rent control, enforcement of housing codes—of the majority of Cambridge citizens, the working-class and student tenants. The local planning board and the zoning board were dominated by real estate people, a phenomenon characteristic of U.S. cities.[73]

Tenant Problems under Housing Capitalism.   Those who rent in America face many problems. Today just as in the past, tenants have been at the mercy of laws favoring property owners and landlords. Owners of apartment complexes sometimes have reputations for not meeting tenants' needs for heating and the like. Slow decay is characteristic of many apartment complexes, even in Sunbelt cities. In large Sunbelt cities like Austin, Houston, and Dallas half the population rents; many people live in new apartment zones with rapid growth-decay cycles. One such area near Dallas has been described this way: "Addison is so new and so sterile that it seems to be wrapped in cellophane, and yet many of its granddaddy apartments, built as long as seven or eight years ago, have already deteriorated into Sunbelt slums with rotting floors, sewage backups, leaky roofs, buckling pavement, mildew, roaches, and rats."[74]

Maintenance is a routine problem for tenants. Both low-rise and high-rise apartment buildings are complex living environments requiring extensive maintenance of public service areas, such as grounds, stairways, lobbies, and elevators. Larger complexes may use a building manager hired by the owner. If for any reason maintenance costs are resisted by owners, because of a desire for higher profits or residents' support of rent control, the apartments and public areas may well deteriorate. If elevators are not repaired, walls not painted and plumbing not fixed, then the apartment complex can become a relatively unhealthy or even dangerous place in which to live.[75]

Maintenance is particularly a problem when apartment complexes are developed by one company and then sold to another. The major tax incentives for owning apartment complexes are short-term, but the maintenance costs are a long-term commitment. Many owners do not seem to care what happens to the project ten to forty years in the future; by that time they will have sold out their interest to someone else.

Tenants' organizations have increased in number and significance in the United States. This organization has not come easily. A barrier to organizing tenants is that they are seldom in an apartment complex long enough for long-term commitment. Acting as individuals, many tenants protest with their feet; they keep moving to find better apartments in need of less repair. Tenants may have to sue to get stubborn landlords to make repairs, and few are willing to do so. According to Kaye Northcott, we are headed toward being "a nation of poorly housed tenants."[76]

Publicly Subsidized Housing.   Unlike European countries, the United States has never had much publicly subsidized housing. The public housing that has been built generally has been reserved for the poor. From the beginning most public housing was segregated in ghetto and poverty areas, built cheaply and with spartan characteristics, and, as Downie puts it, "given all the homeyness of prisons by government officials under constant pressure from real estate interests and homeowners who fear the alternatives."[77] Many projects have been poorly designed and cheaply constructed; they have housed concentrations of the poorest families. Suburban governments have worked vigorously to keep public housing out. Scattering public housing in smaller complexes around cities would mean that middle-income and upper-income people would have to live next to moderate-income families. Better facilities and construction in public housing would mean higher taxes. Publicly financed housing for moderate-income families would compete with private real estate interests. The many problems and failures of public housing have been used by the real estate industry to support their idea that private enterprise can serve poor families better than can government. Yet the private market has *not* in fact provided fully adequate, sound housing for tens of millions of moderate-income Americans.[78]

In contrast, in numerous European countries a significant proportion of middle-income families live in cost-rental housing, much of it facilitated or subsidized by government. And there is *no stigma* attached to being a tenant in such housing.

One European Alternative to Single-Family Homes. David Popenoe's study of suburban development in Europe and the United States led him to the conclusion that the United States is atypical, that sprawling suburbanization is not an inevitable development in industrialized cities. The United States does not have much high-density suburban development; European cities do. Popenoe studied a large suburb of Stockholm called Vällingby, a residential area where people live in apartments, mostly three-story buildings with garden apartments spaced out around acres of public spaces such as parks and playgrounds. Great emphasis is given to pedestrian and bicycle paths, although there are streets and parking lots. Each cluster of low-rise buildings is centered around a bustling town center. Facilitating access to all parts of the city, a subway links this inner suburb, inhabited by middle-income families, to other parts of the city. Extensive retail, day-care and youth, and recreational facilities are in Vällingby, in excess of those found in most U.S. suburbs.[79]

Popenoe also studied Levittown, Pennsylvania. In comparing it with Vällingby he concluded that Vällingby was a better housing environment for women working outside the home, because of its extensive child-care facilities. Vällingby provided easier access to the rest of the city in the form of mass transit. Leisure-time activities were more varied in Vällingby; there was less TV watching and more walking, biking, and interacting with children than in Levittown. Vällingby was a pedestrian-oriented subject; because of its high density it was built closer to the downtown area. Both communities were found to be family centered.[80]

Vällingby is built on land that is publicly owned; long-range planning by the Stockholm government resulted in *public* ownership of 70 percent of the suburban land within the city boundaries, as well as large areas beyond. This city control made careful planning—a first-rate mass transit system, many playgrounds and parks—of suburban development possible. Moreover, much building in these suburbs has been done by publicly owned development corporations similar to public utilities. Public involvement not only made possible large-scale higher-density housing environments with excellent facilities but also kept the rental costs below what they would have been if private speculators had been involved in land dealings and private developers had been the only group involved in building.[81]

Interestingly, growing economic pressures in the United States make the Swedish kind of low-rise garden apartment buildings in multiple-amenity developments attractive alternatives to single-family homes, because the cost of land, materials, and financing have put new homes out of sight for a growing number of American families.

NOTES

1. John Keats, *The Crack in the Picture Window* (Boston: Houghton Mifflin, 1956), as quoted in Herbert Gans, *The Levittowners* (New York: Random House, 1967), p. xvi.

2. Cf. Gans, *The Levittowners*, pp. xv-xxix; Kathryn P. Nelson, *Movement of Blacks and Whites between Central Cities and Suburbs in Eleven Metropolitan Areas, 1955-1975, Annual Housing Survey Papers*, Report No. 2 (Washington, D.C.: U.S. Department of Housing and Urban Development, 1978); and Larry H. Long, "Back to the Countryside and Back to the City in the Same Decade," in *Back to the City*, edited by Shirley B. Laska and Daphne Spain (New York: Pergamon Press, 1980), pp. 61-75.

3. Gans, *The Levittowners*, pp. 5-13; Barry Checkoway, "Large Builders, Federal Housing Programmes, and Postwar Suburbanization," *International Journal of Urban and Regional Research* 4 (March, 1980), 26-28; and Mark Gottdiener, *Planned Sprawl* (Beverly Hills, Calif.: Sage Publications, 1977), p. 96.

4. Gans, *The Levittowners*, pp. 6, 5-13.

5. Checkoway, "Large Builders," pp. 21-25; S.J. Maisel, *Housebuilding in Transition* (Berkeley and Los Angeles: University of California Press, 1953); J.P. Herzog, "Structural Changes in the Housebuilding Industry," in the *Dynamics of Large-Scale Housebuilding*, edited by Real Estate Research Program (Berkeley and Los Angeles: University of California Press, 1963).

6. "Straight Talk from a Builder," *Housing* 59 (June, 1981), p. 29; see also President's Commission, *Urban America in the Eighties*, pp. 24-25.

7. Curtis T. Bell, *Shopping Center Development Guide* (Washington, D.C.: National Association of Homebuilders, National Housing Center, n.d.), mimeographed, p. 11. Checkoway, "Large Builders," p. 25.

8. James Lorimer, *The Developers* (Toronto: James Lorimer and Co., 1978), pp. 85, 90-96.

9. Robert L. Steele, "Big Builders Getting Bigger," *Builder* 4 (April 1, 1981), p. 66. See also pp. 66-68.

10. Ibid.; and U.S. Home, *Annual Report*, 1981.

11. Woodlands Development Corporation fact sheet, in author's files.

12. Woodlands Development Corporation, "The Woodlands," brochure in author's files.

13. Leonard Downie, *Mortgage on America* (New York: Praeger, 1974), pp. 154-172.

14. Lillie Mikesell, "Challenges of the New Community," *Buildings* 74 (January, 1980), p. 49.

15. Richard A. Walker and Michael K. Heiman, "Quiet Revolution for Whom?" *Annals of the Association of American Geographers* 71 (March, 1981), pp. 80-81.

16. Michael E. Stone, "Federal Housing Policy: A Political-Economic Analysis," in *Housing Urban America*, edited by Jon Pynoos, Robert Schafer, and Chester W. Hartman (Chicago: Aldine Publishing Co., 1973), pp. 424-427.

17. Checkoway, "Large Builders," p. 21. Checkoway cites examples from the social science literature.

18. Edward Eichler and Marshall Kaplan, *The Community Builders* (Berkeley and Los Angeles: University of California Press, 1967), pp. 9-10.

19. A 1978 HUD survey is reported in Martin D. Abravanel and Paul K. Mancini, "Attitudinal and Demographic Constraints," in *Urban Revitalization* (Beverly Hills: Sage, 1980) pp. 31-39.

20. W. Parker Frisbie, "Urban Sociology in the United States," *American Behavioral Scientist* 24 (November-December, 1980), pp. 177-214.

21. Checkoway, "Large Builders," p. 37.

22. Ibid., p. 22.

23. Richard A. Walker and David B. Large, "The Economics of Energy Extravagance," *Ecology Law Quarterly* 4 (1975), pp. 963-985.

24. Jeffrey Schrank, *Snap, Crackle, and Popular Taste: The Illusion of Free Choice in America* (New York: Delta Books, 1977), pp. 122, 123.

25. See Lorimer, *The Developers*, p. 126.

26. Ibid., pp. 99-114.

27. Mikesell, "Challenges of the New Community," p. 47.

28. Pearl Janet Davies, *Real Estate in American History* (Washington, D.C. Public Affairs Press, 1958), p. 221.

29. "News," *Builder* 4 (March 1, 1981), p. 11.

30. Carla Freeman, "Housing Costs: A Builder's Bibliography," Prepared for Special Committee on Costs and Material Supply, National Association of Home Builders, January, 1981.

31. "News," *Buildings* 74 (April, 1980), pp. 16-17; Sy Nicholson, "Long Term Mortgages: R.I.P.," *Buildings* 74 (May, 1980), p. 36.

32. Quoted in Downie, *Mortgage on America*, p. 29; see also Stone, "Federal Housing Policy," pp. 424-427.

33. "News," *Builder* 4 (February 1, 1981), p. 13.

34. Carol Anderson, "Coping with the Recession," *Builder* 4 (June 1, 1981), pp. 16-19.

35. Joseph Ackerman, Marion Clawson, and Marshall Harris, eds., *Land Economics Research* (Baltimore: Johns Hopkins University Press, 1962), p. 9.

36. Marion Clawson, *Suburban Land Conversion in the United States* (Baltimore: Johns Hopkins University Press, 1971), pp. 8-10 and passim.

37. Bruce Lindeman, "Anatomy of Land Speculation," *Journal of the American Institute of Planners* 42 (April, 1976), pp. 142-152; Downie, *Mortgage on America*, p. 88.

38. Downie, *Mortgage on America*, p. 6; Lindeman, "Anatomy of Land Speculation," pp. 150-151. This section draws on Joe R. Feagin, "Urban Real Estate Speculation in the United States: Implications for Social Science and Urban Planning," *International Journal of Urban and Regional Research* 6 (March, 1982), pp. 35-60.

39. Davies, *Real Estate in American History*, pp. 138, 166; Mark I. Gelfand, *A Nation of Cities* (New York: Oxford University Press, 1975), p. 59; Peter Drier, "Tenants as a Minority Group" (unpublished manuscript, Tufts University, March, 1981), pp. 10-11.

40. Davies, *Real Estate in American History*, pp. 95, 140.

41. Robert Goodman, *After the Planners* (New York: Simon and Schuster, 1971), pp. 58-59.

42. Charles Abrams, *The City Is the Frontier* (New York: Harper and Row, Colophon Books, 1967), p. 231.

43. Nathaniel S. Keith, *Politics and the Housing Crisis since 1930* (New York: Universe Books, 1973), p. 30.

44. Stone, "Federal Housing Policy," p. 430; Richard A. Walker, "A Theory of Suburbanization: Capitalism and Construction of Urban Space in the United States," in *Urbaniza-*

tion and Urban Planning in Capitalist Society, edited by Michael Dear and Allen J. Scott (London: Methuen, 1981), pp. 404-405.

45. Abrams, *The City Is the Frontier,* p. 72.
46. Checkoway, "Large Builders," p. 34.
47. Abrams, *The City Is the Frontier,* p. 73; Stone, "Federal Housing Policy," pp. 423-433.
48. Abrams, *The City Is the Frontier,* p. 36; see also pp. 71-72; Goodman, *After the Planners,* p. 58; "How Safe Are Your Savings," *Newsweek,* March 15, 1982, pp. 50-55.
49. Downie, *Mortgage on America,* p. 53.
50. Cushing N. Dolbeare, National Low Income Housing Coalition, "The Need to Limit Homeowner Deductions," *Statement to Committee on Ways and Means, House of Representatives,* Washington, D.C., 1981, p. 8; Rolf Goetze, "The Housing Bubble," *Working Papers for a New Society* 8 (January-February, 1981), pp. 48-51.
51. Dolbeare, "The Need to Limit Homeowner Deductions," p. 8.
52. Goetze, "The Housing Bubble," pp. 49-51.
53. Wesley, Marx, *Acts of God, Acts of Man* (Coward, McCann, and Geohegan, 1977), pp. 108-114.
54. Ibid., p. 114.
55. Ibid.
56. Jerry Ruhl, "Builders Suppress Soil Problem Study," *Rocky Mountain News,* March 6, 1980, pp. 1, 68.
57. Henry Aubin, *City for Sale* (Toronto: James Lorimer and Co., 1977), pp. 349-351.
58. Downie, *Mortgage on America,* p. 10.
59. President's Commission, *Urban America in the Eighties,* pp. 32-37.
60. Ibid.
61. Walker, "A Theory of Suburbanization," p. 409.
62. Ibid., p. 410; see also J. Ullman, ed., *The Suburban Economic Network* (New York: Praeger, 1977).
63. Manuel Castells, *The Urban Question* (Cambridge; MIT Press, 1977), p. 388.
64. Jim Kemeny, *The Myth of Home-Ownership* (London: Routledge and Kegan Paul, 1981), pp. 8-46.
65. Quoted in ibid., p. 11.
66. Ibid., p. 63. See also pp. 8-46.
67. Ibid., pp. 63-64; J.A. Agnew, "Homeownership and the Capitalist Social Order," in *Urbanization and Urban Planning in Capitalist Society,* pp. 458-475.
68. Anderson, "Coping with the Recession," pp. 18-19. The quotation is on p. 19.
69. "News," *Buildings* 75 (May, 1981), p. 16; "News," *Buildings* 75 (March, 1981), p. 16.
70. "Multi-family Housing Forecast," *Buildings* 75 (January, 1981), pp. 43-45.
71. Jack Newfield and Paul Dubrul, *The Abuse of Power* (New York: Viking Press, 1977), pp. 113-120; Lorimer, *The Developers,* pp. 132-135.
72. Oscar Newman, *Community of Interest* (Garden City, N.Y.: Doubleday, Anchor Books, 1980), pp. 101-118; Kaye Northcott, "In Ten Years They'll Be Slums," *Texas Monthly* 7 (November, 1979), pp. 163-265.
73. John Mollenkopf and Jon Pynoos, "Boardwalk and Park Place: Property Ownership, Political Structure, and Housing Policy at the Local Level," in *Housing Urban America,* pp. 55-65.
74. Northcott, "In Ten Years They'll Be Slums," p. 164.
75. Newman, *Community of Interest,* pp. 101-119.
76. Northcott, "In Ten Years They'll Be Slums," p. 265.
77. Downie, *Mortgage on America,* p. 58.

78. Keith, *Politics and the Housing Crisis since 1930*, pp. 108-221; Newfield and Dubrul, *The Abuse of Power*, pp. 113-114; see also Joe R. Feagin, Charles Tilly, and Constance W. Williams, *Subsidizing the Poor: A Boston Housing Experiment* (Lexington, Mass.: Lexington Books, 1972).

79. David Popenoe, *The Suburban Environment: Sweden and the United States* (Chicago: University of Chicago Press, 1977), pp. 61-63.

80. Ibid., pp. 29-43, 176-224.

81. Ibid.

9

THE GROWTH COALITION: POLITICIANS, DEVELOPERS, AND ALLIED CAPITALISTS

INTRODUCTION

In the early 1970s public relations releases extolled the virtues of a government-assisted urban renewal project in central San Francisco: a "center city redevelopment to include a sports arena, 800-room hotel, office buildings, and parking for 4,000 cars...going up only a few blocks from the San Francisco Hilton."[1] The area at issue is a central-city area called South of Market, adjacent to the downtown corporate center of San Francisco. Beginning around World War II, San Francisco became a center for multinational corporations, with headquarters for such giants as Southern Pacific, Standard Oil of California, Transamerica Corporation, Crown Zellerbach, the Bechtel Corporation, and the Bank of America, to name a few. A major administrative and financial center, San Francisco has a growing corporate need for support facilities such as office buildings, convention centers, and hotels. In the South of Market case several thousand people, mostly retired working people, would be forced out of their apartments and homes as buildings were torn down to make room for new buildings. In downtown redevelopment clichés the common justification for pushing working-class residents, including the elderly, off their land is that the land can be put to a "higher and better use." As Justin Herman, director of the Redevelopment Agency, put it: "This land is too valuable to permit poor people to park on it."[2] Official justifications for this type of large-scale land clearance argue that new buildings will improve the city's tax base, make the city look better, and bring new jobs.

In the 1950s a San Francisco Planning and Urban Renewal Association was created, a private planning group dominated by corporate executives and designed to generate business interest in urban renewal. In the association's "Prologue for Action" the effects of the changes desired by this corporate business elite were made clear.

> If San Francisco decides to compete effectively with other cities for new "clean" industries and new corporate power, its population will move closer to "standard white Anglo-Saxon Protestant" characteristics. As automation increases, the need of unskilled labor will decrease. Economically and socially, the population will tend to range from lower middle-class through lower upper-class.[3]

Working through the local governmental redevelopment agency, these business executives intended to accomplish that class-biased goal. Governmental assistance is critical to the downtown projects of these business-oriented growth coalitions. This particular project was approved by the San Francisco Board of Supervisors and went through a number of stages: from the issuing of a plan for the area in 1954 to resident displacement and building demolition in the late 1960s.[4]

The San Francisco Redevelopment Authority (SFRA), like other large renewal agencies, had the power to coordinate private and public action. Carrying out renewal plans, it moved urban residents around, bulldozed areas, and advertised its projects with little democratic input. In the 1960s several large renewal projects had been carried out, resulting in the displacement of 4,000 families, mostly working-class blacks and Japanese.[5]

Called "Yerba Buena Center," the development in the South of Market area was designed to expand the corporate business district to the south; it gained the support of corporate executives and investors. Selling the plan to the public was more difficult. Speculative real estate operators and adjacent landowners stood to gain from this land clearance, but getting public support for governmental expenditures required the help of local newspapers. We have previously noted the importance of newspapers in urban growth coalitions. San Francisco newspapers strongly supported the Yerba Buena development editorially and in their news coverage generally supported the points of view of business leaders.

Who are the thousands displaced to provide profits to a few corporations? South of Market had long been an area of retired working men's lodging. Before displacement most of the 4,000 residents of this area were single, primarily older, men living on small pensions. Dozens of residential hotels provided those retired or disabled men with low-rent housing, generally decent and in sound condition. Some of the hotels needed rehabilitation, but the proposed massive clearance was not required to improve the area significantly. It was close to the transportation and other service facilities that these older men needed. The area was home, a place where single men could find friendship and support services.

This area was often described as a "skid row" or "transient area." Media stereotypes were intentionally aimed at these retired workers in an attempt to persuade other people in San Francisco to support the business-oriented urban renewal. The retired workers themselves were conspicuously absent from the planning process for the project. Nonetheless, the people in the area did eventually organize against the problems about to be visited on them. A tenants' group was formed and fought legal battles with renewal agencies over inadequate relocation plans and replacement housing for those displaced. They won a limited victory in the form of an agreement in which the redevelopment agency agreed to develop 400 low-rent housing units as part of Yerba Buena Center and 1,500-1,800 low-rent units in other parts of the city. For virtually the first time in urban renewal history, the developers had to make some major concessions to a people's movement directed against renewal.[6]

URBAN RENEWAL
AS GOVERNMENT POLICY

Until the 1930s the federal government generally took a laissez-faire (hands off) approach to city government, but during the Great Depression many local governments expanded out of necessity, in part because of enormous unemployment problems. Their activities brought many city governments to the edge of bankruptcy, and federal action was soon required to bail them out. Federal jobs programs and housing programs were part of the aid to severely pressed cities. Much of this aid, as we have seen in the FHA programs in the last chapter, took the form of subsidizing ailing businesses as well as assisting ordinary consumers. This type of business welfare state has expanded greatly since the 1940s.

The Business Welfare State: Urban Renewal.   After World War II housing was considered by many Americans to be a major problem that the federal government should address. The 1949 Housing Act authorized the construction of 810,000 public housing units over the next few years and a massive program of urban clearance and redevelopment. In that act Congress explicitly said that the "general welfare and security of the nation" requires "a decent home and a suitable living environment for every American family." Yet the central problem was, and is, that private enterprise builds houses for those who can afford them, not necessarily for those who need them. And the result is that low- and moderate-income families often cannot secure a decent home and suitable living environment.[7]

The 1949 Housing Act envisioned the use of federal money for "slum" clearance and the provision of decent low-rent housing by private enterprise. But this did not happen. As a surprisingly candid report of the National Commission on Urban Problems puts it, urban renewal became a "federally financed gimmick to provide relatively cheap land for a miscellany of profitable or prestigious enterprises."[8] The urban renewal program has provided a tremendous subsidy for numerous private builders. Federal government funds have been used to bulldoze large central-city areas considered "blighted," and the improved land has usually been sold to developers for about a third of what it cost city renewal agencies. Central cities have been redeveloped; downtown construction has been undertaken. But a heavy price has been paid for this government-assisted development. The majority of those forced out of so-called "blighted" areas have been poor and nonwhite. Only a small amount of new housing built in renewal areas has had rents low enough for those displaced to afford. Much more housing has been destroyed than built.[9]

More recently, government renewal programs have been reorganized, and their names have changed, but the results have been remarkably the same.

Alphabet Soup Programs: CDBGs and UDAGs. In the mid-1970s the Community Development Block Grant (CDBG) program brought under one umbrella most federally subsidized urban renewal and revitalization programs. Every city with a population over 50,000 can get a certain share of block grants based on its size, poverty population, and other demographic characteristics. The 1974 law establishing this grant program officially requires that CDBG grants principally benefit low- and moderate-income people; but so far this intent has been sidestepped, with the active encouragement of some federal officials, especially under the Reagan administration. Urban Development Action Grants (UDAGs) are part of the CDBG program; this money is also supposed to provide help for distressed cities.

These grants were originally designed with the idea of improving the lives and housing of low- and moderate-income people in cities. However, in fiscal year 1978 nearly three-quarters of the money was awarded to industrial and commercial projects, not housing projects. These dollars have ended up going into profitable large-scale hotel and shopping center projects in many cities.[10]

Reportedly, in the early 1980s a total of $13 million in government subsidies was provided for the development of Baltimore's 500-room Hyatt Hotel. Of that, $10 million was a federal UDAG. According to an article in *Mortgage Banker*, the Hyatt project would not have been economically viable without the UDAG grant. This means that the level of profit was higher than it would have been without governmental assistance. In the jargon of bankers the situation is described thus: "In general, a real estate project showing a return on cost (or unleveraged yield) of more than 12.5 percent in a normal debt market may be positively leveraged. As the return drops, a more favorable debt market is required. Our more sophisticated customers are now using return on cost as a key measure of viability early in the development process."[11] Such projects as this have been described in business circles as the ideal private-sector-public-sector partnership.

In Chapter 5 we noted the conflict in Detroit's Poletown area, a substantially Polish and black neighborhood. There a planned General Motors project would demolish 1,500 homes, 150 businesses, and numerous churches to construct a new automobile plant. This project has been supported by a $30 million federal UDAG grant, plus millions more in other government subsidies and property tax breaks. As of 1981 alternative areas for the plant had been rejected by GM. Elsewhere in Detroit the world headquarters building of General Motors is near low-income black areas. In the late 1970s GM announced it would buy several hundred apartments and homes in the area to demolish a large number and rehabilitate the remainder. Other developers were working with GM to build new office buildings in the area. To facilitate the redevelopment the city government applied for a federal UDAG grant.[12]

Local community groups, particularly an ACORN (Association of Community Organizations for Reform Now) group, fought the GM proposal. At one demonstration, ACORN members demonstrated with "G.M. Crow" signs and passed out leaflets that said, "Tell G.M. thanks for nothing—displacement with no relocation benefits." Eventually, under pressure from local community residents, GM and the city gave ground and agreed to some of the community demands, including at least one hundred rehabilitated multifamily units and relocation payments for all affected families.[13]

Effects. In many cities local officials have channeled federal money into a variety of urban revitalization programs aimed at reviving—from a business point of view—downtown areas. What residential housing has been built in these projects has been disproportionately for the well-off. Lenders generally provide loans for projects that they can see will make money; these usually do not include housing developments for low- and moderate-income families. By the 1950s it had become clear that much federal money for cities was going into projects most favored by developers—such as airport and highway construction, port improvements, commercial and industrial projects, and the like—not for the housing projects most needed by low- and moderate-income urbanites. Not surprisingly, government redevelopment authorities have largely been from business backgrounds or have been business oriented. Contradicting the goals of the 1949 Housing Act, government action in urban redevelopment projects displaces ordinary working people from neighborhoods and raises the cost of housing for many urbanites.[14]

THE GROWTH COALITION

Developer-Government Corporation. In many cities those capitalists and managers concerned with urban land, development, and redevelopment have organized themselves locally and nationally as a growth coalition. Business "think tanks" such as the powerful national Committee for Economic Development provide research support for advocates of economic growth and development at the local and national level. Active lobbying for growth is carried out by such groups as chambers of commerce.

William Angel has underscored the importance of local "boosterism" in generating corporate development in cities. Boosterism means advertising and marketing a city to business enterprises outside the area. Suburbs, as well as many cities themselves, are advertised aggressively by local business and political leaders as great places to do business. Ads appear in a variety of places, including magazines and newspapers. Boosters press for government services and facilities, such as highways, urban renewal, convention centers, and utilities. Local business leaders work hard, with government assistance, to get facilities that will entice industrial corporations to their areas. They project the image of a favorable business climate. Communities and states vigorously advertise their business climate—lower taxes, lower wages, and government receptiveness to businesss.[15] Harvey Molotch has argued that this organized effort to affect the outcome of city growth distribution is at the center of local government as a political force. Boosterism is part of the everyday politics that decides who gets what, and where, in cities. Local leaders also work to build internal boosterism, to get citizen support for growth, such as for controversial infrastructure, water, sewer, and utilities projects.[16]

In the 1950s David Rockefeller organized New York City leaders into what became the Downtown-Lower Manhattan Association, a typical urban growth coalition. As mentioned in Chapter 4, Rockefeller and his business associates were the force behind the World Trade Center, office space that was to be filled by large corporations. The project displaced residents and destroyed small businesses. With the help of the governors of New Jersey and New York, the latter his brother Nelson, David Rockefeller succeeded in getting New York's Port Authority to put up the center. The Port Authority could float tax-exempt bonds and thus reduce the costs of the project with taxpayer subsidies; it had the governmental powers to condemn land for public use and to speed up the project by evicting present occupants faster than private leaders could working alone.[17]

Provision of Government Services.   Powerful real estate actors regularly receive governmental largesse. Critical to the corporate city is a government-provided infrastructure: the roads and freeways, sewer and water systems, police and fire services, tax and abatement programs. Whether they are building suburbs or shopping centers, developers and builders need city services. In a recent analysis of Milwaukee, Arnold Fleischmann examined the special utility assessments paid by residential developers in the 1950s. He found heavy subsidies. For example, in 1954 the city government charged $3.00 per front foot on a residential housing block for storm and sanitary sewers. By these assessments on residential builders, the city collected $322,000; however, the facilities actually cost the city $2 million. The city thus promoted residential expansion and private profit making by homebuilders. Not surprisingly, in this case developers with large tracts of land outside the city limits were eager to be annexed in order to get subsidized services. Moreover, older neighborhoods of Milwaukee were in effect subsidizing outlying residential areas. One city government report found that neighborhoods near the downtown area paid millions more in taxes than they got back in permanent utility improvements and operating appropriations; but six outer areas got $32 million more in benefits than they paid in taxes. Older neighborhoods were subsidizing developments from which they received little or no benefits.

Moreover, much governmental support for development has become sophisticated and complex. An MXD in Cincinnati opened with a luxury hotel and an office tower as its centerpieces, together with shopping areas and an atrium. The project involved the city government, which bought the land and leased it to the developer and owners to facilitate profit making. The city provided other subsidies—street improvements, walkways, and landscaping. The decision makers there candidly view the project as lasting only a few decades, followed by replacement. Cincinnati's director of urban development noted that "we felt that future citizens of Cincinnati should not have to repeat the process [of packaging the land] when the buildings are replaced in the next century. When the time comes, we will simply take them down and find a new developer for the site." Developers and their political allies do seem to be building for the short term, with a view of for-profit buildings being recycled on government-assisted land every few decades.[18]

Interestingly, city halls are becoming "entrepreneurial" in their dealings with some developers, requiring a piece of the profits in return for providing development subsidies for certain downtown projects. In one Louisville hotel project the city was scheduled to get half of the profits after the developer got a 15 percent return on his equity. The city was to get half of any appreciation in value of the property. Of course, this type of arrangement can be risky for city governments, because developers and others are first in line for any income. Some developers like these arrangements because the governments are taking on expensive front-end development costs, such as land costs, construction loans, and second mortgages. City involvement means that taxpayers are taking major risks if projects fail; and private developers are protecting themselves from the risks they have previously assumed.

Tax Breaks and Bonds.   Governments have provided many tax reductions. Owning property such as apartment buildings and office towers can involve large tax deductions for building depreciation; owners may pay small percentages of their early profits back to government as taxes. A certain percentage (5 percent to 10 percent or more) of a building's cost is taken off as a depreciation deduction each year. This reflects a fictitious notion, because many buildings do not in fact depreciate in worth at that annual rate. The fiction is used as cover for giving huge tax subsidies to developers and owners. Given ever-rising construction costs, some buildings are actually appreciating in terms of replacement value. Depreciation tax deductions can create paper losses for an owner-corporation, which sharply reduce the taxes it pays on its operations unrelated to the buildings.[19]

Powerful businesspeople can get tax concessions or "hardship" reductions from local taxation boards. One New York study by Newfield and Dubrul examined a landowning capitalist family with thirty-three buildings in Manhattan. In a five-year period the family reportedly received two-thirds of the many requests it made for tax assessment reductions. Other owners on the same blocks received just 16 percent of the assessment reductions requested.[20]

Tax-exempt bonds sold to investors by city agencies have been used to finance parking lots, garages, and services for various developments. Bonds have been used to finance factories and office towers. Tax-exempt bonds reduce the taxes of well-off investors (individuals, banks, and other corporations) who purchase them, reducing total U.S. tax revenues. In this way, the taxpayers in general pay, if indirectly, for services and facilities required by urban developers. This device has provided government-assisted subsidies for industrial corporations locating in metropolitan areas, such as Olin Mathieson Chemical, Borg-Warner, Georgia Pacific, and U.S. Rubber.[21]

Another device used by developers is the "special tax district." Special assessment districts are set up by local government authorities, usually for one purpose, such as constructing a water system. Bonds can be issued by this special district at lower interest rates. Assessment districts have long been a way of getting taxpayers to pay (via bonds) for utility and street improvements substantially benefiting developers and allied corporations.

Using such districts, developers are not dependent on city or suburban governments to extend water, sewer, and other utility systems into new areas. This can increase the supply of land for development, as well as the speed of development. Defenders of municipal and other special utility districts (called MUDs in some areas) argue that using tax-free bonds to pay for subdivision utilities lowers the initial cost of housing in the area, because the utility bonds are paid off over a long period of time. However, the special utility districts can have serious disadvantages as well. Eventually, the bonds will have to be paid off, as well as the interest on the loaned money. The total cost, including interest, will usually be higher in the long run. In addition, the districts create many small sewer and water systems that may be less efficient and more costly to maintain than larger regional systems. When such areas are annexed by a nearby municipality, these small systems can be costly to maintain or upgrade. In some states developers have set up special tax districts, voted into existence by a few of their friends and supporters, and have then issued tax-exempt bonds to obtain publicly supported financing for the utilities. There are now tens of thousands of special districts, each with the ability to issue tax-exempt bonds. The existence of many utility districts just outside city boundaries can contribute greatly to the haphazard sprawling out of suburban development.[22]

From the developers' point of view, the key virtue of these districts is that control over growth is firmly in the hands of developers—millions of dollars of taxpayer dollars are spent by developers even though the taxpayers concerned had no voice in the matter.

Bridges, highways, sewers, other utilities, and convention centers tied to government bond issues look good; and long-term bonds make them seem affordable. But the lenders will eventually have to be paid far more than they have loaned to governments because of interest charges. Eventually government-backed bonds must be paid out of a city's revenues or by securing yet other loans. Commenting generally on bonds, Henry Aubin notes that "to be able to sell the bonds in the first place, and to be able to continue to sell new bonds in order to pay back those people who have bought the previous bonds (for this kind of debt is regenerating) the seller [e.g., city government] must jump through various hoops held by the underwriters."[23] Underwriters are usually banks; they help government officials to plan debts and advertise bonds to investors. The underwriters, usually lenders themselves, and other bankers can determine interest rates a government must pay based on how risky they view the city to be; in fact, they can deny money. Borrowing is necessary to finance government programs; direct property taxes are usually not enough. Government officials must be "nice" to their bankers or they cannot get all the financing they need to provide municipal services.

CONTROLLING "CRAZY MIXES"
OF LAND USE: ZONING

Concerned about stopping "crazy mixes" of land use, such as neighboring industrial and residential uses, the national and local real estate boards have been among the influential supporters of zoning laws. These local laws separate land uses, regulate densities, and require case-by-case decisions on zoning variations. By 1920 nearly 90 percent of the country's largest ninety-three cities had zoning ordinances specifying which areas could be used for residential, commercial, and industrial purposes. Real estate organizations pressed for an extension of zoning to entire metropolitan areas and for city planning of roads, parks, and playgrounds. Zoning laws were declared constitutional by the U.S. Supreme Court in 1926, and by the late 1930s every state had passed enabling legislation permitting cities to establish zoning laws.[24]

Why did many in the real estate industry support this type of government intervention in land markets, intervention that interferes with the right of owners to dispose of property as they see fit? Zoning laws were first promoted to prevent land from being used in ways that would reduce adjacent property values. Early real estate industry people saw zoning not as a way of planning cities or of protecting the environment, but as a way of protecting their land values from the destructive actions of neighbors.[25]

Real estate operators often serve on and otherwise heavily influence the decisions of zoning boards. Rezoning a piece of land can mean enormous profits for the owner, as when an area is shifted from residential to commercial use. So it is not surprising that developers have supported zoning, especially when they dominate or influence zoning boards. Early support for such regulations and for deed restrictions came in particular from the larger real estate operators. John E. Burchard, a prominent architectural historian, once told a group of big developers that "'zoning can protect you against the small, inefficient entrepreneur. Zoning can protect the big fellow against the marauding of little guys who have nothing at all in mind."[26]

In recent years a few writers have argued that zoning is costly and unnecessary. For example, Bernard Siegan's book-length analysis of zoning is filled with comments such as "zoning is a failure and should be eliminated." In his view, zoning restricts housing production, and elimination of zoning will greatly increase more efficient use of land.[27] Nonetheless, city land-use patterns are very similar in zoned cities and nonzoned cities. This is because real estate actors create patterns of land use that are about the same under zoning as without it.[28]

One reason zoning has limited effects on patterns is that zoning laws and commissions are frequently influenced or manipulated by powerful land-oriented actors. Variances have often been liberally granted to developers and other entrepreneurs by local zoning boards. A study of Suffolk County suburbs in New York City by Mark Gottdiener concluded that local governments are heavily influenced by powerful business interests. Some rezoning decisions were made in terms of the political costs and gains to elected officials. Campaign contributions and other direct political contributions were a major category of rewards provided by developers and bankers and commercial firms. Payment was not made for every zoning or other government decision favoring a business, but exchanges of favors happened often enough to show that local zoning and other political officials were supporters of profit-making development.[29]

Large corporations, until the 1950s, were content with the existing patchwork quilt of local zoning ordinances, but in the decades since there has been growing pressure for zoning reform to permit higher-density, larger-scale development projects. Much public discussion of zoning reform has been led by planners and professors who see zoning as too inflexible in practice. But change in the housing and development industry really underlies this renewed discussion of zoning reform.[30] The growing importance of large developers and other corporations is responsible for new pressures for changes in zoning laws. Development interests have pressed for statewide zoning laws, so that regulations will be similar across a large geographical area. They have pressed streamlining and reduction of local land-use regulations. Smaller developers and builders as a group have not in fact been vigorous supporters of these zoning reforms, because they operate quite well at the local level and on a smaller scale.[31]

A network of corporate-oriented organizations, including the Rockefeller Brothers Fund and other Rockefeller family organizations, the Urban Land Institute (with multinational and developer corporations dominating its board of directors), and the Real Estate Research Corporation, have spearheaded the zoning reform movement in the United States. The Urban Land Institute, has pressed hard for revising zoning laws so that larger projects can be built more easily. These corporate-oriented groups are not primarily seeking the public interest in pursuing reform, though they may describe their activities that way. Rather, they push land-use policies that serve their business interests, clothing those interests in the guise of planning principles.[32]

FISCAL CRISES IN CITIES

Cities are centers for profit for capitalism, but many working people continue to pay a price for the way cities have grown and died. In the last decade numerous northern and midwestern cities have faced serious government fiscal crises, with a few coming to the brink of bankruptcy. The costs of city services—highways and streets, fire and police services, city hospitals—have been rising rapidly in recent years, even while some of these services have been deteriorating in quality. Some conventional analysts have explained the problems of cities in terms of factors such as excessive union demands, unnecessary city services, corruption, and inept government management. Although there is some truth to this view, it misses broader trends in U.S. capitalism.

The federal government has neglected northern cities such as New York by pumping out more taxes from them than it pays them back. The core dilemma of such cities is not the absence of money to cover wages and services. It is the unequal distribution of available money. Substantial local and federal government money goes to support the projects of industrial corporations and developers; services suffer, and moderate-income housing becomes scarce, in part because public money is channeled to these corporate needs. Corporate officials have been moving their industries and capital to Sunbelt cities; many middle-income workers have moved South as a result, leaving behind local government with fewer people and industries to tax to pay for city services. The problems of Frostbelt cities stem in large part from class conflict; city governments are caught between the demands on the one hand of powerful corporate capitalists for a favorable profit-making climate and on the other of municipal workers for a better standard of living and city residents for good services. Pressures build to reduce wages, business taxes, and city services, so costs of doing business will be reduced. Otherwise capital will leave for the Sunbelt.[33]

Economic stagnation from 1974 to the early 1980s made it difficult for many cities outside the Sunbelt to cope adequately without a heavy dependence on financial institutions.[34] What this dependence means can be seen in New York City's financial crisis, which came to public attention in 1975 but has persisted. Because of sharply rising expenditures and declining taxes, New York borrowed heavily from banking institutions. New York banks, already in trouble because of shaky foreign and other loans, had a sizable proportion of their assets in New York City securities. If the city's government failed, the banking institutions might fail. In the spring of 1975 the city government was unable to meet its payrolls and pay the interest on past loans. On the verge of complete bankruptcy, New York was bailed out by immediate state and federal government action. The state government created a Municipal Assistance Corporation, which could sell its own securities to help cover the city's debts. When this was not completely successful, the state legislature took a more drastic step in the fall of 1975 and established an Emergency Financial Control Board (EFCB).[35]

Made up of bankers and corporate capitalists, the EFCB directly administered the finances of the city, taking over from democratically elected officials. It was headed by chief executives from such corporations as N.Y. Bell Telephone and American Airlines, as well as from banking institutions. The board was supposed to balance the city's budget by 1978. Its authority had the look of putting the "fox in charge of the chicken coop," because banks hold so much of New York's municipal securities. In addition, a new city government management office, staffed by business executives on loan from corporations, was charged with supervising productivity goals for government agencies.

In a speech to a conference of the National Municipal League in 1980, William Ellinghaus, president of AT&T, bragged about bringing fiscal responsibility to New York City by slashing city employment, controlling city worker wages, reducing services, and getting it to run more like a business. Moreover, he recommended that other cities be run even more along business lines than they presently are by a fiscal plan acceptable to investors and by using business management practices. He urged business executives to become even more involved in government management.[36]

Expanded business control over cities is not new. In the 1930s many big cities were faced with severe financial problems. Cities such as Detroit and New York worked out agreements with financial institutions to suspend interest payments. The cost was high in new interest charges and in expanded bank capitalists' control of government expenditures. Even then many cities were under the control of what Mark Gelfand has called the "financial dictators."[37]

Workers and their families paid a heavy price for the financial salvation of New York City. Austerity was the plan. City services to residents were cut significantly, and taxes were increased. "Free tuition and open enrollment at the City University, library hours, sanitation pickups, city hospitals, day-care centers, the city work force—were cut back or eliminated."[38] City transit fares were raised 40 percent, the city parks began to decay, and the streets became even dirtier. Thousands of employees were laid off, and thousands more who resigned were not replaced. A disproportionate number of those laid off were minority and female. There was a major pay freeze for workers. Municipal unions agreed to give back millions in fringe benefits they had won in earlier years, to defer wage increases, and to accept the laying off of thousands of city employees. Bank and other corporate officials used New York's fiscal crisis to scare the working people of New York into accepting this plan as the only solution to the crisis.[39]

Austerity as a Long-term Strategy.   Many business leaders and their political allies believe that a northern renaissance can occur, that northern cities can recover economically. But to do this workers in northern cities must accept a favorable business climate as have workers in the South. They must accept austerity—the lower wages and benefits, weaker unions, cuts in government services to residents (but not to capitalist projects), reduced taxes for businesses, and government subsidies paid out of taxes to attract business to northern cities. Cooperating with capital often means human suffering.[40]

Urban Enterprise Zones: Restoring the Favorable Business Climate.   In the early 1980s President Ronald Reagan argued at a press conference that people living in troubled cities could vote with their feet. If they didn't like their conditions, they could pick up and move to more prosperous cities in the Sunbelt. This was the same theme articulated in the *Urban America* report. Reagan's approach emphasized reliance on unrestrained market mechanisms for solving problems. Although earlier government urban programs, such as urban renewal, have been oriented to the needs of capitalists in the private market, this approach proposed an even more radical implementation of that ideology. Reportedly, powerful advisers to President Reagan wanted no urban policy at all. David Stockman, Reagan's budget director, wanted to do away with most urban development grants and revenue-sharing programs. Pressure from urban mayors forced Reagan's advisers to back down and come up with a plan.

In the spring of 1982 the president's major approach to cities was put forward in the form of an "urban enterprise zones" proposal. The idea was to give huge tax cuts and other subsidy incentives to persuade businesses to locate plants in inner-city areas. Corporate income tax and property taxes would be reduced, and cities would be required to waive many building code, safety, and zoning regulations. Some neighborhood services would be transferred to private companies. Twenty-five zones a year would be created, for three years. An earlier administration proposal to do away with minimum wage laws was abandoned. By early 1983 this was the only official urban policy of the Reagan administration, but the implicit policy seemed to be intentional neglect of city problems. As one commentator phrased it, this approach was "Social Darwinism applied to the cities."[41]

NOTES

    1. Chester W. Hartman, *Yerba Buena: Land Grab and Community Resistance in San Francisco* (San Francisco: Glide Publications, 1974), p. 13. The next few paragraphs draw heavily on this book.
    2. Quoted in ibid., p. 19.
    3. Quoted in ibid., p. 43.
    4. Ibid., pp. 23-27.
    5. Ibid., pp. 48-50.
    6. Ibid., pp. 93-97.

7. Diana Klebanow, Franklin L. Jones, and Ira M. Leonard, *Urban Legacy: The Story of America's Cities* (New York: Mentor Books, 1977), p. 350.

8. National Commission on Urban Problems, *Building the American City* (Washington, D.C.: U.S. Government Printing Office, 1968), p. 153.

9. Klebanow, Jonas, and Leonard, *Urban Legacy,* pp. 351-353.

10. Christopher W. Kurz, "Public/Private Leveraging of Urban Real Estate," *Mortgage Banker* (November, 1980), p. 13.

11. Ibid., p. 15.

12. Chester W. Hartman, Dennis Keating, and Richard LeGates, *Displacement: How to Fight It* (Berkeley, Calif. National Housing Law Project, 1982), pp. 147-148.

13. Ibid., pp. 145-146.

14. Mark I. Gelfand, *A Nation of Cities* (New York: Oxford University Press, 1975), pp. 112-114; Robert A. Beauregard, "The Redevelopment of the Advanced Capitalist City," paper presented to Conference on New Perspectives on Urban Political Economy, Washington, D.C., American University, May, 1981, p. 8.

15. William D. Angel, "Beggars in Velvet Gown," (unpublished Ph.D dissertation, University of Texas, 1977), p. 21.

16. Harvey Molotch, "The City as a Growth Machine," *American Journal of Sociology* 82 (September, 1976), p. 313.

17. Jack Newfield and Paul Dubrul, *The Abuse of Power* (New York: Viking Press, 1977), pp. 88-96.

18. "Cincinnati's Fountain Square South: From Historic to Commercial Asset," *Buildings* 76 (February, 1982), p. 65; Robert Guenther, "Cities Getting Part of Profits," *Wall Street Journal*, September 29, 1982, Sect. 2, p. 31; Arnold Fleischmann, "The Political Economy of Annexation and Urban Development," Ph. Dissertation, University of Texas, Austin, Texas, forthcoming, 1983, chapter 3.

19. James Lorimer, *The Developers* (Toronto: James Lorimer and Co., 1978), pp. 64-66; cf. Mark Gottdiener, *Planned Sprawl* (Beverly Hills, Calif.: Sage Publications, 1977), pp. 111-119.

20. Newfield and Dubrul, *The Abuse of Power,* pp. 134-135.

21. Charles Abrams, *The City Is the Frontier* (New York: Harper and Row, Colophon Books, 1967), pp. 221-227.

22. Ibid; Rice Center Research and Development Corporation, *Houston Initiatives: Phase One Report* (Houston: Rice Center, 1981), pp. 13-14.

23. Henry Aubin, *City for Sale* (Toronto: James Lorimer and Co., 1977), p. 373. See also pp. 372-374.

24. Pearl Janet Davies, *Real Estate in American History* (Washington, D.C.: Public Affairs Press, 1958), pp. 77-80, 146-147.

25. Downie, *Mortgage on America,* pp. 89-90.

26. Quoted in Robert Goodman, *After the Planners* (New York: Simon and Schuster, 1971), p. 147; see also Davies, *Real Estate in American History,* p. 66.

27. Bernard Siegan, *Land Use without Zoning* (Lexington, Mass.: Lexington Books, 1972), pp. 128-129, 247.

28. Ibid., p. 23.

29. Gottdiener, *Planned Sprawl,* pp. 82-83.

30. Richard A. Walker and Michael K. Heiman, "Quiet Revolution for Whom?" *Annals of the Association of American Geographers* 71 (March, 1981), p. 68.

31. Richard F. Babcock, *The Zoning Game* (Madison, Wis.: University of Wisconsin Press, 1966), p. 139.

32. Walker and Heiman, "Quiet Revolution for Whom?" pp. 72-83.

33. Traditional experts are quoted in "Urban Experts Advise, Castigate and Console the City on Its Problems," in *The Fiscal Crisis of American Cities,* edited by Roger E. Alcaly and

David Mermelstein (New York: Vintage Books, 1977), pp. 6-9; also see Jacob Epstein, "The Last Days of New York," in The Fiscal Crisis of American Cities, pp. 61-62.

34. Kenneth Fox, "Cities and City Governments," in U.S. Capitalism in Crisis, edited by Bruce Steinberg et al. (New York: Union for Radical Political Economics, 1978), p. 179.

35. Roger E. Alcaly and Helen Bodain, "New York's Fiscal Crisis and the Economy," in The Fiscal Crisis of American Cities, pp. 31-38; Ken Auletta, The Streets Were Paved with Gold (New York: Vintage Books, 1980), pp. 278-280.

36. William Ellinghaus, "Urban Management: A Businesslike Policy for City Planning," Houston Business Journal, November 24, 1980, p. 4.

37. Gelfand, A Nation of Cities, p. 51.

38. Auletta, The Streets Were Paved with Gold, p. 278.

39. Ibid., pp. 276-291.

40. David Mermelstein, "Austerity, Planning and the Socialist Alternative," in The Fiscal Crisis of American Cities, p. 354.

41. Timothy K. Barkenov, Daniel Rich, and Robert Warren, "The New Privatism, Federalism, and the Future of Urban Governance: National Urban Policy in the 1980s," Journal of Urban Affairs 3 (Fall, 1981), p. 3.

10
THE PEOPLE VERSUS THE DEVELOPERS: DEMOCRATIZING URBAN DEVELOPMENT

INTRODUCTION

September 1981. Two thousand riot police are called in. Tenants in eight houses who are there illegally as "squatters" are being evicted. The police charge without warning into a crowd that gathered outside the houses to protest the evictions. An eighteen-year-old tenant is killed by a bus in the turmoil. This incident is one of many clashes between tenants and police in a city with a severe shortage of affordable rental housing units, a city where the local government has a program of land clearance for "blighted" areas. That clearance program has brought destruction of sound housing, many evictions, housing standing vacant for long periods of time, and replacement of older housing by more luxurious construction. The place is West Berlin. There police, government, and landowners have been battling a cross section of German young people who cannot find affordable housing because of a severe shortage. Numerous housing riots like this one have occurred in European cities.[1]

Can this happen in the United States? That question has been answered "yes" by those observers who point to a growing U.S. housing crisis. In the 1980s, 14 million new households will be created, but housing construction —both new homes and apartments—at current rates will fall far behind that predicted growth. There is now an estimated shortfall of a half million (some say one million) housing units each year in the United States. Those hit hardest are low-income and middle-income individuals and families. About the same time that the West Berlin housing riot took place, a citizen's protest group (ACORN) moved four low-income families into abandoned buildings in Philadelphia and Detroit. This "squatting" protest was a tactic designed to pressure government officials to take action to meet a severe housing short-age. These housing activists suggested that more abandoned houses would be occupied unless more such housing was made available to families desperately in need of it.[2] Illegal squatting could become a major trend in the United States, with even middle-income whites joining in, if the housing crisis persists.

Many middle-income Americans have been forced out of housing markets they are accustomed to. With average home prices in the $70,000 to $80,000 range in the early 1980s, and with continuing high interest rates, the average income of homebuyers skyrocketed from about $28,000 in 1978 to $39,000 in the early 1980s. Without outside assistance most American families can no longer afford to buy an average American house; many young families, white and nonwhite, can look forward to never owning a house. Renters too face severe problems. There is a growing shortage of affordable rental housing. Even in the Sunbelt, where there was substantial apartment construction in the 1970s and early 1980s, occupancy rates were quite high—above 95 percent. Moderate-rent apartment housing sometimes has an occupancy rate above 100 percent because of families doubling up in one apartment. Relatively small numbers of moderately priced homes and af-fordable rental units have been built in recent years. This type of housing development remains neglected by the movers and shakers of modern cities.

CAPITAL FOR DEVELOPMENT

Today many developers, builders, and their bankers are not much interested in providing housing for average or low-income Americans. If challenged, they complain that the housing shortage is not their fault, that they do not have the capital or incentives for such development. But capital is available for shopping centers, office towers, business parks, MXDs, and the like. Why not for affordable housing? One problem is that developers, bankers, and other powerful real estate interests look at housing in a different way than tenants and most homeowners do. Tenants look at an apartment as shelter—it is housing and home. But for most apartment investors, developers, and owners many of whom are large corporations—the units are only housing investments, with level of profit being the primary concern.

Much investment converting existing apartment complexes into con-dominiums has aggravated housing problems of tenants. Conflict between owner-developers and their affluent condominium clients, on the one hand, and tenants already in the housing targeted for condominium conversion is becoming commonplace in U.S. cities. Recently in Arlington, Virginia, across the Potomac River from Washington, D.C., most buildings in one of the last large apartment complexes, Buckingham Community, were sold to a Chicago developer who specializes in conversion. Because one-quarter of the garden apartments in Arlington have been converted to condominiums in recent years, the residents feared the worst. Many tenants will probably have a difficult time finding alternative housing units they can afford to rent. Reportedly a seventy-year-old amputee needs a ground floor apartment. A middle-income divorcée with two sons needs an affordable multibedroom apartment. An eighty-year-old tenant who has lived there twenty-six years fears the disruption of a major move.[3]

The tenants organized to resist displacement. A 1981 Washington *Post* story noted that "one strategy tenant leaders are considering is forming a corporation, finding investors and buying the property themselves. A more probable tactic is to legally challenge any zoning changes" by the developer. As a local activist put it, "Buckingham is really the Custer's last stand for low- and moderate-priced housing in Arlington County." But the developer has a different view, as he commented, "I can understand the yelling and screaming. They can do whatever they want. But I didn't buy with the intent of keeping it like it is. In my opinion, it's substandard and in some form, it has to be recycled."[4] Much moderate-rent housing has been recycled at a profit to provide housing for the most affluent fifth of Americans. Capital can be found for some types of development but not for others.

PROTESTING DEVELOPMENT
BY THE GROWTH COALITION

The growth coalition composed of developers, lenders, other powerful business interests, and allied politicians has been at the center of our discussion throughout this book. This powerful coalition has made and remade our cities; it is oriented toward development and redevelopment projects, many of which have been subsidized by government assistance. Yet much development has been resisted and protested by citizens. Over the last two decades citizens' groups have questioned the actions of growth-oriented leaders; they have attacked the idea of ever-accelerating growth and private development. Much protest has targeted the *social costs* of urban development, the costs that are paid not by the developers and owners but rather by community residents who are displaced, who pay higher taxes, or who cannot find affordable housing.

Highways.   Major highway and expressway projects in cities such as Boston, New York, Philadelphia, and Washington have generated major protest. Thousands displaced by projects have protested in various ways, including mass gatherings and civil disobedience. Lawsuits have been filed, but in most cases the citizens have lost. For the most part judges have ruled in favor of road construction. With only minor alterations most highway construction has been permitted.

Yet in a few cities, such as Boston, citizens' pressure has periodically forced developer-supported highway construction to be canceled or delayed significantly. In the 1970s local and state governments in Massachusetts rejected a commitment to certain long-planned expressways in the Boston area and committed the state to spend $2 billion on mass transit. Community and neighborhood groups, as well as environmental groups, pushed for this moratorium and were pleased with the decision. Business leaders were angry. A key citizens' group was the Greater Boston Committee on the Transportation Crisis, a federation of community groups opposed to expressways; different types of people were included. For a time the chair was a priest from East Boston who had helped earlier with protests against the expansion of Boston's airport into East Boston neighborhoods. The citizens' federation argued that the planned expressways would benefit suburban developers and suburbanites at the expense of central-city residents, whose densely populated neighborhoods would be destroyed or cut apart by the highways. Many of these people did not have cars; public transit was their greatest need. In the Boston case, citizen pressure successfully won out over pro-highway development interests, for a time at least.[5]

Redevelopment.   Intense opposition to redevelopment and gentrification has come from a variety of people's organizations in cities from Seattle to Boston. In Washington, D.C., the Capital East Community Organization and the Adams-Morgan Community Organization joined together to fight gentrification. Trying to stem the tide of speculative real estate development, these citizens' groups pressured the city council to pass a bill called the Real Estate Transaction Tax, which would have restricted speculative buying and selling. Developers and speculators organized to resist the "Speculator's Bill." Calling it "socialism in our time," real estate interests organized an effective lobby, and the bill that passed in 1978 was so watered down that most developer-builders could avoid the speculation taxes. In this case a community-based group was only partially successful in its attempt to bring housing decisions of developers and speculators under democratic control.[6]

To counteract central-city speculation and gentrification in the mid-1970s the St. Ambrose Housing Aid Center in Baltimore set up a counseling service for neighborhoods faced with private real estate speculation and later went into the business of buying and repairing homes for sale to lower-income people on a nonprofit basis. The Seattle Displacement Coalition, composed of many community groups, was formed to help tenants fight eviction in condominium apartment conversion situations. In Chapter 9 we discussed the role of a tenants' organization in fighting urban redevelopment and displacement in the central city of San Francisco. There citizens were successful in getting developers and public officials to agree to provide some low- and moderate-income housing to offset partially the social costs of development primarily benefiting large corporations.

The head of the National Association of Neighborhoods has argued that the benefits of most redevelopment are not being felt by low- and moderate-income households and that government officials are "not facing the realities of the injustices."[7] He argues that developers should be required by governments to relocate those displaced by redevelopment within their original neighborhoods. Such views signal the emergence of neighborhood associations which are willing to take on powerful development interests. One objective is to pressure governments to help incumbent city residents stay in their homes, using a variety of government aid programs—such as those facilitating home repairs, rehabilitation, loans, and utility lifeline measures. A number of neighborhood group leaders and their policy analysts have called for government aid for "rehousing banks," that is, programs that can buy and hold existing units of modest-cost central-city housing under local government control as a permanent reserve of moderate-rent housing supply.[8]

Malls.   Industrial parks and shopping malls have been protested by citizens' groups, a fact signaled in discussions of citizen protest in developers' handbooks. There have been numerous attempts, and a few successes, by citizens' groups seeking to stop large mall developments. One such attempt was in Burlington, Vermont, where the citizens fought against a nearby mall to be built there by a large corporation. Citizens protested against the traffic congestion and accelerated decline of the downtown area that the new mall would bring. In Hadley, Massachusetts, another citizens' group took on a national mall developer corporation (see Chapter 7). A seventy-store mall was planned for thirty-five acres of farmland there. At issue was the questionable need for another mall in this small town and the air, water, soil, and traffic problems that a mall would create. The mall was to be constructed by a corporation that had already built twenty-eight malls across the United States. This group slowed down the mall development but was unable to stop it. They lost this battle, but won greater support. The activity of an antigrowth minority raised the consciousness of most townspeople, and at later town meetings citizens took action to create toughter zoning restrictions to prevent future malls; several proposed development projects were defeated. The idea of fighting developers was made legitimate.[9]

As we noted in Chapter 7, in the last few years in cities in eastern Canada there have been several citizens' movements to stop or control the location of shopping centers, in part because of the destructive effects of competition from malls on downtown areas. There citizens concerned over corporate development in their cities have turned out numerous hard-line pro-development politicians and replaced them with opponents, or less enthusiastic supporters, of unbridled urban development. This in turn has led to a number of development control laws, including a moratorium on shopping malls on Prince Edward Island and freezes on development in the province of Ontario. Today in Canada elected government officials are less enthusiastic about shopping centers. One result of this is that major developers moved from Canadian to U.S. cities looking for profitable investments where antigrowth sentiment, they feel, is not so strong and where most public officials are more business oriented.[10]

But the intensity of feeling against development in U.S. cities may be growing. There is the dramatic case of the Uptown area in Chicago. At the heart of this northside area is a multiethnic community of black, white, Hispanic, and Native Amercian families—a logical target for corporate redevelopment. A developer (Mayor Richard Daley's ex-son-in-law) proposed for this area a large shopping center and residential complex with 100,000 square feet of shops and two high-rise office towers. Demolition of older buildings for this large-scale project was underway when a residents' organization filed a class action suit, *Avery* vs. *Landrieu*, targeting the developer, the federal Department of Housing and Urban Development (HUD), and local government agencies. The suit was designed to fight the displacement of these moderate-income residents and argued for "the existence of a historic conspiracy by which the city and private developers, acting in concert, fulfilled the demand for upper- and middle-income housing by the destruction of low cost housing in 'target areas.'"[11] The lawsuit contended that the displacement would increase racial segregation because it would destroy one of the few integrated neighborhoods in Chicago. A lawyer for the neighborhood group argued in the April, 1980, issue of *Chicago Lawyer*, that this major project was part of a "plan to destroy the racially integrated nature of the community. The developer could not afford to build a very expensive high-rise building and have poor black people half a block away."[12]

Early in 1979, after losing an attempt to have the judge dismiss the lawsuit, the developer agreed to important concessions desired by residents: (1) at least one-fifth of the new housing would be reserved for moderate-income families, with preference to local residents; (2) affirmative action hiring programs would be implemented in the construction; (3) the total number of high-income apartments would be reduced; (4) a large grocery store would be built in place of planned specialty stores, with a majority of its employees drawn from the local community; and (5) $60,000 in damages would be paid for evicted tenants and for a legal defense fund. Negotiations were also carried out with HUD, the city of Chicago, and the Chicago Housing Authority to provide 1,200 units of government-subsidized housing in the Uptown area.[13]

Tenants' Protests.   Tenants' movements have sprung up across the nation, protesting condominium conversions by developers, the lack of development of moderate-rent housing, and the ever-rising rents that the short supply of rental housing seems to generate. The surge of tenants' organizations is typified in New Jersey. There tenants' movements began in the 1960s, and by 1970 the New Jersey Tenants' Organization (NJTO) had organized 20,000 tenants in forty-three rent strikes. The strikes were generally effective in reducing rent levels or improving conditions. The NJTO was successful in part because it maintained aggressive organizational and voter registration drives, which led to the election of sympathetic politicians and the passage of rent control laws. Similar movements have developed in other states. By the early 1980s more than two dozen towns and cities in California had passed rent control laws, under pressure from tenants' groups. There were statewide organizations for tenants spanning the continent, in the states of California, Texas, Indiana, New Jersey, New York, and Massachusetts.[14]

In the same period the National Rental Housing Council, an organization of landlords and housing developers, changed its name to the National Multi-Housing Council to reflect the large number of condominium developers and converters who were members. This organization has provided local business groups with information and aid in opposing rent control and other tenants' movements. On the other side, in 1980 tenants' groups joined together to form the National Tenants Union.[15]

A major issue for tenants' movements since the mid-1970s has been "condomania," the extensive apartment conversion process in cities discussed in Chapter 5. By the early 1980s condominium conversions totaled about 500,000 units, and tenants' groups were organizing politically to fight those developers. There was some type of legal protection for tenants in two dozen states. Some laws require six months (or more) notice to existing tenants from condo-converters. Real estate groups have organized to fight such laws as interfering with "free" market production of housing. The solution, they argue, is to let the "laws of supply and demand" be "honestly observed without interference." Observing the laws of the market doubtless means that more condominium conversion will take place, and that more moderate-income Americans will be displaced into unsuitable or unsafe housing.[16]

Because more and more Americans, unable to afford houses, are becoming permanent tenants, one of the traditional barriers to tenant organizations is thereby lessened; apartment life is no longer a temporary way station for many families. The future will probably see larger and stronger tenants' associations. Large-scale apartment buildings are becoming more commonplace; there is currently a trend away from the smaller apartment complexes in which a majority of renters have traditionally lived to larger complexes and high-rise apartment towers. Massing tenants in one place can lend support to tenant organization.[17]

WHAT ABOUT TRADITIONAL URBAN PLANNING?

Reflecting on discontent over development, some believe that what is needed is more effective work by urban planners. The argument is that the knowledge of planning and allied urban professionals can be used to deal with the problems of highways, displacement, malls, and condominiums. Urban problems have long been regarded as amenable to change at the hands of the social engineers, the professional planners. Yet, on the whole, planners and allied professionals have not been of great help to ordinary citizens facing problems of development and displacement in cities.

Efficiency Planning. Originating in the "City Beautiful" plans around 1900, by the 1920s urban planning had shifted to a greater emphasis on efficiency in the physical form of cities and on maintaining homogeneous land uses by zoning. Later, government renewal programs reinforced the planning orientation toward the efficient shaping of central-city space for development. With an emphasis on technique (cost-benefit analysis, modeling, systems analysis) and a technical-expertise approach to urban development, conventional planners have operated as expert facilitators who do not analyze or respond to the social justice problems created by a profit-centered development system whose urban goals they have helped to implement.[18] Prominent planners have accented this technical expert-client approach to urban redesign, sometimes with an added emphasis on the role of educating clients on what is good design. As a recent review of the planning profession puts it, planners have traditionally "lacked access to the decision-making process ...have tended to avoid political conflict, have been technique-oriented rather than goal-oriented, and are facilitators rather than initiators."[19]

Robert Goodman suggests that most urban planners today are "soft cops," that they are experts who use what they view as "value free" and "scientific" methods to shore up a social structure that is class-stratified, inegalitarian, and, for many low-income urbanites, oppressive. Most practicing planners are so committed to building existing cities that they become the handmaidens of the powerful real estate actors who shape race and class inequality. City planners have been useful in the implementation of business-oriented renewal and redevelopment programs, many of which have displaced large numbers of the poorer residents of cities.[20]

Architects and urban planners play a role in providing the necessary technical rationalizations for projects whose character is determined elsewhere by developers, builders, and bankers. This type of servile planning has led to congested complexes of high-rise buildings in downtown areas, with many sunless streets and sterile offfices; these buildings are not seen in terms of the needs of those who work in them or walk between them, or those displaced by them. Good architects defend what they build in terms such as this: "As professionals, it seems that architects should try to make the best of the world *as it is*—before somebody else fouls it up even further."[21]

Goodman suggests that this was the defense the German official Adolf Eichmann used for his efficient organization of the imprisonment and destruction of Jews and dissidents in Germany. Providing inhumane development with efficient architectural and planning tools does little to change its fundamental character. Architects and planners speak of their buildings as monuments to this or that planning perspective. Less often do they see themselves as providing *humane* places for *ordinary people* to live in and prosper in.[22]

In a study of a massive commercial mall development in a southwestern city Claire McAdams found that urban planners entered into the development process in two ways, as private consultants for the developer and as staff planners for the city's planning commission. The first phase of development was hidden from the general public; a hired-hand planner helped the developer prepare a profitable mall development plan in secret. When the city's planners saw the plan, several raised objections to its environmental impact. In spite of the misgivings of some, and pressured to improve the "business climate" of the city, the city's planners recommended approval of zoning changes with a plea that the "applicant continue to recognize" the environmental impact of the project. City planners play an important role in legitimating the land development process that usually proceeds more or less as the developers intend.[23]

Advocacy Planning.   Small groups among urban planning professionals have begun to advocate and implement more democratic planning. Although a minority, people-oriented "advocacy planners" have given greater emphasis to social justice ideals. Advocacy planners are more likely to recognize and criticize the character of the power-privilege structure of the cities within which planning takes place. This neglect, they have argued, leads to naive urban planning.

Emerging since the late 1960s a more radical planning movement has explicitly emphasized the political nature of land use and urban planning. Robert Goodman's book, *After the Planners,* was perhaps the first sustained attack on mainstream planning in the United States. Goodman argues for advocacy planning, for city and architectural planning that pleads for the needs of minority and moderate-income Americans in the halls of government. Modern capitalism has co-opted most planners for its own purposes. Moderate reforms mean cosmetic changes making a project easier to market to the public. Giving the poor more access to traditional planning experts does not increase their incomes or improve their housing significantly. Chester Hartman has, moreover, suggested to a planners' conference that planning from the bottom up will require recognition of the skewed power structure shaping urban land use and will require development of political procedures that provide for real *democratic* control over land-use decisions.[24]

A move toward more democratic planning requires more than new developments in planning theory. It necessitates putting that theory into actual practice in planner-aided efforts for working-class people in cities. Advocacy planners have made attempts to provide planning skills for the "have nots" in the urban revitalization process. One advocacy planner, Chester Hartman, has provided aid to the residents in San Francisco's South of Market area, where the previously mentioned tenants' association successfully forced multinational executives, developers, speculators, and builders to revise their development plans. In this case the advocacy planner and the tenants' association came in too late to stop the revitalization process, but they did force significant changes as the project was built.

In two more recent struggles in San Francisco advocacy planners have developed the information and financial plans for incumbent residents attempting to fight the bulldozing of major buildings that developers wish to redevelop. Moreover, the rise of the "Planners Network" (an advocacy planning group), various conferences by radical planners, and the emergence of new radical planning organizations attest to the growing politicization of the planning field.[25]

PUBLIC BALANCE SHEETS: TOWARD CONTROLLING DEVELOPMENT

Writing in *Scientific American* a decade ago, Edward T. Chase noted: "For all the glories of free markets, market prices simply don't reflect the social costs of bad planning, or no planning. These costs aren't in anyone's books and thus go unaccounted. The public interest is lost among competing narrower interests."[26] Some leaders in people's movements and advocacy planners have suggested new analytical tools for looking closely at the social costs of private-sector development.

As we noted in Chapter 1, one of these tools is the *public balance sheet*, a way of tallying up, as David Smith puts it, the "tangible, measurable, quantifiable costs being imposed on citizens individually and collectively by the actions of the private sector."[27] Social costs such as traffic congestion and displaced renters should be factored into the overall costs of urban development projects.

Counting Social Costs. Traditional urban economists and other social scientists see social costs as "externalities" for which private enterprise is not responsible; or they grope along asking for specific government solutions for some costs without a comprehensive view of who is actually responsible for them. The truth is that the social costs of privately controlled development are *not* external to modern capitalism, but rather are an internal part of its everyday working. Public tax losses from development bonds bought by wealthy investors, job losses from industries seeking a better business climate in Houston or Taiwan, and developer choices about what type of housing is or is not built are features of modern capitalism intimately tied to private profit seeking, which neglects social needs and social costs. Ordinarily a company's accountants do not figure in these costs on their internal budget sheets: "These costs don't show up on any firm's ledger; no accountant writes them down. They're not charged against the income the firm makes from selling its products and services."[28] Yet *someone pays* these costs of location and development. It is ordinary Americans who pay the most heavily.

Tax concessions for development and the direct government subsidies for development amount to billions of dollars. These expenditures and tax losses are mostly paid for by taxpayers in general, less so by the corporations involved. Using the public balance sheet concept, however, one concludes that these substantial social costs should be directly paid for by those powerful real estate interests guiding urban development.

Interestingly, recent studies have shown that tax credits and tax-exempt bonds are available to industrial and development capitalists in most urban areas, so special subsidies have only a mild effect on location and investment decisions. The aggressive bidding by communities for industry only improves private profit margins. The subsidies simply make development less expensive for industrial and development capitalists, wherever they go, and thus more expensive for taxpayers.[29]

Apologists for the present system of privately controlled profit making argue that industrial and development corporations have a right to spend their capital as they see fit—it is *their* money. However, much of what they spend is *not* their money, but rather money loaned to them by banks, insurance companies, and pension funds—and much of this money comes from the savings of ordinary working people. Moreover, the profits of corporations that are reinvested in new plants and development also come from the hard work of workers in the companies and from the consumers who buy their products. So profits and investment capital are not sacred cows that should not be closely examined. Under close scrutiny their publicly generated character becomes obvious. Much so-called private capital is the general public's hard-earned money.[30]

Strategies to deal with the problems of urban development can take many forms. One is to eliminate some government programs, which encourage the waste of publicly generated capital. For example, taxing mechanisms now encourage the destruction of older but still serviceable buildings and their replacement with newer buildings. The overbuilding of office towers and shopping centers is encouraged by irrational depreciation deductions for owners and investors, as well as local, state, and federal governmental subsidies of various kinds. Buildings tend to be discarded before their time, creating unnecessary waste of U.S. resources. Rewriting the tax laws to discourage rapid and unnecessary development might be one step in the direction of a more democratic development process. Moreover, citizens' groups around the country have pressed financial institutions to invest savings from local savers locally, to use local resources for local housing needs.

One Striking Example.   Another strategy would be for government officials to require something in exchange for the zoning decisions, direct grants, and tax subsidies they give to industrial corporations and urban developers. In the early 1980s the people of Santa Monica, California—a satellite city of Los Angeles—elected a progressive city council committed to reshaping development. Many of these were the same voters who had been considered conservative voters in past elections. (They voted for Ronald Reagan in the 1980 presidential election.) In the early 1980s, the new government was trying to create a new development program incorporating major developer concessions to community needs. One developer came to the council for permission to build a multistory office complex. The council agreed, but only after the developer committed himself to meeting major community needs as part of the project: an affirmative action program of hiring, a public park, thirty units of low- and moderate-income housing, a 1,500 square foot community room, and a free day-care center.[31]

In addition, an agreement between the city of Santa Monica and another real estate firm specified that a significant portion of a proposed commercial-office project be constructed to house low- and moderate-income citizens, including units for senior citizens and families with children. The negotiated provisions are to remain in effect for forty years from date of completion. Energy conservation features including solar water heating are also part of this project. In another agreement with a real estate developer, Welton Becket

Associates, the Santa Monica city council reportedly reshaped a 900,000-square-foot commercial-office-hotel complex to include the following: one hundred rental units in new (or existing) buildings for low- and moderate-income renters (including the aged and handicapped), three acres of landscaped park areas with athletic sport facilities, a day-care center, promotion of car-pool, bicycling, and flex-time arrangements to reduce traffic problems, energy conservative measures, affirmative action and job training programs, and an arts and social services fee.[32]

Reviewing these Santa Monica proceedings, Dave Lindorff notes the extraordinary and progressive character of such negotiations between a city council and important developers. These are rare agreements because in big cities, such as New York "developers routinely threaten to drop projects if the *city* doesn't give *them* something (usually a height exemption and a giant tax abatement)."[33] As we have documented throughout this book, the usual procedure is for city councils and other government officials to rush to the aid of developers with a bag of subsidies and services and to require no negotiations with developers for contributions to community needs or meeting social costs. The basic idea of this innovative Santa Monica city council is to have developers pay for some of the problems of housing destruction and increased service expenditures they create. Working against tremendous odds, this council may or many not succeed over the long term.

Interestingly, Santa Monica is a city where the majority of voters are renters; these renters put the new progressive council into office. According to Lindorff these voters threw out a business-oriented government tied to the local chamber of commerce. The new council was not beholden to developers, because they did not depend heavily on developers for campaign contributions. Committed to rent control and to community control of development, the majority of the city council seem to be fighting the current development trend, which neglects the broader housing and community needs of the local population of renters and homeowners.[34]

Many suburban and central-city governments face the process of office building and luxury apartment building construction that reduces available housing, puts new demands on city sewerage and other services, and overloads the already crowded streets and transit systems with new workers. The actions in Santa Monica suggest one way to deal with development: require developers to provide community services and housing and to pay substantially for city services as a part of the negotiated agreement for unbridled private development. Not surprisingly, city council members across the country have shown interest in the Santa Monica progressive movement and have reportedly been working to place some limitations on developers.

Other Communities.   In other cities progressives have been elected to office, men and women centrally concerned about the social costs of private real estate development and industrial location decisions. In 1977 Ken Cockrel was elected to the Detroit City Council; he and his associates developed a citywide political coalition (DARE), which put together proposals for the humane reindustrialization and reform of Detroit. The proposals were an attempt to offset the social costs of auto company decisions to disinvest in the area. About the same time the democratic-socialist mayor of Madison, Wisconsin, Paul Soglin, set up a city-owned development corporation to provide assistance to cooperatives and worker-owned businesses that had had difficulty getting money through private lenders.

In March, 1981, Vermont's largest city, Burlington, elected a democratic-socialist as mayor. Bernie Sanders beat a political veteran for the mayor's office; Sanders was backed by an interesting coalition of homeowners, antiwar activists, and low-income families. Sanders won by opposing large-scale real estate developments, which many felt would have a negative effect on the city's quality of life. He attacked the close linkage of the prior mayor to growth coalition proposals for building a new highway through an older city neighborhood and for shopping mall and condominium development projects.[35] An article in the *Rolling Stone* noted that Sanders and his coalition intended "to press vigorously for some form of rent control, to tax medical and educational institutions in Burlington, and to block 'downtown revitalization' schemes."[36] Subsequently, in a spring election one year later Sanders's coalition won a number of seats on the board of aldermen, an electoral victory showing solid citizen support for Sanders's goals of creating a more democratic local government, of avoiding increased property taxes for homeowners while raising taxes on private hotels, restaurants, and other businesses, and of controlling development and revitalization schemes.

Taxing Corporate Location: A San Francisco Movement.   We have seen that corporations that decide to locate in central cities or in suburbs create social costs that they do not pay. Often they are under-taxed compared to middle-income homeowners, renters, and small businesses. In a number of communities grass-roots organizations have sprung up, seeking to force corporations to pay a greater share of local taxes. One such movement in San Francisco fought for a new ballot proposal called Proposition M:

> We, the people, declare that San Francisco must increase the taxes paid by its largest corporations. It is fundamentally unjust that large corporations, such as giant oil companies whose profits exceed $1 trillion in the 1980's, pay a lower rate of taxes than the average wage earners; and that San Francisco's huge banks and insurance companies pay no local business taxes at all. We pay our share, and so should they.[37]

The proposition passed in a November 1980 election. It required that the Board of Supervisors "increase the taxes paid by its largest corporations."

This victory of a grass-roots movement over large corporations signals how effective electoral participation can be if progressive forces are well-organized. Corporations outspent the "tax the corporations" movement two-to-one. The grass-roots movement successfully used four specific campaign methods: door-to-door canvassing, voter registration drives, street leafleting, and door-to-door leafleting. The electoral success, however, was met by court suits and by a failure of local government officials to implement Proposition M. Because of the inaction of city authorities the tax-the-corporations campaign sued the mayor and city supervisors to force implementation. But this court suit was not successful; and Proposition M was not implemented. City officials did, however, implement another, weaker, measure raising business taxes to 1.5 percent. In the end, then, popular pressure had increased taxes on San Francisco businesses, but only modestly. Although this was not the victory the grass-roots movement had hoped for, it did firmly establish the principle of taxation of large corporations as a partial financial solution paying the social costs leading to urban fiscal crises.[38]

Some New Think Tanks.   Think tanks focusing squarely on the social costs of modern capitalism have been few and underfunded. In 1978 the National Center on Economic Alternatives was created by Gar Alperovitz and Jeff Faux as a progressive "Brookings" think tank in Washington, D.C. Its research associates have issued an impressive and provocative series of research reports and books on the problems in the U.S. economy, with progressive alternatives proposed for current policies.

In the mid-1970s the National Conference on Alternative State and Local Policies was formed as a progressive research center dedicated to provide a communications network for progressive local government officials and labor leaders. The conference has produced major policy-oriented reports supporting progressive policymaking that takes into account the social costs of private decisions. In a 1980 report, *Social Investments and the Law*, Michael leibig shows that federal and state laws generally require pension fund trustees to consider the social effects of their investment decisions.[39] Yet most bankers do not follow the law in this regard. Leibig demonstrates that the usual bankers' criterion of "best financial return" for the dollar, regardless of the social consequences, is not mandated by existing laws. This progressive report is one in a series examining private and public pension funds and advocating people-oriented investments as alternatives to established practices. Public employee pension funds, with more than $140 billion in assets, are a major source of investment capital in the United States. Today most pension funds are under the control of executives in commercial banks and insurance companies, who have invested most of the money in the bonds and stocks of large multinational corporations and, to a lesser extent, in mortgages on large-scale urban development projects such as office buildings, shopping centers, and luxury apartment buildings. The National Conference on Alternative State and Local Policies reports are showing people how they can put these pension funds to work toward meeting more fundamental community needs for moderate-rent housing, for homeownership for moderate-income families, and for worker-community purchase of abandoned plant facilities.

CONCLUSION:
AN ALTERNATIVE URBAN FUTURE
WITH MORE DEMOCRACY

More democratic control over their housing problems. More control over local developers and lenders. More control over the quality of life in their communities. These are the democratic goals of the many citizens' groups we have discussed throughout this book. People are demanding control over companies that too easily abandon communities and create severe social costs for workers with deep-lying ties in the form of mortgages, schools, and community life. Capital flight from one city or region to another, or from the United States to another country has created severe problems for Frostbelt cities such as Youngstown, Ohio, and Detroit, Michigan. Citizens' groups are beginning to fight back, demanding laws that force firms to pay some of the social costs of this too-easy corporate flight. Such laws already exist in European countries including Great Britain, and implementing legislation has already been introduced into the U.S. Congress. As we have seen, citizens' groups are also fighting back against the social costs of urban development oriented to the needs of large retail and industrial corporations. They are attempting to control highway, urban renewal, shopping center, and office complex developments. Sometimes successful, often unsuccessful, these movements demonstrate a thirst for greater control over community life.

The central issue here is *economic democracy*. People's movements are asking for more input into the development decisions that shape their cities. They are asking for bankers, industrial executives, and developers to be less responsive to the demands of profit and more responsive to fundamental community needs. Citizens' groups are pressuring elected government officials to be more active in representing all citizens' interests, whatever their wealth or connections.

Since the Declaration of Independence the principle that people have a right to democratic control over their governments has been clearly etched in basic American documents. This right has often been corrupted because small elites, such as the omnipresent business-oriented growth coalitions, have disproportionately shaped government policies on development, housing, and urban renewal. Citizens' movements targeting the social costs of development, and holding politicians and private elites accountable for those costs, show clearly that the democratic impulse is alive in U.S. towns and cities. For more than two centuries the democratic political ideal has suggested that rank-and-file Americans can make better sociopolitical choices than small unrepresentative elites. Clearly this ideal needs to be put into every day practice in American government, local and national. Beyond that, this same democratic ideal should be applied to the private sphere. If choices are better made democratically than autocratically by an elite in the *political* sphere, why cannot this be the case for the *economic* sphere? Democracy in the private sphere of real estate development in towns and cities is being demanded by many citizen groups. Expansion of democracy into economic decision making—about what gets built or redeveloped in cities—is a logical extension of the early American political ideals in the Declaration of Independence. Whether such expansion occurs will be determined by the citizen struggles now taking place in the cities.

NOTES

1. Tom Sutton, "The Divided City: Squatters and Cops Face Off in Berlin," *In These Times* 5 (October 7-13, 1981), p. 7.
2. Jeanie Wylie, "Squatters Protest Housing Programs in U.S. Cities," *In These Times* 5 (October 7-13, 1981), p. 6.
3. Diane Granat, "A 'Last Stand' Against Condos," Washington *Post*, April 23, 1981, p. Va.3.
4. Ibid.
5. Ralph Gakenheimer, *Transportation Planning as a Response to Controversy* (Cambridge: MIT Press, 1976), pp. 38-50; Allan K. Sloan, *Citizen Participation in Transportation Planning: The Boston Experience* (Cambridge: Ballinger, 1974), pp. 60-72.

6. Eileen Zeitz, *Private Urban Renewal* (Lexington, Mass.: Lexington Books, 1979), pp. 81-84; La Barbara Bowman, "Handbook Guides City Residents in Resisting Displacement," Washington *Post*, July 22, 1979, pp. B4-B5.

7. Quoted in Robert Reinhold, "Reversal of Middle-Class Tide Sets Poor Adrift in Same Cities," *New York Times*, February 18, 1979, p. IV-5; George Grier and Eunice Grier, *Movers to the City* (Washington, D.C.: Washington Center for Metropolitan Studies, 1977), p. iv.

8. Marty Flahive and Steve Gordon, *Residential Displacement in Denver: A Research Report* (Denver: Joint Administration-City Council Committee on Housing, May 1979), pp. 17-19.

9. Jay Neugeboren, "Mall Mania," *Mother Jones* 4 (May, 1979), pp. 21-30.

10. Michael C. Ircha, "Regulating Shopping Centers: Canadian and International Experience," in *After the Developers*, edited by James Lorimer and Carolyn MacGregor (Toronto: James Lorimer and Co., 1981), pp. 70-73.

11. Chester W. Hartman, Dennis Keating, and Richard LeGates, *Displacement: How to Fight It* (Berkeley,Calif.: National Housing Law Project, 1982), pp. 190-191.

12. Ibid., p. 190.

13. Ibid., pp. 190-191.

14. Peter Drier, "The Tenants Movement in the United States: Structural Constraints and Strategic Options," in *New Directions in Urban Political Economy*, edited by Larry Sawers and William Tabb (New York: Oxford University Press, forthcoming), in manuscript, pp. 26-33.

15. Ibid., pp. 23-25.

16. Ibid., p. 34; Joe R. Feagin, *Social Problems* (Englewood Cliffs, N.J.: Prentice-Hall, 1982), pp. 402-403.

17. Drier, "The Tenants Movement," p. 22.

18. Robert W. Burchell and James W. Hughes, "Introduction: Planning Theory in the 1980s—A Search for Future Directions," in *Planning Theory in the 1980s*, edited by R. W. Burchell and G. Sternlieb (New Brunswick, N.J.: Center for urban Policy Research, Rutgers University, 1978), p. xx; see also Melvin M. Webber, "The Urban Place and Nonplace Urban Realm," in *Explorations into Urban Structure*, edited by Melvin M. Webber et al. (Philadelphia: University of Pennsylvania Press, 1964), pp. 84-93.

19. Burchell and Hughes, "Introduction," p. xxvi. Portions of this chapter are taken from Joe R. Feagin, "Urban Real Estate Speculation in the United States: Implications for Social Science and Urban Planning," *International Journal of Urban and Regional Research* 6 (March, 1982), pp. 35-59.

20. Robert Goodman, *After the Planners* (New York: Simon and Schuster, 1971), pp. 12-13.

21. Quoted in ibid., p. 96.

22 Ibid., p. 113.

23. D. Claire McAdams, "Powerful Actors in Public Land Use Decision Making Processes" (unpublished Ph.D. dissertation, University of Texas, 1979).

24. Goodman, *After the Planners*, pp. 171-173; Chester W. Hartman, "Social Planning and the Political Planners," in *Planning Theory in the 1980s*, pp. 76-77.

25. Chester W. Hartman, *Yerba Buena: Land Grab and Community Resistance in San Francisco* (Berkeley, Calif.: Glide Publications, 1974); Hartman, "Social Planning and the Political Planners," pp. 78-79.

26. Quoted in Rodney E. Engelen, "Meeting the High Price of Transportation," *Planning*, February, 1974, p. 13.

27. David Smith, *The Public Balance Sheet: A New Tool for Evaluating Economic Choices* (Washington, D.C., Conference on Alternative State and Local Policies, 1979), p. 2.

28. Ibid., p. 3.

29. Ibid., pp. 4-5.

30. Ibid., p. 6.

31. Dave Lindorff, "About-Face in Santa Monica," *Village Voice*, December 2-8, 1981, p. 20.

32. This discussion is based on copies of development agreements between the City of Santa Monica, California, and H. J. Kendall Associates and Welton Becket Associates (in author's files). The city council has passed ordinances implementing its new limitations on developers.

33. Lindorff, "About-Face in Santa Monica," p. 20. His italics.

34. Ibid.; for a discussion of successful worker and community control, see Feagin, *Social Problems*, pp. 440-442; and Daniel Zwerdling, *Democracy at Work* (Washington, D.C.: Association for Self-Management, 1978), pp. 53-55.

35. Fred Boyles, "Hizzoner the Socialist," *Boston Phoenix*, May 26, 1981, pp. 2, 8.

36. Colin Nickerson, "Red Mayor in the Green Mountains," *Rolling Stone*, May 28, 1981, pp. 13-14.

37. Marlene Dixon, Tony Platt, and Barbara Bishop, *A Case Study: Grassroots Politics in the 1980s* (San Francisco: Institute for the Study of Labor and Economic Crisis, 1982), title page.

38. Ibid., pp. 4-5 and addendum.

39. Michael Leibig, *Social Investments and the Law* (Washington, D.C.: Conference on Alternative State and Local Policies, 1980); cf. also L. Webb and W. Schwecke, *Public Employee Pension Funds* (Washington, D.C.: Conference on Alternative State and Local Policies, 1979).

INDEX

211